THE
SAVAGE
TRUTH
ON
MONEY

THE
SAVAGE
TRUTH
ON
MONEY

Second Edition

TERRY SAVAGE

WILEY

John Wiley & Sons, Inc.

Published by John Wiley & Sons, Inc., Hoboken, New Jersey.
Published simultaneously in Canada.

For general information on our other products and services or for technical support, please
contact our Customer Care Department within the United States at (800) 762-2974, outside
the United States at (317) 572-3993 or fax (317) 572-4002.

Wiley also publishes its books in a variety of electronic formats. Some content that appears in
print may not be available in electronic books. For more information about Wiley products,
visit our web site at www.wiley.com.

Library of Congress Cataloging-in-Publication Data:

Savage, Terry.
    The Savage truth on money / Terry Savage. — 2nd ed.
        p.   cm.
    Includes index.
    ISBN 978-0-470-92416-7 (pbk); ISBN 978-1-118-10045-5 (ebk);
    ISBN 978-1-118-10046-2 (ebk); ISBN 978-1-118-10047-9 (ebk)
        1. Finance, Personal.   I. Title.
    HG179.S2398   2011
    332.024—dc22

                                                2011012026

Printed in the United States of America

10 9 8 7 6 5 4 3 2 1

For Lucy and Allison

CONTENTS

PREFACE

A simple Savage Truth opened the first edition of *The Savage Truth on Money*: *If it were that easy to be wealthy, we'd all be rich!*

A decade ago it seemed there were so many easy ways to get rich—or live as if you were rich. It seemed simple to make a fortune in the stock market. Then it seemed easy to get rich in real estate, not only on your own home, but by buying and "flipping" new homes and condos. And if you didn't invest your way to easy wealth, you could always borrow your way to riches—living beyond your means via home equity loans and credit card offerings.

That all seems so long ago, as our country has endured one of the longest and most devastating recessions in our history. Dreams and illusions have been shattered, and a sense of pessimism abounds. The Savage Truth is that neither extreme is correct, but we are always carried to extremes by our own belief that what is current will continue into the future. That's why we need to understand the basic Truths about money, markets, and human emotions.

Truths don't change like fashion or emotions. The Savage Truths you could have read a decade ago have not been dented by the markets or the recession. That's not to say you could have avoided all the negative impacts of the past decade. But those who were unable or unwilling to see the basic Truths found that their personal finances took a much larger hit than those who had more perspective and more discipline.

The first edition of *The Savage Truth on Money* was written before the dot-com bubble burst and before the real estate bubble burst.

I write now just before the dollar bubble and the federal deficit bubble are about to burst.

America now has a national debt that is more than $14 trillion! It's a number that is impossible for the human mind to conceive and will be almost impossible to repay. (If you want to know the real dimensions of our debt, which includes promises to future Social Security and Medicare recipients, go to **www.TruthinAccounting.org**. The number keeps relentlessly ticking higher, and is more than $75 trillion at this writing!)

We've learned that America is only a cog in a fragile global financial system. There is no longer a way to avoid the impact of one country's profligacy, whether it be Greece and Ireland, or the United States and China. There are few places to hide. So you must remain alert when thinking about what to do with your money.

That doesn't mean you have to be an economic expert or a daily market trader. Quite the contrary; *The Savage Truth on Money* is designed to help you create a financial plan for your future—using all the resources of the Internet, the financial planning industry, and your own good judgment based on sound principles and basic Truths.

Understanding these Savage Truths won't change the economy. That is a function of political power and human nature. But knowledge and perspective *can* change your financial future and allow you to be successful, or at to least survive, the changing times in which we live.

These Truths are even more relevant today. Context may change, but principles remain the same. We've become more computerized, more used to instantaneous access to financial information, and more accepting of the fact that every day brings a new financial decision. But human nature has not changed, especially when it comes to money.

You may be skeptical that these Truths will still work in the "new America." We've seen people who played by the rules lose their homes as real estate values collapsed. We've seen hardworking employees lose their jobs as the economy collapsed. And we've seen students graduate from college with debts, but no jobs to earn the money to pay off their student loans.

Yet, in spite of the headlines, not all of America was devastated by the recession; some were able to create businesses and buy bargains. Some had paid down their mortgages and built up some savings. Even as they were hit hard by the stock market, many held on and watched their fortunes rebound. They had perspective and discipline, and they stuck with the basic principles of success that have survived the test of generations.

Those who were most devastated were living beyond their means, borrowing on their homes, taking on unprecedented debt, and demanding more from their government. It doesn't make today's reality any less painful, but our entire economy—from individuals to state and federal government—violated the most basic Savage Truth that headed Chapter 1 in the first edition of this book and remains unchanged: *Live within your means. Don't spend it all!*

Think of how different our economy would be if we had all learned that lesson, especially both parties in Washington! It's a story as old as the grasshopper and the ant, or the Bible, and the moral remains the same: During the good times, prepare and save for the tough times or they will devastate you.

Now we begin a new cycle. Are you prepared? Have you hedged your bets on your financial future? Are you ready to be a survivor who goes on to become even more successful in the next economic boom?

There *will* be good times ahead for America, make no mistake about that. Surely your grandparents, or great grandparents, who may have lived through the Great Depression of the 1930s must have been pessimistic about the future. Similarly, those who faced a deep recession in the early 1980s—with interest rates at 20 percent and unemployment at 12 percent and the Dow Jones Industrial Average under 800—found it difficult to believe our economy would recover, and even boom.

In the extended bear market of the 1970s, few could see into the future to a technology revolution that would send the stock market soaring to 14,000, push unemployment to record low levels, and create low mortgage rates not seen since the 1960s. Back then, few had enough belief in the future to keep investing in stocks when the outlook was gloomiest. But those who did believe in the future—and invest for it—were well rewarded.

Now if *you* give up in the midst of the current unsettled economy, you're likely to miss out on the next great economic upswing. No one ever got rich betting against America. Sure, you want to hedge your bets—on growth, on the dollar, and on your future. But you never want to give up believing in a better future for yourself, your family, and our country.

This new edition of *The Savage Truth on Money* contains those same Truths that would have saved so many people from so much financial woe, if only they had been heeded. They're as appropriate today as ever. I've included some updated references to drive the point home. After all, if we don't learn from our mistakes, we'll go on making them. It's never too late to start over.

It's also a guide to your opportunity to save yourself and redirect your finances in a new economic and political reality. Whether you're just starting out and are disillusioned about your prospects, or you've watched your fortune go down the drain and wonder how you'll manage your life, this is your roadmap to the future.

By now, we've all learned the Truth about believing that "this time it's different." The financial lessons of the past decade prove a simple Savage Truth: *Human nature never changes.*

To be financially successful requires that we withstand the emotions that destroy financial plans and goals. We must understand the lessons of the market and then create plans that control our natural tendencies to be motivated by fear and greed. But as I said in the original *Savage Truth*, all of that is a waste of energy if we don't have the self-discipline to believe in the future and stick with well-made plans.

Perspective is critical. We can always see our mistakes in hindsight. Now it's time to look forward, recognize the new realities, and apply the Savage Truths to prosper in the Savage Future.

THE SAVAGE TRUTH ON MONEY

CHAPTER 1

THE SAVAGE TRUTH ON GETTING RICH

Financial Security Demands Smart Choices

Everyone wants to know the secret of getting rich. And lately, people are wondering if it's even possible to "get rich"—or at least to live well and then retire confidently. America faces real challenges, given our country's burden of debt and our political infighting, not to mention the current economic situation. It's tempting to give up, to forget that this is not the first time America has surmounted challenges and gone on to prosperity.

So here's the Savage Truth: *The American Dream is not over.*

Achieving financial security will require a fresh start and a new approach. If you're willing to try, or try again, you can succeed. You need only to understand the basic Truths, which have not changed despite market volatility and economic uncertainty.

It's a tribute to America that there are many roads to wealth in this country, and they are open to all. Stories of young technology entrepreneurs abound, but age is no barrier. Michael Dell founded his computer company at the age of 19, and by age 34 his personal stock ownership in Dell Computer was valued at $16 billion. Ray Kroc, on the other hand, didn't start McDonald's until he was in his mid-fifties. Great fortunes were started in the Depression years of the 1930s.

In case that seems like ancient history, consider the fortunes built in the last few years. Facebook made its founder, Mark Zuckerberg, a billionaire even after the tech bubble had collapsed. Groupon's founders tapped into the social-networking, bargain-hunting mentality of the recession to create a successful technology company with a value exceeding $6 billion in 2011.

The Savage Truth: *Even in tough economic times, entrepreneurs with good ideas can build companies that defy the most pessimistic mood of the nation.*

There is no one template for success in America, but building a business does require an entrepreneurial spirit born of optimism. In America, age, race, and gender do not stand in the way of success— nor does the economic climate.

As entrepreneurs build businesses, they create opportunities for others—either by creating jobs or by selling shares to public investors. Groupon had just 50 employees in the summer of 2009, and more than 3,500 by year-end 2010. You don't have to create a new business to build financial security, but you do have to be aware of the growth opportunities around you. That's how success spreads, and an economy grows.

One of the fastest routes to financial success has always been through sales of a product or service. Today, technology allows start-up companies to compete without the investment capital that was traditionally needed to gain a foothold in markets. In other eras, real estate developers used borrowed money to amass wealth. All of these roads to success involve the risk of uncertain compensation. And not everyone has the desire or can afford to trade a regular paycheck for the potential riches of entrepreneurship.

It is also possible to become wealthy by investing in the business-building talents of others, but that requires patience, attention, and self-discipline. That's why the stock market exists. First, though, you need the capital to invest. That's a matter of simple mathematics.

You *Can* Get Rich on a Paycheck If You Don't Spend It All

There are two simple rules for amassing investment wealth:

1. Spend less than you make.
2. Invest the difference—both money and time—to maximum advantage.

Here are two stories that illustrate these truths:

RETIRED SECRETARY LEAVES $18 MILLION TO HOSPITAL

CHICAGO SUN-TIMES—A secretary who made her fortune investing bonuses from her salary, which hit an estimated high of $15,000 a year before she retired in 1969, left her fortune to Children's Memorial Hospital. Few friends suspected that Gladys Holm, who lived in a modest two-bedroom apartment, was wealthy.

Holm's boss, the company's founder, had advised her to invest her yearly bonuses in the stock market, a longtime friend said. "If he bought a thousand shares of some company, Gladys would buy ten shares of the same thing. Nobody gave her that money; she earned it."

NEW YORK UNIVERSITY TO GET ONE-FOURTH OF COUPLE'S $800 MILLION ESTATE

ASSOCIATED PRESS—Professor Donald Othmer and his wife, Mildred, lived modestly in a Brooklyn townhouse and rode the subway. In the 1960s, they each invested $25,000 with an old friend from Nebraska, Warren Buffett. In the early 1970s, they received shares in Berkshire Hathaway, then valued at $42 a share. When the couple died recently at ages 90 and 91, the stock was worth $77,200 a share—making their fortune worth an estimated $800 million.

All of these successful investors lived modestly all their lives. At no point did they decide it was time for an expensive vacation, an impressive vacation home, or even a new car. Thus, they were able to accumulate, invest, and leave behind a huge fortune. Surely, there must be a happy medium between living daily on credit card debt and dying with a huge fortune. Most people I know would like to live in that middle ground.

There is one other similarity to note: Neither Gladys Holm nor the Othmers had children. Children may be nature's way of making sure that we can't possibly die with a fortune!

Most important—neither Gladys Holm nor Professor and Mrs. Othmer ever sold any of their stock. Think of the temptations. As their fortunes grew, there was surely the temptation to spend just a little of their profits. And at times of stock market crisis, surely there was a temptation to sell and cut their losses. But they stuck to their long-term plan.

Don't doubt that this kind of investment success can happen again in the coming decades. Think what a great leap of faith it was for these ordinary people to invest in an uncertain future. Their profits were built slowly, but were accelerated by the fact that they were investing when others were skeptical.

Today's true headline success stories are the current generation of technology entrepreneurs. They built businesses, and their wealth is scored by the value of the stock they sold to the investing public and the shares they still hold. But behind each "overnight" success story is the truth that they followed the two principles at the top of this chapter. They lived frugally—primarily because they were too involved in their businesses to spend time on recreation and consumption. They also invested their resources, mostly their time, in building their businesses.

Steven Jobs, who founded (and later rescued) Apple Computer, is renowned for starting the business in his garage. Only *after* his company proved itself did he share in the rewards. Bill Gates built his mansion after he built his company, Microsoft. And then he started giving his money away through strategic philanthropy. Facebook, which today has half a billion participants, including the Queen of England, was another college venture, but Facebook cofounder Mark Zuckerberg famously was not in it for the money!

As one successful entrepreneur remarked to me on the occasion of a new accomplishment: "After a certain point, it's not the money. It could be lollipops. It's just the way you keep score!"

For most of us, it *is* the money. We need it to take care of our families, to put our children through college, to plan for retirement. But we can take lessons from these success stories. And even if we may not reach that pinnacle of great wealth, we can participate.

There's no question that their inherent brains and timing (sometimes referred to as luck) helped make these entrepreneurs rich. Their success stories are notable because they took a relatively short time to build dramatic wealth. But they followed the basic principles: They invested their time and money *before* they reaped the rewards. Yes, they dreamed, but they didn't buy lotto tickets or create extravagant lifestyles before they were financially successful. They worked to turn their dreams into reality instead of living as if their dreams had already come true. And they didn't quit when things got tough. Many of those tech multimillionaires (even billionaires) saw their paper fortunes melt away in 2001. Others lived through the decline and went on to amass even greater wealth.

It's a Savage Truth: *Persistence pays!*

So, how can the Savage Truths in this book get you on track—or back on track—to financial security? Life doesn't come with guarantees, but it does come with opportunities.

The secret of getting rich is to make choices that help your money work *for* you and stop working against you. If your money works at least as hard as you do, and if you have a sensible plan you can stick to, over time you'll come out a winner. And that's the Savage Truth.

THE SAVAGE TRUTH ON YOUR RELATIONSHIP WITH MONEY

Money Is Power

Before you make any investment or saving decision, before you set financial goals or choose a career, you must come face to face with the power of money in your life. Your relationship with money must be reevaluated as you reach different stages in life. Only by facing money issues directly can you become comfortable with so many other personal decisions that confront you.

A decade ago it might have been possible to coast along, expecting pay increases and a comfortable lifestyle that would lead to retirement. Now we've all seen a compelling demonstration of the importance of financial security, and the importance of financial planning. This generation will be forever changed by the longest recession since the Great Depression. Today's children will never take money for granted the way their parents might have done. And out of these experiences comes a new respect for the power of money.

Recognizing the power of money can be exhilarating or intimidating. If other people have money, and therefore a degree of power over your life, you may react negatively. If your boss holds the power of the paycheck, you may feel forced to work certain hours or perform unpleasant tasks. If your parents hold the power of the purse, you may feel coerced into making concessions about your lifestyle.

However, if *you* have the money, you are empowered to choose how you spend your time as well as your cash. You may choose to work even harder, to enjoy more leisure, to become philanthropic or artistic, or to devote more time to making your fortune grow. Money certainly isn't the only powerful force in your life, but having money can empower you to take greater control over your lifestyle.

Saver or Spender?

You know who you are, when it comes to your money personality. Are you a *saver* or a *spender*? I'm not quite sure where our money personality is created. It could be from the experiences you had as a child. But, then, how do you explain two children, growing up in the same household, who have completely different money personalities? Give each an allowance, and one hoards every penny while the other can't wait to go to the store!

Whether it's determined by heredity or environment, by this stage of your life your money personality is firmly ingrained. If you realize how hard it is to change yourself, you'll know how impossible it is to change your spouse or partner. So the entire concept of money management is to set up systems to deal with your inner self—your fears, your compulsions, and your desires. If you can channel all that energy into a disciplined plan, you can be successful financially no matter what your basic personality traits.

The Most Powerful Money Emotions Are *Fear* and *Greed*

Decisions about money unleash these two powerful emotions, which are frequently the cause of financial downfall. Noticing the symptoms and gaining the courage to surmount these emotions is the first task in managing money. Lack of emotional control will negate all the benefits of good advice and good planning.

Greed is understandably dangerous because it is the emotion that makes us take risks we cannot afford. Greed convinces us that we "need" instead of simply *want* to make that purchase. Greed urges us to spend for today instead of investing for tomorrow. It can distort investment decisions and blind us to long-term consequences and risks.

Fear can be equally dangerous. Fear keeps us from taking appropriate risks or making changes to improve our lives. It paralyzes us and blinds us to opportunity. Indeed, this paralysis can be an actual physical reaction to making money decisions. It's as difficult to conquer a fear of money as it is to rein in overwhelming greed.

These emotions may be triggered by our childhood conditioning about money, by cultural expectations, or by recent experiences with money decisions. There's no doubt that people have money personalities. By nature or nurture, they become savers or spenders.

Inside each of us is a small persuasive voice that dictates how we respond to fear and greed.

Those twin emotions assault even the wisest investors and smartest traders. Taking control of your financial life requires not only knowledge of money, but also the self-discipline to use your knowledge to conquer fear and greed. What good is a financial plan if you don't have the self-discipline to stick with your decisions?

Self-Discipline Is the Essence of All Decision Making

Self-discipline should not be confused with self-denial. Self-discipline means making knowledgeable decisions based on a rational assessment of likely results and then sticking to your decisions in the face of emotional upheaval. That principle applies to every financial decision—from buying a car or a dress to investing in a stock or mutual fund. People recognize the importance of discipline when they turn to financial advisors for help—not only in determining the appropriate investment, but in sticking to that decision in the face of market reversals. It's human nature to seek advice, reassurance, and counsel about when to alter a decision based on new realities.

Can you do it alone? Most people are capable of managing their own finances, given the knowledge and tools that are now easily available. You'll learn how to use Quicken or Mint to gain control over your everyday spending and to plan for the future.

However, I know that many people who write to me or post questions on my blog at **TerrySavage.com** are overwhelmed by their relationships with money. Just as all the desire in the world cannot help alcoholics or gamblers to overcome their compulsions, all the investment books and rules cannot make the fearful bold, or the greedy self-controlled.

Help is available in many forms. As you'll see in Chapter 3, there are several national, nonprofit consumer credit and spending counseling services. Your local community college may offer classes or help in setting up a budget and managing your money. Later in this chapter I'll show you how to find a qualified and certified personal financial planner. Automatic monthly investment plans can create the structure to override your emotions and build an investment program, just as automatic deductions can be used to cope with debt repayment.

Keep in mind that knowledge is one ingredient of your relationship with money, but conquering your emotions is quite another aspect of financial success. Smart people do fail, but failures can always be overcome. Impulsive and irrational people rarely find financial success.

Bulls, Bears . . . and Chickens—Your Relationship with Money Is Unique

No matter how smart your advisor, or how sophisticated your investments, your personal relationship with money is unique, and it affects the decisions you make. No one else has quite as much insight into your desires, anxieties, and tolerance for risk. The most difficult task is to step back from your emotions and calculate the risk it is appropriate for you to take.

This is a process of self-discovery that I have long referred to as "sorting out the bulls, the bears, and the chickens." In any financial market, the *bulls* invest believing that prices will move higher, while the *bears* sell out in fear that prices will drop. But the *chickens* stay on the sidelines, unwilling or unable to risk their capital. There's a little bit of chicken in all of us, and it's nothing to be embarrassed about. In fact, those who had adequate savings were cushioned from the impact of the recession and job loss.

Sometimes it's wise to be chicken because you have a very short time horizon. If college tuition is due next fall, or if you're saving for a down payment, you don't want to risk investing in the stock market. Short-term losses could jeopardize your important long-term goals. It's important to sort out the portion of your finances that can, and should, be exposed to the opportunities that risk provides. But it also takes discipline to set aside a portion of your assets and keep them safe from risk.

Sometimes you're forced to be a chicken because this is the only money you have. While it's tempting to risk doubling your resources in some exciting investment, you can't afford to lose even a portion of your capital. There's an old saying in the markets: "Desperate money never makes money." The world is littered with losing tickets from racetracks and lotteries. Long-shots and jackpots make news when they pay off because it's so rare. Those huge lottery pools are created by all the people who buy losing tickets.

Risk and reward are two sides of the same coin, but unlike a coin toss, on which the odds are always 50–50, risk and reward are not always equally balanced. The science of money management is understanding your own tolerance for risk and acting when the rewards can objectively be considered to outbalance the risks. Unfortunately, this is not a subject for intuition.

At the top of the market, an investment seems least risky and most enticing. At market bottoms, it appears most risky to invest your cash—but hindsight shows that's just when you should have taken the risk. The big money is made—and lost—at the extremes. But an ongoing and disciplined program can keep you from being wrong at those turning points. And some "chicken money" sitting on the sidelines can give you courage to follow your plan.

Never be chicken out of ignorance. There are objective ways to balance risk and reward. Nobel Prize–winning economists created the concept of *beta,* a way of measuring inherent risk and volatility in individual investments. And computers can theoretically measure and limit portfolio risk, when markets run true to form. But no one has yet developed a way to measure the risk inherent in human emotions. So let's just set aside some "chicken money" and follow the old market saying: "Sell down to the sleeping point." If it keeps you awake at night, it isn't worth the risk.

THE SAVAGE TRUTH ON THE CONSEQUENCES OF CHOICES

Little Choices Have Big Consequences

In the midst of life's turbulence, you're reminded of the consequences of the big choices you made over the years: the choice of a college, a marriage partner, or a career, or a decision about having children. These turning points stand out as defining moments that changed the direction of your life. But small decisions, compounded over time, can have an equally significant impact on how your life turns out—especially when it comes to money.

Your money can work *for* you or *against* you. It all depends on the choices you make. If you make the correct choices, even a small amount of money can grow to become a powerful ally. If you make the wrong choices, your money will leverage its power against your own best interests. One thing to keep in mind: It's never too late to change course for the future.

Every day we're faced with money choices: *Spend or save, buy or sell.* They may appear to be decisions of the moment, but today's choices can have long-lasting consequences. That's because the consequences of our financial decisions are magnified over time.

Think of the problems NASA has in sending a rocket to Mars. Sure, the planet is a huge target. But if the navigation calculations are off by just a fraction of a degree at the launch, the rocket will miss Mars by millions of miles. Small errors, magnified by distance or time, can take you very far off course.

This advice, given a decade ago, reached too few people. By mid-2005, the U.S. savings rate went negative, as people borrowed on their home equity and financed their lifestyles on their credit cards. It's no surprise, then, that the impact of the housing market collapse was so devastating to so many.

Even as we move into the second decade of this century, Americans now have nearly a trillion dollars revolving on their credit card bills, many making only minimum monthly payments. The recession forced millions of consumers into bankruptcy. And, despite a 24 percent decline in the number of credit cards outstanding, there were still 378 million cards being used at year-end 2010. The debt habit—and the burden of carrying debt—are hard to shake.

American families remain burdened with debt taken on during the boom years. They purchased things they wanted or needed *now,* without regard to the long-term consequences of those choices. Then, during the recession, they were forced to incur debt, simply to purchase basic necessities. With no savings, Americans have been digging a deeper hole, despite write-offs of balances in bankruptcy.

My favorite story about choices shows the long-term effect of time on money when it comes to spending decisions. Suppose you charge $2,000 on your credit card this month and make only the required minimum monthly payments on your bill. At an annual finance charge of 19.8 percent and a $40 annual fee,

It will take you 31 years and 2 months to pay off that $2,000!

Along the way, you could pay an additional

$8,202 in finance charges.

If you had made a different decision, the results would have been equally dramatic and far more pleasing. If you had *invested* that same $2,000 in a stock market mutual fund that returned the historical average of 10 percent and placed your investment inside a tax-sheltered individual retirement account (IRA), in 31 years—about when you'd be paying off your final credit card bill—

Your IRA would be worth $38,389.

If you made that same spending-versus-investing decision every year and set aside $2,000 in your IRA for 31 years at the same rate of return,

Your IRA would be worth $364,000.

Special attention to twenty-somethings: If you started your annual $2,000 IRA contribution *now* and averaged a 10 percent annual return, in 50 years

Your IRA would be worth nearly $2.5 million!

This is a classic example of how small choices, leveraged over time, can change your life. You may not remember every small spending or saving decision as you look back over your life. They may not compare with the major life-changing choices you agonize over. But these small decisions reveal one of the greatest money secrets: the power of time in compounding money. Money makes money.

The CARD Act of 2009 offered some protections against many credit card practices, including requiring higher minimum monthly payments. Still, the average rate being charged on outstanding balances is nearly 16 percent, and many consumers who have missed payments or charged over the limits are paying rates over 30 percent.

Despite your skepticism about stock market returns, the average long-term annual rate of return, including dividends, on large-company stocks remains 9.9 percent at year-end 2010, according to Ibbotson, the market historians.

The basic Savage Truth is more valid than ever: *Debt will destroy you.* If you'd invested that money in stocks—over the long run—you would have come out far ahead, despite the scary setbacks in the market. Sadly, too many people learned the lesson about the dangers of debt the hard way. Fortunately, America does not have debtors' prisons. Bankruptcy—a last resort—allows you to start over. But this time, learn the lessons and do things differently to get different results.

Here's an important Savage Truth: *The lessons that cost the most teach the most!*

It's Easier to Find Money than It Is to Find Time

I've often told this story of how you could easily turn a $2,000 IRA into a million dollars or more by investing conservatively in a mutual fund that just matched the performance of the stock market averages. (For details on getting started, jump to Chapter 6.) But some people who come to my seminars are buried in debt, wondering whether to take the bankruptcy route or continue to struggle with bills. Where would they ever find the money to make a monthly investment in the American Dream?

That's the problem with big numbers like "a million dollars." They're so overwhelming. So let's make it more realistic. Just in case you were intimidated about finding that $2,000 a year to set aside in your individual retirement account, let me point out that

$2,000 a year is only $38.46 a week!

Surely, you can adjust your spending—or your earnings—to find an extra $38.46 a week.

If you're already buried in debt, then an extra $38.46 a week will pay down $2,000 of your debt within one year, to say nothing of the interest payments you'll save. Perhaps finding that weekly sum will require working in a restaurant instead of dining out. A weekend or part-time job may bring in more money if you can't possibly cut back your spending. In recent years, even these temporary jobs have been hard to find. But don't give up, because it's always easier to earn more than to cut back.

Do you still think you can't afford to get out of debt and start investing for your future? Take a quick look at your paycheck. For sure, there's a deduction for Social Security taxes that's much larger than your $38.46 weekly target. You get along fine without that money—and you're not likely to see much, if any, of it at retirement. Doesn't it make sense to put an equal amount away every paycheck in a savings and investment plan that will pay off in the future?

A $2,000 debt seems relatively insignificant now, in an era when families routinely find themselves $20,000 in debt, and students graduate from college with an average debt burden of $25,000. But the principle remains the same: Break it down into monthly and then weekly chunks and attack the problem one step at a time.

In Chapter 3, you'll find specific resources for dealing with debt—from counseling you can trust, to bankruptcy procedures, to recognizing and avoiding scams such as debt "negotiation" offers. And even if bankruptcy is your only way out, you'll want to do things differently next time, so read on.

Time Is Money

You may have heard the story about the boy who was asked whether he'd rather have $5 million in 31 days—or 1 penny doubled every day for 31 days (see Figure 1.1). The boy chose wisely.

Day	Dollar Amount
1	$ 0.01
2	$ 0.02
3	$ 0.04
4	$ 0.08
5	$ 0.16
6	$ 0.32
7	$ 0.64
8	$ 1.28
9	$ 2.56
10	$ 5.12
11	$ 10.24
12	$ 20.48
13	$ 40.96
14	$ 81.92
15	$ 163.84
16	$ 327.68
17	$ 655.36
18	$ 1,310.72
19	$ 2,621.44
20	$ 5,242.88
21	$ 10,485.76
22	$ 20,971.52
23	$ 41,943.04
24	$ 83,886.08
25	$ 167,772.16
26	$ 335,544.32
27	$ 671,088.64
28	$ 1,342,177.28
29	$ 2,684,354.56
30	$ 5,368,709.12
31	$10,737,418.24

Figure 1.1   Growth of a Penny Doubled Daily

**One penny, doubled every day for a month,
will grow to $10,737,418.24.**

That's certainly a huge consequence from a small choice. Although this book won't show you how to double your money every day, you will certainly learn how to invest very small amounts regularly to create dramatic long-term growth.

Taxes Impact Tomorrow More than Today

No one likes to see the bite that taxes take out of a paycheck or to compute the amount owed to the government every April. And if you think the overall burden of taxes is rising, it's not your imagination.

In 2000, federal tax receipts were 20.6 percent of the economy (gross domestic product)—the highest since 1944, during World War II. It is projected that government spending as a percent of GDP will rise to 25 percent by 2030. And as our population ages, more of this annual spending becomes nondiscretionary.

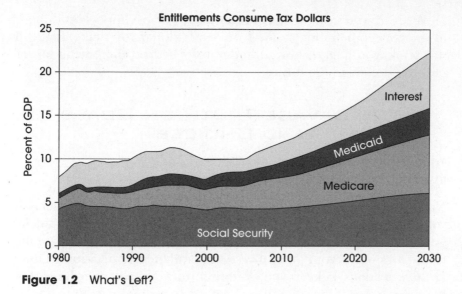

Figure 1.2 What's Left?

Within 20 years, government spending on mandated programs and promises such as Social Security, Medicare, Medicaid—and interest on the national debt—will consume every penny of this 25 percent tax levy on the economy. That will leave nothing for national defense, roads, education, or any of the other programs we'd like government to provide. Figure 1.2 shows this graphically.

We confront some devastating choices as a nation. While income tax *cuts* would help our economy grow out of its problems, the political reality is that Congress is likely to increase taxes in your lifetime. Or they will push the Federal Reserve System to create more money, devaluing the dollars you've saved for retirement.

That turns some standard investment advice on its head! You'll want to plan ahead for the potential impact of inflation on your retirement savings. Since we save and spend in dollars, it will become very important to consider what those dollars will buy in 20 years or more.

When it comes to tax decisions, you'll also have to reconsider your historic plans. Traditionally, the idea was to invest in tax-deferred programs such as an IRA, because you assumed you'd be in a lower tax bracket at retirement when the money is withdrawn.

But if you believe income tax rates will rise in the future, you'd want to pay taxes now, and invest your money for tax-free growth, in a Roth IRA, for example. At the very least, you might want to split some of your retirement savings into before- and after-tax types of plans.

Whether you save pre-tax or after-tax, the most important thing is to *save*. Set some money aside from every dollar you make. Later in this book, you'll learn how to hedge your bets on the buying power of those dollars in the future.

THE SAVAGE TRUTH ON GOALS AND CHOICES

Your Goals Are Your Most Important Choices

Now that you know financial independence is within your reach—if you make the correct choices—it's time to set some personal financial goals. These are your most important choices because they create the framework for all your other investment and lifestyle decisions. These are the beacons to keep you on target; they are the guardrails that keep you from taking emotional wrong turns. Your goals are your most personal financial decision.

Whether your goal is getting rich or having financial security, it's important to define that goal on your own terms. Take a moment to think about your own definition of being secure enough to not worry about money on a daily basis.

For some people, financial security is defined by being out of debt; others total up the amount of their investments to get a perspective on their current and future situation. Some people define financial security as being able to live for six months to a year without a job; others define it as having their money last as long as they do—a secure retirement income.

Some may put a specific dollar figure on their target; others recognize that the possibility of inflation or changing health needs requires a flexible financial cushion. For some, getting rich implies having enough money to do whatever they want—and they have an extravagant list of "wants." Still, most multimillionaires will tell you that money can't buy freedom from problems.

The best—and worst—thing about setting goals is reaching them. That means you have to set new, higher goals. Keep in mind when setting goals that you're posting both a target and a direction. You may reach milestones along the way to your ultimate goal of financial freedom. The day you've paid down all your debt will certainly be an exhilarating one. Now you can travel further down that same road, using the money you set aside to pay bills to start investing. I never heard anyone complain about retiring with too much money! I hope your biggest problem is that you've reached all of your financial goals.

Set No Goal You Can't Control

The key in setting goals is to set targets you can control. If your goal is to set aside a certain amount of money every month to pay extra on bills or to start investing, don't count on a pay raise to make it happen. A raise is up to your boss. But you could reach your goal by spending less on dining out each month. That's a decision under your control.

Since the whole idea of goal setting is to motivate yourself, you'll need some financial targets that you can reach in a far shorter period of time than it will take to hit more distant targets such as retirement. Start by listing your short- and long-term financial goals.

Your short-term goals might include paying off all your credit card bills or student loans. You might set a goal of saving enough money for a car or a down payment on a first home. Short-term goals might take anywhere from six months to five years.

At the same time, you should also be setting longer-term goals such as college for your children or retirement savings. Those numbers may seem larger, and more intimidating—but you have the advantage of time on your side if you start working toward those long-term goals now.

Tape your list of goals to your mirror, where you'll notice it every morning and evening. Your goals should be motivating, not intimidating. Be realistic about your expectations, and set goals in manageable increments. Your short-term goal of paying off your credit cards might start with paying off the highest-rate card, or the largest balance, first. Then move on to the next objective.

Remember: No matter what the time horizon or size of your financial goals, you'll never reach them if you don't get started. The first two letters of the word *goal* are "go."

A Goal without a Plan Is Just a Dream

Only in fairy tales do castles get built without a plan. In real life, you have to hire an architect to create a drawing and then engage the services of a builder to help you achieve your dream home. Then you have to have a reasonable financial plan to make your mortgage payments, consider rising property taxes, and have savings to pay for repairs. And as millions of Americans have now learned, you can't plan for rising home prices to automatically take care of these needs.

A financial plan is not engraved in stone; it can always be adjusted to fit your circumstances. But having a plan is the only way to put the odds of achievement on your side.

Life doesn't come with guarantees. When you define financial security for yourself, you'll need to make some assumptions. How long will you live? How much money will you need to maintain your lifestyle? How much will your investments grow? How much will inflation erode your savings?

Those projections will change as you redefine financial security and as the economy changes. You may have lifetime goals but be forced to revise your plan because of current events. Always keep your actions on track to meet your goals.

In Chapter 3, you'll find links to programs that can help you plan for the impact of inflation, or changing tax rates or investment returns, to help you decide how much you should be saving now.

Your financial plan is a framework that needs to be adjusted— but not entirely replaced—as circumstances change. If you are self-disciplined and willing to invest the time to stay current, you can certainly do this yourself. But you are likely to decide that you need professional help, if only to mitigate the emotion that can overwhelm you in both bull and bear markets, in good economic times and bad.

Finding the Right Planner Is the Most Important Part of Your Plan

Financial planning is an art as well as a science. When hiring a financial planner, it's important to discuss the scope of the plan and have mutually agreeable expectations about the outcome.

Before you start your search, you need to consider what type of advice you need. Do you only want investment advice for your IRA rollover? Or do you need a more complete projection of whether you're on track to reach your goals, be it the first home, or college for your children, or retirement? Have you considered the impact of estate and life insurance planning?

It will be important to find an advisor to cover all your questions, although you may continue to work with your own lawyer and accountant. But if you're just getting started, don't think you have to wait until you accumulate a huge pile of assets to need a planner. In fact, setting up an annual consultation with a planner can help you accumulate those assets and avoid making mistakes at the beginning that could derail your future.

Financial planning is important for *everyone*—young or old, rich or poor. The most basic spending and saving plan doesn't have to cost you a thing. In Chapter 3, you'll see how to reach the nearest office of the National Foundation for Consumer Credit. They'll work with you to create a spending/saving plan (okay, a budget!) and it won't cost you anything.

But if you have goals, or want to set goals, you'll be better off working with a *certified financial planner*. Don't be led astray by salespeople who call themselves "planners." Here's how to find the real thing:

- There are several good sources of referrals to financial planners. The Certified Financial Planner Board of Standards created the registered mark *CFP*. It designates licensed planners who have taken a rigorous examination covering not only the financial planning process, but also insurance, investments, tax planning, retirement planning, employee benefits, and estate planning. The board also investigates candidate backgrounds and requires adherence to a code of ethics. To search for certified financial planners near you, go to **www.cfp.net**.

- Some planners work only for a fee and do not accept commissions on the investment and insurance products they recommend. Fee-only planners belong to the National Association of Personal Financial Advisors (NAPFA). Check in at **www.napfa.org** or **www.feeonly.org** for a list of fee-only planners in your state.

- Many banks, insurance companies, and mutual fund companies also employ certified financial planners to offer advice, either on investments only, or on a wider range of topics. Look for the CFP designation, because these planners are held to a higher standard of responsibility. They must disclose any conflicts of interest, and they are required to put their clients' interests ahead of their own. Stockbrokers, financial consultants, and others who may sell financial services are not bound by these fiduciary obligations, although that type of regulation is being considered.

- It's important to know how your financial advisor is compensated, and it is imperative that you ask whether she or he is bound by the CFP fiduciary standard. Many brokers or salespeople have a high degree of integrity and set their own high standards in their relationships with clients. But you should be aware of the differences between the two categories.

■ To check on a *broker*'s disciplinary history, go to **FINRA.org** and click on the "Broker Check" tool. To check on disciplinary history of an *investment advisor*, go to **AdviserInfo.sec.gov**. Go to **CFP.net/search** to check out *financial planners*.

The Outcome of Your Plan Is Only as Good as Your Input

Just as you'd choose an architect for your dream home based on references and examples of his or her building style, you'll have to do some interviewing and investigating before you settle on a financial planner. References, preferably from someone you know and trust, are a must. And you'll have to determine if you feel comfortable after an initial meeting or two. Don't be afraid to ask questions about the planner's fees and style. Equally important are the questions the planner should be asking of you. He or she should be willing to listen to your hopes and fears and to your short- and long-term goals.

Just as you accept responsibility for determining your own goals and seek help in reaching them, you must accept ultimate responsibility for the financial plan you mutually agree upon. A special note to couples: It's unlikely that you have exactly the same money styles or personalities, but it's important that both of you feel comfortable with the plan and the planner you choose.

No matter how much each member of the family contributes financially, this plan will affect your current and future lifestyle equally. Just as an architect might meld styles to suit the eclectic tastes of clients, the planner must create a product that encompasses the personal traits of the individuals. If you don't speak up during the initial meetings, the planner will not have the information to build upon.

Plans Change

Whatever dollar amount you put on financial security, your goals will inevitably change as your personal circumstances change. Flexibility in planning is not to be confused with an emotional reaction to changing life events. A plan exists to provide context for change, yet nothing changes circumstances like a change in the economy. That's why you need to understand some basic truths about the economy and politics—and how they affect your financial plans.

THE SAVAGE TRUTH: NO PLAN IS AN ISLAND

No man's fortune is safe while Congress is in session.

—Mark Twain

No one has said it better than this eminent observer of our society and its politics. Although the words were written generations ago, they ring true in our economy even today.

All the goals you set and the plans you make are affected by the general state of the economy. And that is determined by two separate sources of economic power. The legislative and executive branches have the power to tax and spend, while the independent Federal Reserve System governs banks and sets monetary policy by controlling the supply of credit and its price (interest rates). That's why it's so important to keep an eye on Washington and how actions there are affecting your future wealth.

As a result of the global financial crisis in 2008, both the Fed and the government have assumed new, greater economic powers justified by the need to "resecure" our financial system. The government "bought" one of America's largest companies—General Motors—as part of its rescue plan. Then the government "sold" part of its holdings, when the company became profitable again, retaining a large interest. Had I written of this possibility 10 years ago, you would been astounded, but now we take government intrusion into the financial markets as a "necessity."

The Federal Reserve System became more intimately involved in the economy than its historic role of dual responsibilities of keeping inflation low and employment high. During the financial crisis of 2008, the Fed expanded its mission beyond buying only Treasury securities. The Fed bought many "assets"—including mortgages guaranteed by Fannie Mae and Freddie Mac, and commercial paper from money market funds—in its effort to keep the U.S. financial system from collapse. As for Congress, after helping to create the housing bubble by requiring Fannie Mae and Freddie Mac to buy lower-quality mortgages to provide home ownership to those who could least afford it, Congress went on to "reform" the financial system. In one of the great ironies of American history, the financial reform bill—Dodd/Frank—was named after two members of Congress who did the most to facilitate the disaster in the first place!

The past few years have given you even more reason to keep an eye on the politics of Washington, if you're trying to plan for your own future! While you don't have to be an economic forecaster, you should understand the basic forces that will impact your investments and retirement plans.

Sound Money Is the Key to Creating Wealth

The Federal Reserve has the power to create more money and put it into circulation. It's a little more complicated than running the printing presses, but easily understandable if you've ever played Monopoly. Suppose the game is moving slowly, so the banker decides to change the rules and give everyone an extra $500. Whenever someone lands on a property like Boardwalk or Ventnor Avenue, an auction is held and the highest bidder gets the property.

Suddenly, with more money in the game, property prices rise as extra cash goes into purchases. The value of the old money you saved—just in case you landed on Park Place—declines. With more money in circulation, your savings have less buying power. Prices go up, even though the illusion of wealth had been created only because the banker distributed more money.

That's the phenomenon of *inflation*: money creation pushing prices higher. Thirty years ago, the United States had a taste of how inflation can destroy a country. Given the amount of money the Fed has created in the wake of the financial crisis of 2008, we may get another close-up look at what happens when too much money or credit is created. We should learn from past experience.

Inflation was rampant in the early 1980s, rising to double digits and causing people to trade their cash for real assets that would hold their value. Everything from soybeans to houses to gold coins increased in value as more dollars purchased fewer goods. People were fearful that money held for the future would continue to lose value.

It took a decade of total discipline, along with a deep recession and high interest rates, to regain people's faith in the future value of their money. Under Fed Chairman Paul Volcker, people came to trust the future value of the dollar. Proof of that was the fact that savers demanded less interest on the money they loaned to the government and to corporations—believing that the money would still be worth nearly its current value when their loans were repaid.

Truly, a belief in the future value of the currency is the key ingredient in real economic growth. Even a small amount of inflation can have devastating long-term consequences, as seen in Table 1.1.

If you think you need $100,000 today to maintain your lifestyle, take a look at the long-term impact of even a relatively small amount of annual inflation—3 percent. In 10 years, you'd need nearly $135,000 to match today's spending power. In 20 years, the number jumps to over $180,000. That's why you must make plans that include the impact of inflation on your retirement, on your life insurance benefits, and on the cost of anything you will need to purchase in the future.

A belief in the future value of the currency is still a key ingredient in real growth. But after several years of concern about the long-lasting recession, and jobless recovery, the Fed started to act like that banker in the Monopoly game—throwing more money on the table in an effort to get things moving. They called it *stimulus* or *TARP* or *quantitative easing*—all terms for creating money and credit out of thin air. The Fed simply buys government securities or other assets, and pays for them with newly created credit on the books of the banks.

As of this writing the jury is still out on whether this latest round of money creation will keep the economy from falling deeper into

Table 1.1   Effects of Inflation

**How Inflation Impacts $100,000 Over Time
(Amount required to equal today's
spending power)**

Years	Inflation Rate	
	3%	5%
1	103,000	105,000
2	106,090	110,250
3	109,273	115,763
4	112,550	121,551
5	115,927	127,628
6	119,405	134,010
7	122,987	140,710
8	126,677	147,746
9	130,477	155,133
10	134,392	162,889
15	155,797	207,893
20	180,611	265,330
25	209,378	338,635
30	242,726	432,194

recession or stimulate recovery. Ultimately, there is little doubt that down the road the value of the dollar will fall, as it looks more and more like "Monopoly money." That is the very definition of inflation, which can devastate all your financial planning.

The Inflation–Deflation Debate

For a generation, Americans worried about inflation, the declining purchasing power of their dollars. Then, the growing spread of global *deflation* created new concerns. Deflation is reflected in falling prices for assets, typically as buyers are fearful of spending money. But deflation is not always a negative force.

Sometimes deflation is caused by innovation, as when technology led the way to change. The economy reaped the benefits of ever-lower prices for chips and other computer components. As prices fall, new inventions are easier for everyone to afford. And those new technologies create new and better jobs for those who are prepared to take advantage of them. That was Henry Ford's philosophy when he started manufacturing automobiles on his assembly lines, and as a general principle it holds true today.

However, deflation can also be a dangerous negative force in the economy. Deflation is a tremendous burden to those who must repay debt. While inflation makes debt easier to repay in cheaper dollars, deflation makes dollars more valuable and harder to come by. As an economy slows and workers are laid off, people find it harder to repay their mortgages and their credit card debt. That leads to bankruptcies and write-offs. Money literally "disappears" down the black hole of lower asset values and loan write-offs.

Perhaps the most negative aspect of the deflationary process is falling prices on those assets, such as homes being sold after foreclosure. Everyone figures prices will continue to fall, so they wait to buy—leading to a downward spiral in prices, and in attitudes. Fear rules as people worry about losing jobs, so they stop buying in spite of lower prices. Deflation is a dangerous downward spiral, and the Federal Reserve is quite aware of that fact.

So if you picture the economy as a giant see-saw in a child's playground, you can see the effort it takes to balance out the forces of inflation and deflation. That's the job of the Fed, using its monetary tools of credit creation. And it's also the job of the government, using its fiscal tools: government spending and taxation policies.

Adding to the problem is the fact that these tools work with a lag. Injecting new credit into the economy may take a while before it creates growth And if the deflationary fears are too great, the money may sit on the books of the banks and corporations because they're too worried to lend or invest for future growth that might not come.

Then add politics! Politicians on both sides of the aisle are afraid to offend their constituents by cutting spending or raising taxes. Compromise is hard to reach—and when it comes it often makes for the worst kind of irrational legislation. And, in that context, you have to make some important financial plans for your future!

It's a Small World, After All

Walt Disney may have created that refrain to demonstrate how interconnected we are with the rest of the world, but the past decades gave an economic demonstration of its truth. When you're making financial plans and investment decisions, you must look beyond America's borders.

Technology has created a globally interdependent financial system. With the click of a computer key, vast amounts of money can rush into a country to purchase its stocks or to invest in its real estate or industry. Similarly, money can be transferred out easily when prices move too high for economic reality.

Overvalued currencies in mismanaged economies are sold by investors and speculators who transfer their assets to a currency that will preserve its value. Loans are defaulted, and banks fail. Interest rates are raised to lure speculators to hold on to the weakening currency. One positive side effect emerges when a country devalues its currency: Its exports appear cheaper to the rest of the world.

For many years, the dollar's strong buying power meant lower-cost imports for Americans, keeping a lid on domestic price inflation. But those cheap imports provided competition for domestic manufacturers of the same goods. As business slowed, domestic manufacturers were forced to lay off workers. The jobs went overseas, destroying much of our traditional industry.

Fear of global competition raises the issue of restrictions on imports—something that hurts both U.S. consumers and foreign producers. A decline in world trade because of protective tariffs has the potential to create a global depression. The financial crisis of recent years has been a very frightening demonstration of how small and interrelated the global financial system has become.

The Danger of America's Debt

The ongoing financial crisis that was ignited in 2008 has created a new Savage Truth: *You have to think beyond the dollar.*

That's because the United States is so much in debt, and because so much of that debt is held by foreign central banks. China and Japan each hold nearly a trillion dollars of our IOUs. How did that happen? Well, actually, you helped the process along every time you went shopping.

Those low-cost imports, so much in demand by U.S. consumers, eventually caused a great economic imbalance. We buy "stuff" from China and send them dollars to pay for our purchases. Chinese exports to the United States rose from $100 billion in 2000 to $365 billion in 2010, while their imports from the United States rose only from $16 billion to $92 billion.

Chinese companies deposited those dollars in their bank, in exchange for the local currency, which they used to pay their workers. Then the Chinese central bank used the dollars it held to buy U.S. government securities: Treasury bills, notes, and bonds. In effect, China has been financing the U.S. budget deficit.

By the end of 2010, it was estimated that the Chinese central bank held more than $850 billion of U.S. government debt, slightly more than Japan's holdings. The two countries hold more than 44 percent of our foreign-owned debt.

In effect, the Chinese, Japanese, and other foreign central banks that hold dollar debt have become a potentially powerful force in the U.S. economy. They could demand higher interest rates if they saw that the Fed was creating too much new money—*inflation*. And higher interest rates could devastate the U.S. economy.

The United States has become the world's largest debtor. Since the U.S. dollar is the world's "reserve currency," the entire world is watching. Many countries have their own debt problems. The U.S. economy is still the largest in the world, but China is now running second. Europe, which united to compete with both economic superpowers, is now in the midst of its own financial crisis. Even as the United States copes with its growing budget deficits, several European countries are being forced into austerity, much to the anger of their citizenry.

Those who do not learn from history are destined to repeat it.
—*George Santayana*

We are often so caught up in our current economic circumstances that we forget to take a step back and gain perspective. Unfortunately, history never repeats itself in exactly the same way. We know from nature that there are regular cycles. Spring inevitably follows winter—no matter how long winter drags on. Many historians and market technicians perceive long- and short-term cycles in the economy and the stock market, which serve as a guide to the future.

Others refuse to acknowledge any patterns of repetition. Over the centuries, there have been many claims to a "new era"—whether it was discovering the riches of the New World, the promise of the Industrial Revolution, or the potential of technology. Indeed, these discoveries changed the direction of the future. But were they a "new paradigm" or just part of the continuing upward spiral of human progress? And can economic progress overcome human nature?

Those are the challenges faced by optimists who believe in the future, who believe that intelligent planning can build on lessons from the past, instead of repeating past disasters.

Paradigms Change, but People Don't

There's no question that scientific knowledge and technological developments have the power to create and redistribute both power and wealth. But one factor that remains constant over history is human nature.

Those two basic forces—fear and greed—always rise to the surface when it comes to making money decisions. How else to explain the extremes to which markets always swing? When human nature gets involved in the decision-making process, all the rules of behavior are set aside along with all of the facts and statistics that determine where markets "should" go.

Market technicians use charts that smooth out the variations in behavior caused by emotional extremes. Historic averages blend in the highs and lows of price and emotion. But when you are living through one of those extreme periods, it is difficult to resist joining the crowd in either buying or selling at exactly the wrong time. After all, it's only human nature!

So that is your challenge today—to develop perspective both historical and global to withstand human nature and make sensible plans for your future. One thing is sure: The future will come. Will you be ready?

TERRY'S TO-DO LIST

1. Examine your attitudes toward money: power, fear, and greed.

2. Set three realistic financial goals—some short-term and some longer-term targets.

3. Think about whom you should consult for good financial advice—a financial planner, broker, banker, accountant, lawyer, rich uncle—and start asking for advice. Then consider that advice carefully in terms of your own financial personality and goals.

4. Pay attention to what's going on in the economy, politics, and the financial markets. All will affect your best-laid plans!

CHAPTER 2

THE SAVAGE TRUTH ON MONEY MANAGEMENT

Knowledge Is Power

Money management has become an even more compelling personal responsibility in the wake of the Great Recession. You may have less money, but more choices. Should you still contribute to your retirement plan? Can you refinance at lower rates if your home value has fallen? What's the best way to deal with student loans? Is bankruptcy your only way out? These decisions are painful and demanding.

No matter what your financial condition, you're faced with a multitude of choices and products. You may still receive at least three or four credit card solicitations in the mail every week. Banks now compete for your business by offering a variety of products and services, not all of them under FDIC insurance protection. Brokers offer more than traditional stocks and bonds. Exchange-traded funds compete with traditional mutual funds. Insurance agents sell annuities—and you'll find annuities offered under the roof of your bank, as well. Your employer probably now "defaults" you into investing in the company retirement savings plan. But you must then choose the investments you want to make *within* the plan.

Think of all the money decisions you must make every day. Technology promised to make life simpler and more efficient. And technology has made financial advice easy to find. The problem is sorting through all this information and getting some basic guidance in making choices. A huge financial services industry has grown up in the past decade to influence your decisions and sell you products and services. Still, *you* must make the ultimate decisions about whom to trust and where to allocate your money.

As we move into the second decade of this century, there's a call for "financial literacy"—a sense that the recent huge debt bubble and subsequent collapse would not have occurred if only consumers had been more educated. There are new regulations and even a new federal watchdog agency designed to protect consumers—an acknowledgment that existing agencies such as the Securities and Exchange Commission (SEC) and Federal Trade Commission (FTC), not to mention banking authorities and state regulators, all fell down on the job.

Certainly, financial education is important. But so is a dose of skepticism and a willingness to consider potential consequences, as well as tempting rewards. Even consumers who considered themselves financially astute fell prey to the slick salesmen selling home equity loans and adjustable-rate mortgages. The "common wisdom" that you could leverage your way to prosperity through debt brought down many who should have known better. They had access to the most sophisticated technology but were led astray by emotion.

The Truths are the Truths and always will remain so. But new technologies give you more power over your personal finances if you choose to use them wisely. In this chapter, you'll learn about some of those tools, which now revolve around not only your personal computer, but your handheld mobile devices as well. They give you new ability to access information and make transactions instantaneously, from almost any location.

In the first edition of this book, I was leading you by the hand to the programs available on your computer. Today, your hands are leading *you* to online knowledge and resources that are typically either free or very inexpensive. We've moved past many concerns about information safety, to a new world of sharing and communicating though social networking.

It's up to you to pick and choose how to put technology to work on your behalf. But you can't hide from these opportunities or be intimidated by them. It's not a generational issue; many seniors take advantage of learning programs at community colleges and computer stores, and are active participants in the use of financial technology. Yes, you can live with pencil, paper, and file folders—just as the Amish live with horse and buggy. It's quaint, and probably effective. But few would deny that it's a lot easier to use the modern conveniences brought on by technology.

Take a deep breath if you're new to this subject. But if this chapter is already well-known to you because you grew up in this new era, then use your proficiency to help your parents or grandparents make their financial lives more efficient. What a great gift you can give. And at the same time, their experiences with money might prove helpful, if you can bring yourself to listen.

THE SAVAGE TRUTH ON USING TECHNOLOGY TO CONTROL YOUR MONEY

Technology Is the Tool, Not the Answer

Opening your mind to technology is a key ingredient in your quest for financial independence. By now you know you can find mutual funds, low-cost life and car insurance, best deals on credit cards and mortgages, and instantaneous stock market analysis with a click of your mouse. But if that were all it took to be financially successful, we wouldn't have seen fortunes lost in stocks, real estate, and consumer debt. The Internet is just the first step to financial planning and security.

You can use your new knowledge and information to converse intelligently with your financial planner, stockbroker, insurance agent, or accountant. A good advisor is always worth the fees you pay for advice, reassurance, and a balance to your own instincts. But you'll find it's much more empowering to act from the strength of knowledge, rather than merely following instructions blindly.

Here's something to keep in mind: Computers are the tool, not the answer. Technology may change our lives in untold ways, but human nature stays the same. We will always confront those two basic emotions when dealing with money: fear and greed. Our ability to make rational decisions based on knowledge, not emotion, will ultimately determine our financial success. Being knowledgeable requires having information, and a link to the Internet is today's best tool for gaining information. But that still leaves you with the job of figuring out which information you can trust, and which advice is appropriate for your situation.

The Savage Truth: *Technology is empowering—but only you have the final control over your money.*

Throughout this book, I'll mention various websites where you can get financial information, services, and tools. If you get lost, just come home to **www.TerrySavage.com** and you'll be directed to my latest columns and links. At my website, you can click on my blog to post your personal finance questions and receive a prompt online response.

Online Money Management

A decade ago, people were intimidated by things we now take for granted—online bill payment, money management software, online tax preparation, and programs that aggregate personal financial information from different sites. Now those tools are the basis for successful money management.

The starting point is a program that sits securely password-protected on your desktop or laptop computer—the popular Quicken money management software. Instead of buying it in a box, you can simply download it from **Quicken.com** onto your personal computer, paying with a credit card. This program will reach out to all your financial providers and securely download the latest information, such as your credit card purchases, account balances, and investment portfolio prices. The drawback is that you have to be sitting in front of that particular computer to access and manage the information.

Once you have Quicken on your computer, its easy for even "non-techies" to set up the automatic connection to your banks and card issuers. When you update those accounts with one click of your mouse, the latest transactions are downloaded and categorized. You'll easily be able to see how much you spent in a certain category—perhaps dining out or entertainment. And you can see how much you paid to anyone, making it easy to track medical bills, for example.

Quicken's Deluxe program costs just $59.99, and Quicken Premier costs slightly more, but adds features to track your investments. If you're new to online money management and concerned about maintaining control over your data, this is an excellent place to start. It integrates with QuickBooks for small businesses and with the popular TurboTax software.

But even as Quicken remains the leading software provider, it recognized the importance of mobile online money management by purchasing one of the most successful companies in the field—**Mint .com**. The resources of Quicken have enhanced Mint.com, and vice versa. You can give this program a test run at Mint.com. Amazingly, it's *free*.

Once you sign up for Mint.com, you can access all your financial information from multiple providers on *any* computer or on your mobile device. You're not limited to the one computer where you maintain your Quicken files.

No matter where you are, you can check your bank account or credit card balances so you don't end up paying for an overdraft. Your transactions are downloaded and categorized every day, so you can graphically see where your money has been going. Mint even has a "Get out of Debt" goal feature, which helps you prioritize and pay down credit card balances and student loan debt.

More important, you can set financial goals and budget in real time using Mint. If you're about to exceed planned spending in a certain category, such as clothing or entertainment, you'll receive a reminder. And Mint will reach out to you with e-mails or text messages warning that limits are near or regular bills are due to be paid. The company says it sends out 20 million e-mails every month, ranging from monthly summaries to bill payment reminders to suggestions for improvements. You can't move money with Mint—at least not yet. But you can find out everything about your money, instantaneously.

When you join Mint.com, you become part of a community of nearly five million users, able to compare your spending style against others in similar stages of life and similar income brackets. It's all done with complete security, but you can learn from others or from their advisors.

How can all this value come to you for no charge? Mint.com is constantly offering you ideas for products and services that can improve your financial situation. For instance, it could suggest a lower-rate credit card, or savings on auto insurance or life insurance, or higher rates on CDs. Their algorithm uses all the information from your spending downloads to offer suggestions to improve your financial life. The financial services companies that participate support the site.

You can also find helpful tools at your bank's online bill payment website. Banks want to keep their customers at their own sites, so they're enhancing their online bill payment services to include money management. A recent survey by Intuit found that more than one-third of bank customers are now managing their finances using online solutions provided by their financial institution.

As if all these options to control your money weren't enough, there are a growing number of new "apps" (applications) for the iPhone and other smart-phone users that give you "anytime, anywhere" access to your finances and help you better manage your money on the go. They can be downloaded free, or very inexpensively. For example, Loan Shark ($5) helps you decipher and compare the real cost and repayment terms of various types of loans. And for $9, Portfolio RT gives you instant access to stock quotes. There are a quarter-million apps, many related to personal finances, enabling you to track your finances, invest, and even send money via PayPal to the contacts in your iPhone.

The point is not to be overwhelmed by financial technology. Take it one step at a time, and you'll find it can be easy and inexpensive. Start by paying your bills securely from your bank's website.

Online Bill Payment: The Starting Point

Online bill payment is the starting point for using technology to control your finances. In the decade since the first edition of this book, which served as an introduction to online bill payment, the Federal Reserve has closed many of its check processing centers. The U.S. Treasury requires that anyone applying for benefits on or after May 1, 2011, must receive their payments electronically, while anyone currently receiving paper checks will need to switch to direct deposit by March 1, 2013. And the U.S. Postal Service is lamenting the decline of first-class mail and closing post offices. Think of all the trees that have been saved by the advent of electronic bill payment! If you haven't started paying your bills at your bank's website, there will never be a better time.

When you start banking online, you no longer have the burdensome chore of writing and mailing checks or paying for postage stamps. Almost every bank website offers an easy signup for secure online bill payment. With a click of your computer mouse, you can pay every bill.

Most bills are paid by electronic transfers from your checking account to major billers such as credit card issuers, utilities, auto loan payments, and retailers. For some payments (think paying your brother the money you borrowed), the bank prints paper checks and sends them to your designated recipients by mail.

If you have your paycheck direct-deposited to your checking account, you'll always have the money to pay regularly scheduled bills. You can easily set up automatic bill payments for recurring regular amounts like your car loan or mortgage payment. Within a few years, it will be common for bills to be presented to you online instead of arriving in the mail.

In fact, there is one company that will already provide that service for you. You can have all your bills sent to the mailing address of **Paytrust.com**. They'll scan those bills into a secure Internet mailbox or accept electronic bills. You can go online at any time to view the actual bill, and click to pay it. And you can pay those bills from different banks and different bank accounts. You can even schedule regular monthly payments, such as a mortgage or rent, to be paid automatically.

The cost is $12.95 per month, which includes 25 transactions per month, with additional payments at $0.65 each. This is a perfect service for long-distance caregivers who want to manage accounts for an elderly parent, or for those who travel or spend winter months in a warmer climate. You can simply redirect the mailed bills to Paytrust, and then pay them remotely, online.

Once you've started paying your bills online, you can easily download all that information into your Quicken desktop program if you want to use the data. Or you can pay your bills from your Quicken software via a direct online link to your bank. Quicken will create a check register and reconcile cleared checks and keep you in balance. You can even print that check register if you still want to keep paper files. Otherwise, you'll just do an automatic backup to a separate disc in your computer. It's all very safe and amazingly easy to get started.

If you have that information downloaded to Quicken, or have signed up to the financial planning tools offered on the bank's website, you can track, organize, sort, and use the information to help you reach your own personal goals, whether debt repayment, saving for future events, or managing your investments. You can access the latest information from your bank at any hour of the day or night. You see everything on a real-time basis. No more wondering when the check clears; a click of your mouse will let you instantly see where you stand. ATM withdrawals show up immediately as debits to your account, making it easier to see where your money is going—before you go overboard.

Total Knowledge Yields Total Control

Online banking is just the first step toward getting control of your finances. All of this information is secure and private, and you can update it as often as you wish. These days, almost every financial services company will allow you to link in and download your information once you provide a secure PIN to gain access.

When you download your credit card information or view it securely online, you'll never be surprised by the balance on your bill at the end of the month. If you've set up your stocks and mutual funds in the portfolio section of your program, you'll know about your gains and losses as soon as you download daily market information. Your money management program can manipulate all of your spending, saving, and investing information to help you manage future financial decisions. And it can be used in conjunction with a financial planner or other financial advice websites.

At **www.Simplifi.net** you can set up your own free financial plan, complete with an interactive spending plan. This website is an independent, SEC-registered investment advisor, so you get unbaised advice on everything from budgeting to investing. Like Mint.com, they keep their services free by partnering with providers and getting paid only if you choose to use some of those services.

Simplifi.net is not an alternative to getting help in overall financial planning, but it can help you prepare for a meeting with your planner. After all, you don't want to waste your advisor's expensive time figuring out what you've been spending and why you aren't saving enough. Like Quicken, it is designed to help you understand your cash flow.

And you know that old Savage Truth: *Cash flows easiest down the drain!*

Knowledge gives you the power to redirect your money before it disappears. And, that same detailed knowledge of your spending and saving can help you take advantage of tax-planning opportunities.

A Taxing Opportunity Exists

One of the best money-saving opportunities created by managing your finances on your computer occurs when it comes to taxes. All of your checking, savings, and investing information can be downloaded immediately into popular tax preparation software programs such as TurboTax, TaxCut, or TaxSaver. You can even file your return online and get your refund that much quicker. TurboTax even has an iPhone app.

There's also a tax advantage to using these programs throughout the year. They allow you to predict the tax implications of selling a stock at a profit or loss. You'll never pay a penalty for underwithholding when you use the program to help make quarterly tax estimates. Since the online connection picks up the latest tax law changes, it's like having an accountant at your side, prompting you to take deductions and plan ahead.

You may never give up your longtime accountant, but he or she probably uses the professional version of TurboTax to process your returns. You can save on accountants' fees by handing over your annual financial package on one disk instead of a file folder or shoebox full of paper receipts. Or become even more tech-savvy and do your return online, giving access to your accountant to make changes. Now your accountant can spend more time advising and less time processing your return.

The Challenge: Getting Started

If you are already using technology, it's a short leap to becoming empowered by it. Don't assume that access to information is a substitute for action. And if you're still intimidated by technology, ask for help. Each of the websites I've mentioned offers help, both online and by a toll-free number, to guide you through the process. You'll look back and be amazed at how easy it was to get started—and how much more empowered you've become.

The true advantage of using a computer to compile, track, and update all aspects of your current financial life is that you can create scenarios for your financial future. Are you saving enough for retirement? Do you know how much you'll have to save to send your child to college? Can you reach both goals at your current pace? Information that's already in your plan from the savings and investing section will be transferred automatically to the planning section of your program. You'll be able to see how a slight change in amounts, timing, taxes, or rates of return can affect your future.

Are you ready to take control of your finances? It's not just a matter of having the tools or getting organized. This is a mental challenge and it requires you to stay on top of your finances on a regular basis. Knowing where you stand with all of your personal finances, being able to organize that knowledge, and being able to access the latest information to make decisions are key parts of the Savage Truth—the parts that set you free.

If you're ready, it's time to get started—or start over!

TERRY'S TO-DO LIST

1. Purchase the latest version of Quicken financial planning programs. (The cost should be about $60, either online for a direct download or at an office supply store.)

2. Contact your bank to set up online banking. They'll explain how to download your check payments into your Quicken software.

3. Go through your banking information for the past few months and assign each purchase a budget category. (You can use the categories supplied by Quicken, or create your own.)

4. Consider mobile applications like Mint.com to put your money info at your fingertips.

5. Ask your accountant how you can be more efficient in preserving and presenting tax records, perhaps by using TurboTax, as well as Quicken.

CHAPTER 3

THE SAVAGE TRUTH ON SPENDING AND DEBT

You *Can* Control Your Cash Flow

Getting control over spending is the first step toward wealth and financial independence. For many people it is a larger hurdle than the second half of the formula: making money. Indeed, some people earn far more than others even dream of, but they still spend their lives in financial bondage. Creating financial independence starts with exerting control over your own cash flow.

If only more people had taken heed when I first wrote these Truths, I'm quite sure the bankruptcy rate would be much lower. The following section is mostly unchanged from the original edition. My advice still stands. The Great Recession has made it more important for you to understand these Savage Truths, whether you're digging out from under or just starting on the journey to financial independence.

THE SAVAGE TRUTH ON SPENDING

We Can All Spend as Much Money as We Make

Did you ever think that if you earned as much money as you're making today, you'd be in great financial shape? Somehow our list of wants and needs always seems to grow faster than our paycheck. That's just human nature. There's always a way to spend the money we make, and rarely any left over at the end of the month. And if you don't currently have enough money to pay for your purchases, it's all too easy to create money by simply charging them.

Where does all that money go, and how can you reorganize your finances to make sure you reach your goals? If you're just starting out in your working life, the opportunity to set goals and make a plan is exciting. If you're one of the millions of Americans who are buried in debt, it's tough to contemplate your present situation, yet it must be done if you want to move forward. And if you're starting over, it's important to do things differently this time around.

The first step is the hardest because it requires making the commitment to take charge of your financial life, instead of being carried along by circumstances. It's also the easiest because the first step is simply figuring out where you are right now. Start by creating your own personal balance sheet—and don't be surprised if it doesn't balance!

Money Flows Easiest Down the Drain

Take a sheet of paper and draw a line down the middle. (Or use your online money management program for this task.) At the top of the left column write the words *I Own,* and at the top of the right column write the words *I Owe.* Then list the items in each category.

For instance, many people would immediately list their largest asset—a home or condo—in the left column. In the right column, under "I Owe," you'll list the amount of your mortgage balance. This is your personal balance sheet, even if it doesn't exactly balance.

Not everything you've purchased over the years counts equally as an asset. On the "I Own" side of the page you may list your car, furniture, clothing, jewelry, retirement plan, savings bonds, or anything else you've been spending money on over the years.

You'll notice that some assets maintain their value over the years, or even increase in value. *Except for very unusual economic circumstances, you can probably sell your home for more than the purchase price.* Similarly, your retirement plan investments should increase in value over the long run.

(*Note:* Since I wrote that sentence in the previous paragraph a decade ago, we've lived through the "very unusual circumstances" that saw home prices decline as much as 30 percent in some areas. But, unless you could not make the mortgage payments or were forced to sell by other circumstances, the drop in value could be managed until the eventual rebound. And there will be a rebound!)

Now look at the other things you own. Your car may lose value each year, yet it contributes to your wealth because you use it to drive to work and earn money. But your old furniture and clothing lose value quickly. Just check the Sunday want ads to see what a used dining room set or "wedding dress, size 8, worn once" will fetch if you try to sell those items! However, you might justify the cost of the business suit you buy to impress a prospective employer.

Some of your past purchases may have an intangible or sentimental value, but for the purposes of this personal balance sheet it's enlightening to see the current cash value of all your assets. Are you surprised at the total? Are you surprised at how little value there is today in things that were originally such expensive purchases?

Debt Weighs More Heavily

Now it's time to list your debts in the "I Owe" column. Your largest debt is likely to be your mortgage—a debt that has some interesting advantages. First, it is probably the lowest interest rate you will pay on any money you borrow. Second, your mortgage interest is deductible on your income tax return. And third, that borrowing supports an asset that is likely to grow in value. Finally, your mortgage payment is likely to be equal to or less than the amount you'd pay in rent, so it's money you would spend anyway to have a roof over your head.

Even with 25 percent of American mortgage holders owing more than the current market value of their home, this advice holds true today.

You can make a similar argument about the debt you take on to finance your education. Student loans also come with some relatively low interest rates and easy repayment terms. (See Chapter 10.) And a good education is important in today's job market. Just don't forget that these are loans, not gifts. Repaying them appropriately is important to maintaining your good credit—and the ability to borrow money for things like a mortgage in the future. Today, student loans have become more of a burden, with relatively higher rates amid soaring tuition costs. (See details in Chapter 10.)

Other debt is less beneficial. Your car payment may come with a higher interest rate, and that interest is not deductible. Still, your car gets you to work, which brings in your income. (If you're not using your car for commuting or business purposes, or if you could easily substitute public transportation, you might reconsider the overall costs of owning a car and decide the monthly payments are not worth the convenience.)

As you continue on down the "I Owe" column, you'll have to confront the rest of your monthly bills, mostly from credit cards and retail stores. Do you know where all your bills are right now? Perhaps some are hiding in your top drawer, and others in your briefcase. A few might have slid into the trash can, but they'll be back next month. So starting now, just pile up all your outstanding bills and make a list. Include the total balance, annual percentage interest rate for the finance charges, and the minimum monthly payment. For many people this is a startling, even frightening, amount.

Your Income Is Not Your Paycheck

If you ask most people how much they earn, they'll probably give you a nice round number—thousands of dollars a year. But think again. That's your top-line number, your bragging income. It's not your *real* income—your *after-tax* spending income. Let's take a closer look at the money that comes right off the top of your paycheck: *taxes.*

In 1948, when your parents or grandparents were just starting out, the median-income American family paid just *2 percent* of its income in taxes to the federal government. In 2010, the median-income American family worked 99 days—until April 9—to reach "Tax Freedom Day." That means they spent more than three months working to pay taxes at the federal, state, and local level. In fact, if Americans were taxed enough to actually pay for *all* government spending (including deficit spending) in 2010, they would have worked until May 17—an additional 38 days of work!

Working the 99 days until Tax Freedom Day means taxes add up to more than the same family spends on food, clothing, and health care combined. It's money that you earn but cannot allocate to either spending or saving.

Here's a hint: If you want to make sure you are taking the optimum amount of tax withholding so you don't owe the government money in April, but aren't making them an interest-free loan by over-withholding, go to **PaycheckCity.com** and use their easy W-4 calculator.

Even with the correct withholding, the bottom line on your paycheck is far from the top line that the company is paying you.

There may be other deductions from your paycheck for insurance, retirement plans, and other company benefits. It might make you feel a little better to know where a huge hunk of your income is going, but you'll have to organize what's left of your paycheck to reach your financial goals.

An Irregular Paycheck Doesn't Justify an Irregular Budget

In this era of recession, downsizing, and entrepreneurship, millions of Americans have given up the security of a regular weekly paycheck— or been forced to survive—by starting their own businesses. Working on your own doesn't alleviate the problem of payroll deductions for taxes, insurance, and retirement plans, but it does make the income side a lot less predictable. It gives you flexibility and the opportunity to reap huge rewards from your efforts.

Whether you consider yourself an entrepreneur or an independent contractor, the inability to forecast your income precisely makes it all the more important that you have a safety margin of savings to provide for the unexpected. That contradicts the entrepreneur's need to be willing to risk it all for the future of the business. Entrepreneurs and their families need to have a lot of faith— and some savings and investments on the side. Or they need to be desperate enough to recognize that this is the only way out of their financial woes.

No matter what the reason you find yourself working for yourself, understanding cash flow is a basic requirement, so don't skip the next section. Remember, even severance pay and unemployment benefits are taxable on your state and federal tax return, depending on your overall income.

All Income Is Disposable

It's possible that more than $1 million, and perhaps as much as $10 million, will flow through your checkbook over your lifetime. Think of it this way: If you make $50,000 a year on average over a 25-year working career, your paychecks will total $1.25 million. You may not have control over about one-third of that cash, which is deducted for taxes. Still, the spending, saving, and investing choices you make along the way will have a big impact on your future financial security.

Economists call what's left of your paycheck after taxes and mandatory deductions your *disposable income*. It's true that all the money is going *somewhere,* but the essence of controlling your money is deciding just where that somewhere is. That involves making choices based on a clear distinction between needs and wants.

One way to make that process easier is to assign a time value to your money. If you work a 40-hour week and take home $500 after taxes (roughly equivalent to earning about $42,000 per year), you must work one hour to take home $12.50 after taxes. You might think twice about spending $50 on a dinner at a nice restaurant if you knew you worked four hours to pay for it.

Try dividing your paycheck—after taxes—by the number of hours you worked each week to get a per-hour value for your time. I call it the *worth quotient.* Think of all the effort that went into your job—everything from smiling at your boss to finishing a project on time. Is what you're about to purchase worth the effort that went into earning that money?

Even worse, if you charge that purchase and make only minimum monthly payments, you may pay one hour's work for the product or service plus another four hours' work in future interest payments. Now consider the alternative: If you invest the money instead of spending it, it could compound in a mutual fund at perhaps 10 percent per year—the average historical average returns of the stock market over the past 60 years. (See Chapter 5.)

At that rate, in 10 years that same $50 you didn't spend on dinner would be worth $129.69. It's as if you worked another 6.4 hours and earned about $80 (after taxes). But *you* didn't do the work; *your money did!*

Suddenly, it's easier to decide how to dispose of your income. In the context of your worth quotient it will be easier to make decisions about what you want and what you really need.

Budget Is Not a Verb

Before you can make changes, you need to figure out where all of your money is going. If you deposit your paycheck in the bank instead of cashing it, you'll have a much easier time tracking your spending: You've written checks, charged your purchases on a credit card, or spent actual cash.

The most frightening financial word is *budget*. It becomes less intimidating if you think of it not as that overwhelming process that implies financial austerity, but as a snapshot of what's currently coming in and what's going out. Yes, there may be a gap in your cash flow. That's probably the part of your lifestyle you're financing on your credit cards. There are some easy ways to fill that gap, but first you need to take a realistic look at what's been happening to that money you work so hard to earn.

To get started, take out your checkbook register and look over the checks you've written for the past few months. It's time to set up some categories. As noted in the previous chapter, it's easier to do this with a computerized money management program, but an inexpensive budget book from an office supply store will suffice if you need to see things on paper. Use Quicken or Mint.com and you can instantaneously categorize your spending and make the task much easier.

Some expenses such as rent or mortgage payments remain the same every month. Other monthly bills will vary. You might spend more on electricity during the hot summer months, or on your heating bill in the winter. Make an average of those amounts for each category and enter it on your budget statement. Then start hunting for expenses that do not arrive on a monthly basis. For example, your auto insurance bill might arrive quarterly. Or you might spend a lot of money on holiday gifts at year-end. All of those "must-spend" items must be factored into your plan.

Track Your Spending

The next step is to count the actual cash that you spend out of your pocket every day. You're probably in the habit of withdrawing cash from an ATM. Remember to keep those receipts and add them up at the end of the week. You may be surprised to see how the money you spend buying newspapers, magazines, coffee, lunch, or lottery tickets can really add up. One solution to the problem of disappearing cash is to use your ATM card instead of cash or a credit card. The purchase amount is withdrawn automatically from your checking account, as long as you have funds available. You won't receive a bill at the end of the month, so you'll never pay interest, but you will be able to track your cash spending more easily. If you're banking online, your debit card purchases will be downloaded with your other banking transactions and automatically categorized into your budget.

If most of your spending is done on credit cards, Quicken or Mint will sort your purchases into categories: clothing, food, dining out, drugstore items, and so forth. You want to know where the money went and how the expenditures fit into—or strain—your budget.

If you've come this far with me, you've done the most difficult part of all financial planning. You've prepared yourself to confront the gap between what's coming in and what's going out. It's easy to say that those credit card balances are the result of unexpected events such as a car repair or the need for a new winter coat, but the unexpected always happens in life. You need to close the spending gap so you can build a savings cushion that allows you to reach your short- and longer-term financial goals.

There Are Only Two Ways to Close the Gap—*Spend Less* or *Earn More*

I'm sorry there's no magic wand to wave. Unfortunately, only the federal government can solve its budget problems by creating new money, and even that eventually has its limitations. You'll have to attack either the spending side or the income side of your budget.

Now, even the federal government is being forced to attack both sides of its budget. At least you have plenty of company in dealing with your financial woes! And there are still only two ways out (if you don't count the lottery): You must figure out how to either earn more or spend less.

SPENDING LESS

Once you know where the money is going, it's easier to set up a system to make sure it gets diverted to the proper places. If spending cash is your problem, carry your ATM card only on Monday, when you'll make one cash withdrawal to see you through the week. If writing checks causes the most unplanned spending, take your checkbook out of your purse or briefcase. If dining out is the big problem, set aside one or two nights a week for restaurant meals. Or eat dinner at home and then go out for coffee and dessert.

Sometimes it pays to make major spending adjustments. If public transportation is an alternative to driving to work, you might consider selling your car. You could use the cash proceeds to pay down your credit card debt and simultaneously cut your monthly budget expenditures on insurance, fuel, maintenance, and garage fees. Similarly, it might be smart to take in a roommate or, heaven forbid, move in with your parents while you pay down your credit card debt.

The hardest part about cutting back on your lifestyle is the emotional feeling that you "deserve" to live in the style you've become accustomed to. Cutting back on your lifestyle to pay down debt on past purchases feels like a double emotional punishment. But it is the fastest way to financial freedom.

EARNING MORE

I think it's easier to attack the income side—except in the midst of a recession. After all, you can cut back only so much because so much of your income is going toward basic necessities. But on the income side there's always the potential to earn more money. That might not be so apparent in tough times, when people are out of work.

Obviously, you can't ask the boss for a raise when the company is still planning layoffs. You and your family members might find a temporary evening or weekend job to help pay down your current bills. As difficult as it is to believe, this, too, will pass. The economy will grow again and there will be jobs, better jobs, in the future. The challenge is to keep moving your head above water during the tough times—and to prepare yourself for the next stage of your life.

A decade ago, I warned that if you decide to join the entrepreneurial revolution and start a small business on the side, you should be sure to keep your current job and benefits until you're sure your business can support your family. Today, the challenge is to keep *any* job, and hope you have benefits. We took so much for granted a decade ago. But our resolution to become more self-sufficient will serve us better in the future.

Many people feel they don't have the current skills to join the labor force or to advance on the job and become more highly paid. Look for evening or weekend classes at community colleges in subjects like basic computer skills. Responsible workers who are willing to learn will still be a valuable commodity in tomorrow's labor market. You'll never know what you can achieve if you don't reach toward your goals.

This advice was a lot easier to put into practice a decade ago when unemployment was lower and times were better. But that doesn't mean you can't find work today—if you're willing to do almost anything to dig yourself out of debt. Health-care firms are the first to hire, especially those dealing with seniors, where the demand is rising. You could work as an aide in an assisted-living facility for just a few days a week, or caring for a senior in his or her home. Families may have to combine again when the overhead of living separately becomes too great a burden.

On a personal basis, you may have to revise your self-image while you revise your financial situation. And when you climb out of debt, you'll look back on the experience as a motivating force for the future.

THE SAVAGE TRUTH ON USING CREDIT AND DEBT WISELY

The first critical issue you'll face as you take control of your finances is creating a balance between the wise use of credit and the dangers of debt. Every day you'll be faced with choices whose long-term costs are not readily apparent. The Savage Truth is that unless you look at its far-reaching consequences, it will be all too enticing to accept the temptations of debt.

In hindsight, that original warning fell on too many deaf ears. By now, you recognize those costs that a decade ago were not so readily apparent. The cost of being overwhelmed by debt is a price far too many families are paying through rising bankruptcies and fore-closures. Just because it's happening to so many people doesn't mean it couldn't have been foreseen or avoided. And it doesn't mean that you can't start over again.

Even if you've lost most of your material possessions, you have gained experience. And if you realize how much you once accomplished without the benefit of all this knowledge, think how much opportunity there is ahead of you—if you're willing to work hard and start over.

Many of America's original settlers were refugees from debtors' prisons in Europe. The United States has always operated on a different principle: the chance to make a fresh start. Now, you have your chance if you need it. The following warnings are unchanged from the first edition of this book, and it's never too late to learn. It's as easy to be tempted by debt as it is to be tempted by candy, food, or alcohol. We live in a society that delivers the message that "having it" and showing that you have it are the prime measures of success. In recent years, society has institutionalized debt and democratized credit.

Credit cards first became widely available in the 1970s. During those years, interest on credit card debt was tax deductible to spur spending. At the same time, inflation was pushing prices ever higher, encouraging the buy-now-pay-later mentality. There were few warnings about the dangers of debt overload.

After 1991, interest on consumer debt was no longer deductible. But the habit of incurring debt to maintain a lifestyle became difficult for many consumers to shake. Lenders were often blamed for overuse of debt because they mailed so many credit card and home equity loan solicitations and offered low teaser rates to encourage borrowing.

But the Savage Truth is that avoiding debt is a personal responsibility. Although unexpected events sometimes make it necessary to borrow in order to survive, addiction to debt is a dangerous disease.

Bankruptcy: The Impact

In 2010, more than 1.6 million Americans declared bankruptcy, the latest statistics in a decade that saw more than a million bankruptcies every 12 months. As job growth remains sluggish in the economic recovery, the number of bankruptcy filings may diminish only slowly.

As noted earlier, America gives people second chances. But all of us pay when debt is written off by a lender. We pay in the form of higher borrowing costs and higher prices in future transactions. And we pay when resources cannot be invested in our economy because they have been written off, sent down the drain.

So without casting judgment on the epidemic of bankruptcies, I think we can all agree it's something to be avoided at all costs. Sometimes the causes are beyond our control: illness, divorce, or company layoffs. But if circumstances force you to choose bankruptcy as an alternative, you should at least know the laws and get professional help. At a minimum, a visit to your local National Foundation for Credit Counseling (NFCC) agency (800-388-2227) will explain your rights and the consequences of this decision.

Credit Cards: Dangers and Opportunities

There's nothing inherently wrong with using credit cards to facilitate all your transactions. Credit cards have the advantage of convenience and security. They can simplify record keeping and budgeting. Many offer rewards or discounts or cash back. They give consumers power in disputes with merchants because the card-issuing bank can intervene on their behalf. Credit cards are a basic necessity for making reservations. And credit cards give flexibility to stretch out payments on major purchases.

But credit cards used unwisely can contribute to ongoing financial problems. Making only the minimum required monthly payment is the most expensive way to pay for merchandise and services. You'll wind up paying interest on the interest, building a mountain of debt that will crush you—as many have now learned the hard way.

We've all become far more sophisticated about credit cards and their dangers. Your credit card may have a Visa or MasterCard logo, but the card *issuer* is one of more than 5,000 individual financial institutions that belong to card-issuing associations. Within federal guidelines, each card issuer has its own rules and rates regarding finance charges, over-the-limit charges, and late payment fees. Some charge annual fees. Others compete on offering lower rates, more benefits, or larger credit limits.

Credit card companies make their money on the volume of charges (for which the merchant pays a small fee) and on the finance charges they assess on unpaid balances. So they're all still trying to get your business. They continue to send solicitations for low-rate cards or "checks" to transfer outstanding balances from another card issuer, but these days they're a bit more careful about their target audience. Even if you receive a solicitation, they're checking your credit report carefully before accepting balance transfers or new cardholders.

And the pitfalls remain, despite recent legislation. The fine print is in larger type these days, but you must read carefully to see that the enticing low rate being offered expires after six months. It's still your responsibility to sort out the promises and the pitfalls.

Credit card offers jumped 36 percent in early 2010, coming off a depressed base during the previous two years. And despite changes in regulation wrought by the CARD Act, these offers are still tempting.

If you're looking for more information on the best credit card to use in your circumstances, either based on finance rates, annual fees, or reward points, go to either **Bankrate.com** or **LowCards.com** to begin your search.

No Such Thing as Easy Credit

You've seen the commercials and mail solicitations promising easy credit. The Savage Truth is that extending credit is a big business in America. To a lender, interest is income. To a borrower, interest on unpaid balances creates more debt, upon which more interest must be paid—enriching the lender even more. That's how used-car dealers make their money—on the interest, not on the purchase price of the car.

If you're already in debt, you might be wondering how you got caught in the trap of easy credit. It was so easy to get in—and seemingly impossible to get out. The word *credit* made you think you were qualifying for a wonderful asset: the ability to borrow. In reality, you walked into the trap of debt: a liability for you and your family. That liability will continue to grow and burden you until you take steps to reverse the process.

Well, the two previous paragraphs were my warning in the first edition of this book, written in 2000. Now, more than a decade later and with consumer bankruptcies soaring, there are new warnings to offer.

The CARD Act of 2009 was designed to protect consumers from some of the "tricks" that card issuers used to increase the cost of credit. Here are some of the provisions:

- Card issuers have to give 45 days' notice before they raise rates, unless you have a variable rate card or are at least 60 days late on your payment.

- They cannot abruptly change annual fees or make other significant changes in terms.

- You have the right to tell your card issuer not to accept transactions that would trigger "over-limit" fees, and that fee can be charged only once per monthly billing cycle.

- Borrowers under age 21 now need a cosigner, or must demonstrate the ability to pay their balances through a work history.

- Your monthly statement must illustrate how long it will take to pay your balance using only the billed minimum payments.

- Two-cycle billing, which cost you interest on new purchases if you carried balances from the previous month, has been prohibited.

Despite the latest credit card protections for consumers, unwary spenders will still be caught in the trap of buying more than they can afford and shouldering a huge burden of interest until the balance is paid off. Others have little choice, needing credit to keep a roof over their head and food on the table. After reaching a peak in 2005, card usage and outstanding balances are declining. Part of that came from the recession, job loss, and bankruptcies. In 2010, total consumer credit outstanding (including mortgages) was $2.451 trillion, down 2.3 percent for a third straight year of declines, according to the Federal Reserve. But that's still a huge increase from 1991, when consumers carried only $750 billion in total debt.

Truly, Americans piled on the debt during the easy-credit years. Paradoxically, by the time mortgage rates fell to below 4 percent in 2010, many could not take advantage of the opportunity to refinance to 30-year mortgages with rates of 4 percent or lower. Consumers had so ruined their own credit (and home prices had fallen so far) that they couldn't qualify.

THE SAVAGE TRUTH ON GETTING OUT OF DEBT

In tough times, there are always scam artists who prey upon desperate consumers. Some offer to "negotiate" your debt, while others urge you into a premature bankruptcy. Mortgage scams abound, charging up-front fees for refinancings that never occur. Desperate consumers dig themselves a deeper hole when they fall for these deals.

The *only* debt counseling services I recommend are those affiliated with the National Foundation for Credit Counseling. You can reach the nearest agency by calling them at 800-388-2227. They will meet with you either in person or over the phone. The meeting is typically free, or at a nominal cost. These NFCC member agencies can offer several services. Sometimes, a simple meeting is enough to put you on course. They can help you organize your bills, suggest expenses to cut, and help you track your progress.

They also offer a debt-repayment service. This is not help in reducing your balances. But they will contact your creditors, which will sometimes reduce interest rates, waive late charges, or "re-age" your account. Then you will send one monthly check to the agency, and they will pay an agreed-upon amount to each of your creditors.

The NFCC member agencies receive a fee from the credit card issuers for providing this service at no, or very low, cost to consumers. In recent years, these programs have helped nearly four million consumers repay $2 billion to their lenders, through counseling and payment plans.

If you simply meet with a member agency to discuss your situation, it does not go on your credit report. If you do enter a repayment program, it will be reported on your credit report, but it doesn't carry the stigma of a bankruptcy. Sometimes, your situation is so dire that the agency will recommend bankruptcy and introduce you to an attorney you can trust to handle the process.

Beware Debt Negotiation Scams

The latest scams in the world of consumer debt revolve around "debt negotiation" firms that were charging high up-front fees until the Federal Trade Commission created some new rules in late 2010. But even those rules against up-front fees haven't eliminated some of the scam artists.

Debt negotiation can work—*if* you have money set aside to tempt your creditor to settle. Unfortunately, many of these services suggested you stop paying your credit card bills and put the money in a separate account so you could negotiate a lower-balance payoff. In the meantime, the cardholder's credit was ruined, and in some cases card issuers went to court to get judgments against the borrower, garnishing wages and posting liens against personal property.

When the FTC took on these services and decreed that no up-front fees could be charged until a negotiation was successful, some of these companies changed to a "legal" model—collecting fees for legal services that were not covered by the FTC rules. Others started selling debt negotiation "kits" to get around the fee prohibition. Some legitimate services remain, but the Savage Truth is that you cannot negotiate a balance without some leverage. If you do have cash set aside, a debt negotiation service is worth a try. But you might be just as successful negotiating on your own!

When You're in a Deep Hole, Stop Digging

If you want to handle your debt woes on your own, it can be done. There are two aspects to getting out of debt. The first is to stop digging yourself into a deeper hole. Don't take on any more debt—and don't fool yourself into thinking that switching to lower-cost debt is solving your problem.

To get on the debt paydown track requires taking extra cards out of your wallet and no longer using them for any purchases. In the interim, you can achieve the convenience of plastic by using a debit card.

A debit card looks just like a credit card and can be used almost anywhere a credit card can be used. Unless you announce that it is a debit card and enter your PIN on the merchant's keypad, the merchant has no idea that your plastic is a debit card. You can simply sign for your purchase as on a typical credit card. (The only exceptions are car rental agencies, which want access to your entire line of credit to cover the deductible in case you get into an accident.)

The debit card works just as if you had paid by check—but much more conveniently. When your card is swiped, your bank is contacted electronically to make sure the balance in your account is large enough to cover your purchase. The purchase is then deducted either immediately (when you use your PIN) or within 48 hours, if you have signed for the purchase. You have no bills at the end of the month, no minimum payments, and no interest is charged on your purchase.

If you're banking online, your purchases show up immediately when you download your checking account information. A debit card allows you to break the credit overspending habit. If there's not enough cash in your account, your purchase will be denied right at the merchant's register unless you've authorized your bank to create an overdraft feature. And your debit card is more secure than carrying cash. Here's the promise written on Visa's website:

> If your Visa Debit card is lost or stolen and fraudulent activity occurs, you are protected by Visa's Zero Liability policy. That means 100 percent protection for you. Whether purchases occur online or off, you pay nothing for fraudulent activity.

A Minimum Effort Won't Solve the Problem

The second, and equally important, aspect of getting out of debt is to pay down the outstanding balances as part of a regular plan. It's a sad truth that the minimum required monthly payments on an outstanding credit card balance are designed to maximize the interest to the lender over the life of the loan, while making credit seem affordable to the consumer.

That minimum monthly payment may be as low as 2 percent of the outstanding balance. But if you're paying down 2 percent and adding on 18 percent in annual interest to your balance (about 1.5 percent interest per month), then you're really only paying down one-half of 1 percent of your balance every month. At that rate, it will take most of your lifetime to repay your debt. Recognizing this issue, the CARD Act now requires disclosure of how long it will take to pay down your debt and what the total interest cost will be. Most card issuers have raised the minimum to 4 percent of the outstanding balance amount, but that still creates a lengthy repayment term with plenty of interest.

In our earlier example of the $2,000 credit card debt that would take you 31 years and two months to repay (and would cost an additional $8,202 in interest), the implied minimum monthly payment is about $41.

- If you added $10 a month, you would repay that debt in 12 years and pay $2,085 in interest.

- If you added $25 per month, you would repay your debt in six years and pay $1,051 in interest.

- If you doubled your minimum monthly payment to $82 and kept paying that same amount every month, you would repay your loan in 2.5 years.

Paying more than the minimum is the most realistic way to fill in that deep hole of debt and rise to level financial ground. Paying *double* the initial minimum monthly payment every month should make you debt-free within three years.

If you'd like to see how much you'd have to repay on your own debt, with specific numbers that reflect your outstanding balances, finance charges, and minimum payments, there are several excellent programs that can help you create a plan and act upon it.

The Quicken money management program has a special section that talks you through a debt reduction program, based on your own spending habits as reflected in your checkbook register. And the free online software from Quicken's Mint.com also allows you to work through your debt repayment issues, with helpful hints about lower-cost credit cards and other tools.

One of the best free online debt reduction calculator tools can be found at **PowerPay.com**—a free resource from the University of Utah. It can help you create alternative payment scenarios to accelerate your payments and become debt-free.

Your Debt Is No Secret

Debt used to be a privately guarded secret—something people never discussed. Now it's a public conversation and a force in social networking. Can there be anyone who doesn't know that every debt transaction—and its repayment—is reported to three national credit bureaus? The information gathered by those credit bureaus is used to make decisions for future credit granting, but it can also be used to screen job applicants and price insurance policies.

Your credit report and the several credit scores that are calculated based on your credit report become the most important numbers in your financial plan. They impact your access to financing and its cost, so it's worth keeping track of your credit report and scores.

There are three major credit reporting agencies. You can access their information at **Experian.com**, **Equifax.com**, and **Transunion .com**. They typically have all the same information, which is reported to them by your creditors. However, there could be discrepancies, which is why you should check all three—a process that is free, easy, and secure.

The *only* way to get the federally mandated free credit report is at **www.AnnualCreditReport.com**. That provides instant links to the three credit bureaus. Do not be misled by other websites that have the word "free" in their names; they all want to sell you some sort of credit monitoring and protection against fraud. (More on that to come.)

You might have some concern about how your credit report could be secure and still allow you instantaneous online access. The questions you're required to answer go far beyond information that would be easily accessible to anyone else. You can be sure that accessing your credit report has a level of security that is well-tested.

Since you're allowed one free report from each company every year, it might be wise to space out your requests, getting one report every four months, each time from a different company. That way you'll stay on top of any changes. There's an easy way to dispute any information that you believe is incorrect. But basically you'll have to deal with the merchant that made the disputed report to get the information removed.

Credit Scores Your Life

Your credit score is a way of placing all the information on your credit report into one easily compared number. The best-known credit score is called the *FICO* score, from the name of its parent, Fair Isaac Corp. The other credit bureaus offer their own version of scores—none as widely used as the FICO.

It's easy to get your FICO score at **www.MyFICO.com**. Beware: Although the word "free" is all over this website, the FICO score comes with a subscription to their monitoring service. If you don't cancel within 10 days, you'll receive a monthly billing.

All of the credit scoring models use a slightly different range of numbers to indicate your status. FICO scores range from a high of 850 down to below 600. The impact of a lower score can be dramatic. For example, on a $300,000, 30-year mortgage, the monthly payment (principal and interest) for those with a score over 760 would be $1,404. A score of 700 to 759 could add nearly $40 a month to that payment. And a FICO score under 640 could jump the payment to $1,689 per month!

There are many companies offering services to "help" you increase your credit score, but avoid them and do it on your own. Length of time at your job and at your residence count in your credit score, so you might want to apply for a mortgage before you switch jobs. Other tips are pretty obvious. Pay your bills on time, since being late is the biggest ding to your score.

There's some debate about closing open but unused accounts. Be sure to hang onto the oldest accounts, even if you don't use them, because they show stability. And if you carry balances, don't close too many accounts because it will increase your percentage of "credit utilization," which could actually lower your score.

Don't apply for a lot of new credit, such as store cards or auto loans, just before you're going to apply for something important like a mortgage. Too many inquiries can also lower your score. (But the scoring model recognizes inquiries initiated by card issuers in an attempt to offer you credit versus those that are initiated when you are seeking credit.) Similarly, keep outstanding balances low, relative to your credit limit.

The most immediate and dramatic way to increase your score is to pay down your debt balances. But beware of offers of temporary, unreported debt paydown loans. These shady deals can wind up costing you money, and your credit score.

If you really need to figure out how to raise your score soon, check the tool at myFico.com that lets you simulate how various moves would impact your personal credit score. Remember, a difference of a few points, moving you into a higher scoring bracket, could save a lifetime of interest payments that really add up.

Protecting Your Credit Is Critical

A decade ago, there were few ways to protect your credit, aside from frequent checks of your credit report. But in the past decade, credit protection has become a big industry. Every credit bureau and a number of independent companies offer some sort of credit monitoring and protection services.

For a number of years I thought this was truly a consumer rip-off. The Federal Trade Commission (FTC) even sued Lifelock, one of the largest providers of credit protection, over deceptive ads. The charges included the fact that consumers could put the same protections, including a credit freeze, on their credit reports without the "help" of this company. As part of the complaint, the FTC noted that this freeze protection is useless against fraud on existing bank accounts or credit cards, and could protect only against newly opened credit accounts. The suit was settled at a reported cost of $12 million in consumer refunds, and the company remains in business.

What should you do to protect your credit? First, be aware of the protections already available to you at no charge. All three of the credit bureaus allow you to put a credit freeze on your account, so no one can get access to your information to fraudulently open a new account. (Be sure you lift this freeze if you're about to apply for a mortgage or car loan!)

Make a list of account numbers for all cards you carry in your wallet, in case it is stolen. And be sure to write the toll-free number of the card issuer to report the theft! (You can get a link to print out the forms for collecting this and other personal information at my website, **www.TerrySavage.com**.)

Never write your PIN on your bank card, and don't put your credit card number on the back of a check. Don't leave your card as a security deposit or for identification purposes. Always take your credit card or ATM receipts and, if you aren't saving them in a file, dispose of them carefully.

Check your online account balances regularly to make yourself aware of unauthorized charges. Every credit and debit card now carries protection against fraud, although it may take a while to get the charges removed.

Then reconsider that overdraft line of credit on your bank account. You're 100 percent protected against fraudulent use of a debit card, but a thief might meanwhile have unlimited access to your overdraft line of credit through a stolen debit card.

If you're still worried about identity theft, you can join the growing numbers who sign up for these programs, typically as part of accessing their not-so-free credit report directly through the credit bureaus. The one aspect of this protection that might be most valuable is a service offered by some of these companies: help *restoring* your identity and credit once your identity has been taken. You see, none of these programs offers a full guarantee that they can protect you completely.

A Secured Card Starts— or Rebuilds—Credit

Perhaps you're ready to start over after a bankruptcy. Or maybe you're a student with no credit history or one who can't get the required parental cosigner. That's where *secured cards* come into the picture. To make it simple, your line of credit is secured by your deposit in a savings account in the issuing bank. The minimum is typically $500. The amount of your deposit becomes your line of credit. If you miss making a payment, the bank has the right to dip into your savings to cover your debt. You'll earn a low rate of interest, but, most important, you'll get a chance to establish a credit history of regular repayments since that information about your account is reported to the credit bureaus. You'll soon be offered other credit cards that do not require a security deposit. Perhaps you could earn more on your deposit money elsewhere, so you'll want to switch to a standard card. Just remember to continue your regular payment habits.

To find issuers offering secured cards, go to **www.Bankrate.com**.

THE SAVAGE TRUTH ON DEALING WITH DEBT

Transferring Credit Card Balances Is Musical Chairs

In an attempt to win market share, credit card issuers have offered tempting low interest rates to those who transfer balances from other cards. There is always a catch: Those teaser rates typically last only six months and then jump far above the average. A borrower who switches too frequently builds up a credit report that is less than desirable. A customer who has too much available credit left over from previous accounts is less desirable to the next lender. When the music stops, there may not be another chair (or credit card) to land on.

As a result of the recession, many card issuers got out of the balance-transfer business, while others decided to get even with consumers who had already transferred balances. Not only did they raise rates on existing customers, but they started charging huge fees for late payments or for exceeding a credit limit. So before yielding to the temptation to dance from card to card to find lower rates, be sure to check out the other penalties you might be facing.

This game has changed since the enactment of the CARD Act, and the recession. But some banks are back to enticing balance transfers with low or no interest payable for the first six months. It's still a trap—because the ultimate rate can be higher than the rates you're paying now. If you don't use that initial period to pay down your debt, you'll be in worse shape down the road.

Overdraft Protection Is Expensive

If you pay your credit cards in full every month, you can pat yourself on the back, but if you do so by dipping into an authorized *overdraft line of credit* at your bank, un-pat yourself. This credit may cost more than the amount you'd pay on a regular credit card. It's nice to have that protection in case of a subtraction error or an unexpectedly large debit card purchase, but regular overdrafting—even if part of a bank convenience plan—is an expensive way to handle your finances. And it's still debt.

You'll Never Get Out of Debt by Taking on More Debt

Managing your debt makes sense. Adding to your debt is nonsense. Paying down high-interest-rate debt first is smart. Consolidating outstanding debt to a single monthly payment is enticing but advisable only if it's done without fees, at a lower rate, and if you've canceled your other cards so you won't build up balances on them once again.

Years ago, you saw commercials announcing that you could consolidate your credit card debt into one lower monthly payment. They promised that the interest would be tax deductible, and you might even have enough money left over to remodel your kitchen or take a vacation! The pro athletes who pitched these home equity consolidation loans surely had no need to borrow, yet they led consumers down a dangerous road.

I wrote that advice a decade ago, when those ads were ubiquitous. I wonder how that pro quarterback feels now that so many were caught in the home equity loan trap, which I warned against at length in the first edition of this book.

The lessons are now very public. But lest you be tempted by current low interest rates, let me point out again that most home equity loans carry a floating rate of interest. If inflation returns, that affordable payment could skyrocket. And most of these loans—if you can still qualify—are for interest-only, leaving you with a big repayment burden down the road.

Even worse, many borrowers who borrow against their homes "reload" (that's the industry's term) their credit cards. After using a home equity loan to consolidate their debt, the temptation of those credit card zero balances becomes overwhelming. But this time, when the economy slows or they lose a job, there will be no home equity to fall back upon. Foreclosure is the only option for those who cannot pay. That's why it's so important to go through a debt counseling program if you are going to take out a home equity loan to consolidate debt.

In the first edition of *The Savage Truth*, I wrote that Americans then had less equity in their homes than at any time in history. That was partly because of new mortgages being made with less than 5 percent down payments and partly because of record borrowings through home equity loans. The foreclosure rate in the late 1990s was the highest since the Great Depression—and that was in the best of economic conditions.

Those warnings, written a decade ago, went unheeded by many. In 2010, at least four million homes received foreclosure notices. The evictions and legal hassles have made headlines, and the fallout continues. Owning a home is still the American Dream. But for too many, it became a nightmare. The silver lining—although not for those who have lost their homes—is that foreclosures have helped push home prices to their lowest level in decades. That will give some people a chance to start over.

Borrowing from Yourself Makes a Fool of the Lender

Your company 401(k) retirement plan—or 403(b) plan for a non-profit organization—may allow you to borrow up to 50 percent of your account value (to a maximum of $50,000), typically at an interest rate of 1 to 2 percent above prime. Since you're borrowing from your own account, the interest you pay will be credited to your account. Because it is a loan and not a withdrawal, there is no penalty or income tax due on the amount borrowed. That leads many people to conclude that borrowing from a retirement plan is the least costly way to pay down consumer debt. That's wrong.

Yes, you're paying interest to yourself. But the amount you borrow from your account is no longer growing at the investment rate you're earning on the balance of your plan. Unless your retirement plan is invested in ultrasafe, low-rate assets, the investment return is not a wash. And when you lose today's investment returns because you borrowed from the plan, you also lose the larger asset base on which your account compounds in the future.

Even worse, if you leave your company (or if the company is sold and retirement plans merge) with a loan outstanding, it is considered a withdrawal, and it results in ordinary income taxes on the amount taken out, plus a 10 percent federal early withdrawal penalty. Also, these loans require regular monthly repayments over five years. If you can't make those monthly repayments, the entire amount may be reclassified as a withdrawal.

The lessons of the dangers of debt have been learned the hard way. Everyone is now aware of the consequences of living beyond their income. But the temptations remain. You must remain vigilant, both against the easy-money offers and your own desires. You *can* live debt-free. And it *is* a better way to live. Whether you're starting over or just starting out, please remember this advice.

TERRY'S TO-DO LIST

1. Figure out where you stand financially right now. Make your personal balance sheet—I Owe, I Own.

2. Make a list of all your outstanding bills, including balances, interest rates, and monthly minimum required payment.

3. Use the simple financial planning software like Quicken or online tracking at Mint.com to track and categorize all your spending.

4. Start using a debit card in place of cash so you'll have a record of your spending.

5. Create a debt repayment plan. Get reputable help in dealing with debt by calling the National Foundation for Consumer Credit at 800-388-2227 and get connected to their nearest local office.

6. Consider alternatives carefully and avoid borrowing more in an attempt to reduce your monthly payments.

7. Get your free credit report using the links at www .AnnualCreditReport.com.

CHAPTER

4

THE SAVAGE TRUTH ON CHICKEN MONEY

Nest Eggs Need Some Safety

Now more than ever, people are placing safety ahead of risk. That's where "chicken money" comes into the picture. We all have a certain percentage of our savings that we absolutely cannot afford to lose. But before you jump to the conclusion that the best way to handle your money these days is to consider only the safest investments, let's put this concept into perspective. First, not all so-called "safe" investments are completely without risk. And second, having some chicken money can give you the resolve needed to ride out the volatility in other investments, designed to bring you growth in the long run.

MAKING MONEY DECISIONS FOR BULLS, BEARS, AND CHICKENS

Bulls think prices are going higher, and they can give you good reasons for buying now—before prices rise. When you hear a bull talking about buying, it's hard to remember that there might be a risk involved in this investment. On the other hand, the bears seem like pessimists. They can give you many good arguments for selling out and staying out. They point out the negatives in the market or in the specific investment, and are fond of telling you how you could lose your hard-earned money. Listening to both sides of an investment argument between the bulls and the bears is like watching a tennis match from midcourt.

Then there's the third category—the chickens. The mantra of the chicken money investor is: "I'm not so concerned about the return *on* my money as I am about the return *of* my money."

Chicken Money Is Not Just Cash

Let's make it clear: Chicken money is not really about cash, although holding some paper money for emergencies is wise. After the tsunami in Japan, safes full of paper money washed ashore, in a country where hiding currency is a tradition. But much of the hidden cash was totally lost, and many safe-owners could not be identified. No, our definition of chicken money revolves around the safest, short-term investments.

Chicken Money Is Money You Cannot Afford to Lose

As noted in Chapter 1, chicken money is nothing to be embarrassed about; it's simply money that you're unwilling to risk. That may be because you have a very short time horizon. For example, you have almost enough for a down payment on your first house, or you received an inheritance and want to save it for your child's college tuition in a few years. That cash does not belong in the stock market, no matter what your enthusiasm for stocks, because of your short time horizon.

Or you may have chicken money because you have a limited amount of assets that must last for a finite period of time. If you're already well into retirement and just want to be certain that your savings last as long as your lifetime, you won't want to take investment risks. After all, without a continuing income you have no way of replacing any losses.

In either case, you'll want to keep your cash in appropriate chicken money investments such as bank CDs, money market funds, Treasury bills, and savings bonds. Those "chicken money" alternatives will be explained in this chapter. But first, step back and consider *why* you are so conservative.

Never Be Chicken Out of Ignorance or Emotion

Some people are chicken because of ignorance. They don't understand how investments in the stock market or mutual funds work, so they leave their money in the bank. Depending on their personal situation, they may actually be harming their financial future. Failure to take appropriate risk may be as dangerous as taking on too much risk. It's one thing to make an informed decision to sit on the sidelines; it's quite another to avoid examining the alternatives and the long-term consequences of a decision.

Other people are chicken out of pure emotion. No amount of reasoning about the importance of taking risks will turn them into investors. Perhaps they had a personal financial loss at an earlier period in their lives, or watched a close friend or family member in that kind of situation. They're unwilling to understand intellectually that chicken money investments have their own inherent risks—namely the exposure to inflation and taxes that eats away at the value of money over time. Even if persuaded to take investment risk, they pay an emotional price by worrying about the loss of principal that may not be worth the potential financial gain. Perhaps the only convincing argument is to set aside in chicken money investments whatever amount is emotionally deemed enough to give peace of mind. The remainder can be invested with some degree of risk in an effort to grow the principal.

Chicken Money Investments Are One-Decision Investments

It's the nature of investing that you must make two decisions, or even three. The first is when to get in, the second is when to get out, and the third is when to get back in again. Chicken money investments are one-decision investments: Once you're in, changes in market circumstances will never force you out. Since you won't have losses, you'll never sell in a panic. Since you won't have gains, you'll never have to decide when to take a profit.

As you'll see, the return on your investment may vary in line with interest rates, inflation expectations, and tax code changes. All of those factors will be relative to changes in the economy, which will have an even greater impact on riskier investments. So, in the end, your chicken money investments will always be the most conservative choice.

There Is One Big Risk in Chicken Money Investments

Chicken money investments are typically low-yielding, government-insured, money market–type investments. What you give up in returns you receive in the assurance that you will not lose your principal to investment risk. But even chicken money investments carry a certain degree of risk: the risk that taxes and inflation will eat away at the buying power of your money.

Part of that risk can be set aside by keeping your chicken money in tax-sheltered accounts such as IRAs or annuities. But when you eventually withdraw the cash, you'll have to pay ordinary income taxes on the earnings, as well as on any of the original investment that was a tax deduction.

Part of the risk of inflation is defrayed because chicken money investments are by nature short-term instruments. If inflation brings with it rising interest rates, the interest rate on the investment will also move higher. But there's rarely a significant spread between the inflation rate and the rate of return on chicken money investments. Think back to when Treasury bills were yielding 15 percent in 1980. It seemed like a very high return, but inflation was running at over 13 percent that year. The true return was less than 2 percent, and taxes consumed a big bite of that return.

Chicken money investments are always *short-term* securities. Even longer-term Treasury bonds issued by the U.S. government have another risk, which will be explained later.

The Rule of 72 Rules the Chicken Money Roost

The Rule of 72 is a simple way to calculate the effects of inflation on the buying power of your money and the effects of interest returns on the growth of your principal.

The Rule of 72 says that if you divide any number that represents your investment return into 72, the result will be the amount of time it takes for your principal to double. If you're earning 7 percent on your money, compounded, your principal will double in 10.2 years. Conversely, if inflation is eating away at your money at an annual rate of 7 percent, the value of your principal will be cut in half in 10.2 years. And if you're earning 3 percent, it will take 24 years for your money to double, or for your spending power to be cut in half.

So it's important to look at both sides of the equation. Interest compounded will build up your principal, while inflation will eat away at its buying power. Of course, if you spend your interest while maintaining your principal, you're just fooling yourself if you believe you're staying even.

Chicken Money: Temporary or Permanent?

There's a cost to holding cash—and it makes for a very lumpy mattress! So these easy-in, easy-out, chicken money investments are often used as a resting place for money in between other investment opportunities. One other notable aspect of chicken money investments is the low transaction costs of getting in and out. Even if you don't consider any part of your investment portfolio to fall into the chicken money category, it's worth learning the ins and outs of these temporary havens.

Then recognize that some of your chicken money is permanently in that category of "can't afford to lose." It may be painful, and tempting, in times of low interest rates to search for higher-yielding but riskier alternatives. Those are the mistakes you regret most, in hindsight. If you truly can't afford to lose your principal, do not chase yield. Self-discipline is a key ingredient in all market decisions—but especially so when it comes to safeguarding a well-defined portion of your assets.

THE SAVAGE TRUTH ON U.S. TREASURY BILLS

U.S. Treasury Bills: The Ultimate Chicken Money Investment

When the world's money gets scared these days, it rushes to the safety of U.S. Treasury bills—short-term IOUs issued by the U.S. government. It wasn't always so, and given the huge debt the United States is building, it might not be that way in the future. Still, in any crisis, such as the financial meltdown in 2008–2009, the world's cash first turns to short-term U.S. government IOUs: Treasury bills. When buyers rush in, they push prices up, causing yields to fall.

But inflation fears can cause these short-term rates to rise rapidly, since the Treasury must auction new bills weekly to repay older, maturing debt—and to borrow more. In the late 1970s and early 1980s, investors questioned the promise and ability of the government to repay its borrowings with dollars that had real buying power. So people rushed to buy gold, soybeans, and real estate. In order to get people to invest in its short-term government securities, the Treasury had to pay high interest rates that reached 15 percent for a period of six months.

Then, under Fed Chairman Paul Volcker, and later Alan Greenspan, the Federal Reserve convinced investors around the world that it would never again inflate the money supply by creating too many dollars. As confidence in the future value of the dollar grew, inflation fears subsided. The combination of confidence in the dollar and fear of declining values of other countries' currencies caused a rush to convert those currencies to dollars and to buy government-guaranteed Treasury bills. As a result of that demand, Treasury bill interest rates fell sharply.

Now, we're potentially at the stage where the world will question the value of the dollar once again. If that fear spreads, the fear of inflation, then interest rates will rise immediately. This time around, that would be particularly expensive for our government because our national debt that must be financed has grown to be more than $14 trillion.

That's why interest rates on Treasury bills have become a true barometer of inflationary expectations. Those rates are set at the weekly government auctions, where huge institutions around the world place bids through Treasury dealer firms. (Smaller individual investors agree to accept the average interest rate set by these public auctions.) The weekly rate is determined by economic conditions, such as inflation expectations, as well as by supply and demand. When there is a great demand for its IOUs, the government can pay a lower rate of interest and still attract buyers. But when buyers are wary of owning dollars, the government must pay a higher interest rate to attract those buyers to finance our debt.

Treasury Bills Are Short-Term U.S. Government IOUs

Treasury bills have maturities of one year or less. *Treasury notes* are initially sold in maturities of from 2 to 10 years. *Treasury bonds* have 20- or 30-year maturities. All are guaranteed by the full faith and credit of the U.S. government, a fact that makes them the safest investments—and the interest rate standard by which all other IOUs are compared.

Treasury notes and bonds pay interest semiannually. Since Treasury bills are sold for such short-term maturities (13-week, 26-week, and 52-week offerings), the interest is actually paid up front in the form of a discount on the purchase price. That is, if you were to purchase a $10,000, 26-week Treasury bill that carried a 5 percent interest rate (as determined at the weekly auction), you would immediately receive a check for $250, which represents the interest you would earn over six months. If you deposited that interest check in your money market fund, you would earn interest on the interest, raising your true yield slightly. And there's a bonus when you buy Treasury securities: The interest is exempt from state and local income taxes, which can be significant if you live in a high-tax state.

It's Easier than Ever to Buy Treasuries

Individuals can easily buy Treasury bills in minimum amounts of $100, through the website **www.TreasuryDirect.gov**. You don't get an actual paper certificate; all transactions are done online and your account is maintained electronically. It's really easy to get started. You'll need your bank account number and the bank routing number, since payment for your purchase and deposit of your interest is done electronically. Your bank will give you its routing number.

You can still purchase Treasury securities by mail with the use of a certified personal check, but the online system is far easier and avoids delay in executing your order. To get information from a customer service representative, call 800-722-2678.

When you purchase your Treasury securities, you can instruct that they be automatically *rolled over* when they mature. That is, the principal amount will be reinvested at the going rate in similar maturity securities. In fact, for shorter maturities, you can authorize automatic renewals when your current Treasuries mature. You can also change your mind at any time, and ask that the proceeds not be renewed, but instead be deposited into your bank account at maturity. But you should not plan to sell small amounts of Treasury securities before maturity, because there is a $45 fee.

Accounts can be registered in the name of one person, two persons, or an entity such as an estate, trust, private organization, or corporation. Instructions about your account can be given online at TreasuryDirect.gov, or through the automated phone system. The only fee charged is a $100 annual fee if your account holds more than $100,000 in Treasury securities.

In recent years, the Treasury has made it much easier for individuals to buy Treasury bills, notes, and bonds at the regular weekly and monthly auctions. However, if you want the safety of Treasuries with daily liquidity, you are better off using a Treasury-only money market mutual fund or money market account in a bank.

Treasury-Only Money Market Funds Offer the Same Security

Banks offer money market deposit accounts that are fully insured up to $250,000. The rates paid on money market accounts change daily to reflect changes in the interest rate marketplace. Since bank accounts are backed by the full faith and credit of the government through the Federal Deposit Insurance Corporation, you're getting the same guarantee as someone who buys Treasury bills directly from the government. But there are occasions when Treasury bill rates might be a bit higher than bank money market rates. If there's little loan demand, for example, the banks will drop rates to make deposits less attractive.

In that case, you might turn to Treasury bills or to a mutual fund that buys only short-term U.S. government IOUs. Every major mutual fund family offers one of these Treasury-only money market mutual funds, with yields that may fluctuate every day based on the market rates for very-short-term Treasury securities. The funds are not insured, but because they invest only in U.S. Treasuries, they are very safe.

The fund families' other money market funds might offer a slightly higher yield because of investments in commercial paper (short-term corporate IOUs) and mortgage-backed securities of a very short term. Treasury-only money market funds typically pay the lowest rate of interest and offer the highest degree of security. It's a distinction that would matter only in times of extreme crisis, but some investors feel more comfortable with that extra margin of safety.

In fall 2008, we saw one of those rare moments when the safety of money market mutual funds that invested in commercial paper was called into question. The failure of Lehman Brothers and their inability to repay their commercial paper threatened the stability of several large money market mutual funds. The government stepped in with a guarantee of those money market funds. The guarantee was lifted a year later, and no money market fund suffered a loss. But for a few weeks, those who had accepted lower yields in Treasury-only money market funds slept better than those whose funds were temporarily threatened.

The Rate Search

When you're searching for the highest rates on insured certificates of deposit, you're likely to find quite a disparity. Even though the weekly Treasury bill auctions set the standard for short-term, risk-free rates, many lenders will offer higher-than-average rates if they are in a geographic area with good loan demand. Conversely, when banks are flush with depositors' money, they may offer lower rates. If you're willing to wire transfer your funds to an out-of-state federally insured institution, the place to search for the best interest rates across the country is **www.Bankrate.com**. Just knowing the competitive situation may help you make a smart decision.

Just make sure that you are buying a certificate of deposit that is federally insured by the FDIC. The standard insurance amount is $250,000 per depositor, per insured bank, for each ownership category. That means you could actually have more than $250,000 in insured deposits in each bank, depending on how the accounts are titled.

You'll find a link to the latest FDIC regulations regarding deposit insurance on the home page at **TerrySavage.com**. And for those who have amounts over the insured level, including small businesses or agencies, there is a way to automatically distribute your cash to a network of insured accounts at different banks. Go to **CDARS.com** to learn more about this valuable service.

You Can Create Your Own Bond Ladder

One problem with investing all your cash at one time is that you might regret that decision if interest rates move higher right after you invest. The solution to that problem is to create your own *bond ladder*—staggering the maturity dates of the securities you purchase. For example, if you wanted to keep your portfolio fairly short term, you could invest in 13-week, 26-week, and one-year Treasury bills. Or you could purchase only 13-week Treasury bills but stagger your purchases every 2 or 4 weeks. That way some portion of your investment would always be maturing, and you could take advantage of higher interest rates.

A bond ladder can also be constructed with longer-term securities, perhaps adding two- to five-year Treasury notes. Under ordinary circumstances, this strategy will add more current yield while preserving the flexibility to take advantage of higher rates. Of course, this process has a downside: If interest rates decline, your overall yield on the portfolio will decline because maturing securities must be replaced with lower-yielding ones.

THE SAVAGE TRUTH ON SAVINGS BONDS

U.S. Savings Bonds Are No Longer a Good Deal

Savings bonds originated as a patriotic way to help the government in wartime. For many years, they were a sensible chicken money alternative investment. But in recent years, the government has changed its formula for paying interest on traditional Series EE bonds. And the Series I bonds, which are designed to offset inflation, can lock you into an incredibly low base rate for the life of the bond. These issues make them less attractive to investors, although billions are invested every year through automatic payroll deductions for savings bonds.

This commentary is a sad one for me to write, since in earlier years I served as a spokesperson for U.S. savings bond campaigns. But today I think you'd be better off buying your child or grandchild an investment in a tax-free college savings plan (see Chapter 10) than giving a bond. And since savings bonds are now sold electronically, you don't even get that official-looking bond certificate, anyway.

Still, you should know how savings bonds work. But the drawbacks of both types of U.S. savings bonds are now significant enough for me to advise you not to purchase them under the current circumstances.

Series EE Bonds

Instead of the interest rate changing every six months based on the market interest rates paid on five-year Treasury securities, Series EE bonds purchased on or after May 1, 2005, now pay a fixed rate for life. That means if inflation returns, you no longer get the benefit of higher rates every six months to offset the impact of inflation. A new fixed rate is set every May 1 and November 1, based on a formula that uses yields of 10-year Treasury securities. Once set, you earn that rate for the life of the bond. And now the maximum annual purchase is $5,000.

EE savings bonds are still sold at a discount to face value, with the interest accruing each year. You don't pay taxes on the interest until you cash in the bonds. EE bonds have a "maturity date" set on the face of the bond, which may have been extended. As a result, some older bonds are worth more than face value because they continued to accrue interest.

The only way to know for sure if your bond has stopped paying interest is to check at TreasuryDirect.gov. Basically, *all* of the old Series E bonds and all Series EE bonds older than 30 years have stopped paying interest and should be cashed in. You'll owe ordinary federal income taxes on the accrued interest. (The government has stopped issuing HH bonds, which at one time allowed you to defer those taxes.)

A warning: *If you have older Series EE bonds, dated before May 1, 2005, they still accrue interest on the old floating-rate formula. So these bonds may be uniquely valuable, and you should think twice about cashing them in before they reach final maturity.*

Also, before cashing in older bonds, make sure you know exactly when the next interest payment will accrue. You want to wait until after the interest is paid, or you risk losing out on the most recent interest earned. If you redeem an EE bond before it is five years old, you will lose three months of accrued interest.

At TreasuryDirect.gov, you will find a "Savings Bond Calculator" tool that will help you find out what your older bond is worth today, based on the issue date.

Among the remaining attractions of savings bonds is the fact that the interest is always free from state and local taxes. Plus, for middle-income families who cash in bonds held in the *parent's name* to pay for college tuition, all the interest earned is tax free. (For this purpose, "middle income" means income of roughly $70,000 on a single return, or $105,000 on a joint return.)

Series I Bonds

In 1998, the Treasury introduced a new series of savings bonds that are indexed to the official rate of inflation, Series I bonds. At the time, I highly recommended them, and the older bonds are still very valuable.

I-bonds earn a fixed base rate that is set for the life of the bond. That base rate changes every six months for newly issued bonds purchased during that six-month period. Each bond also receives a twice-yearly inflation adjustment based on the current annual inflation rate (the CPI for urban consumers). The inflation adjustment is added to the base rate to determine the I-bond yield for that six-month period.

I-bonds issued when the program started in the late nineties are now very valuable, for they may carry fixed base rates as high as 3.6 percent. More recent issues of I-bonds have carried a zero percent base rate, or just slightly higher, reflecting the years of very low CPI inflation starting in 2008. There's no guarantee that the base rate, while set at zero percent, couldn't actually result in a negative return, as happened in the period starting May 1, 2009. And during inflationary times, the consumer price index, which is set by government bureaucrats, might not reflect changes as quickly as the free market in Treasury notes and bills.

If you have a lifetime "zero" base rate, even an inflation adjustment designed to compensate for higher inflation in the future wouldn't make Series I bonds a good investment. My advice: Avoid new purchases of Series I bonds until, and unless, base rates move much higher.

THE SAVAGE TRUTH ON ALL BONDS

The word *bond* conjures up an image of safety and security. Especially during periods of low interest rates on bank CDs, Treasury bills, and other chicken money investments, people are tempted to look at longer-term IOUs, which usually pay a higher rate of interest. But bonds have their own set of risks, and you can lose (or make) as much money in bonds as you can in the riskiest of stocks. So this is a good place to discuss the truth about risk in bonds. These Truths apply to all bonds, including bonds issued by the U.S. government, private corporations, or states and municipalities.

The Risk of Default

The first kind of bond risk is obvious: the risk of *default*. Would you lend money to your brother, adult child, or best friend? It all depends on your affection for them—and on your assessment of the risk that they won't repay. When it comes to investing in bonds, you can rule out affection and make your decision solely on creditworthiness. In fact, there are rating agencies that determine the likelihood of regular interest repayments and ultimate repayment of principal. Triple A is best, and the ratings move downward from there to triple B, the lowest investment-grade rating.

Higher-rated bonds pay a lower rate of interest because people are more willing to lend to governments or companies with stellar credit ratings. Ratings are no secret. Some bonds, called "junk bonds" or "high-yield bonds," have very low ratings and correspondingly high risk, but they also pay higher rates of interest to tempt buyers. If you're willing to take this higher risk of default, you can earn a higher return as long as they keep paying. Just understand that risk and return are opposite sides of the coin.

When I wrote the advice in the paragraphs above a decade ago, I had no idea that investors, including banks and sophisticated money managers, would literally throw caution to the winds and purchase debt backed by questionable mortgages. But it happened—and the losses were huge. Of course, some of those mortgage bonds were backed by quasi-governmental agencies: Fannie Mae and Freddie Mac. Still, the losses were huge as bond sellers could find no buyers willing to take on the risks of default that suddenly became apparent in many of these mortgage-backed securities.

Going forward, you can be sure that there will be much more attention paid to quality of the credit. (Just try to get a mortgage loan today and you'll see what I mean.) But there are still investors who are desperate for higher yields and willing to take on that additional credit risk.The latest concern is for potential defaults in the municipal bond market, as cities and states face huge budget deficits. Now, differences in credit quality are being carefully examined. The "full faith and credit" of a state that cannot pay its bills is hardly comforting. At least the federal government can *print* money to pay its bills and the interest on its debt, while a state can only raise taxes or cut spending in order to have money to pay the interest on its bond obligations.

But risk of default isn't the only risk you take when you buy bonds. There's also the risk that your bonds will lose value in the marketplace because of changing perceptions of inflation. And even federal Treasury bonds are not immune from that risk.

Market Price Risk in Bonds

When it comes to bonds, there's another risk: *market price risk.* Even bonds from top-rated companies or governments can drop in value because of external events such as inflation. Here's a simple example:

Suppose you buy a $1,000, 30-year bond from a triple-A-rated company. The interest rate set on the bond is 4.5 percent—a very nice return compared to today's low inflation rate. That 4.5 percent rate is called the *coupon rate.* Every six months you receive a check for your interest. The company continues to prosper. Then inflation starts to rise. Three years later, when the same triple-A-rated company sells bonds in this inflationary environment, it has to pay investors a rate of 8 percent in order to get them to buy its new 30-year bonds.

Now, suppose you decide you need to sell your bond to pay some bills. Don't assume it is still worth $1,000, even though the company is still doing very well and there is no question it will continue to pay the 4.5 percent interest until maturity, when you will receive your $1,000 back.

In the new inflationary environment, you'll find that no one is willing to pay you $1,000 for your 4.5 percent bond because they could take that $1,000 and get a 8 percent bond of similar quality. What is your old bond worth today if you sell it? About $750.

You've just seen a real-life demonstration of market price risk:

When interest rates move higher, the market value of older,
low-yielding bonds moves lower.

That rule holds true whether you're buying government bonds, municipal bonds, or corporate bonds. Conversely, if you still had one of those 30-year Treasury bonds issued back in the 1980s, with a yield of 14 percent, it would be worth far more than its initial $1,000 cost. (Now, most of those older, very high-yielding bonds have matured. Still, in a period of low interest rates, even bonds from a decade ago have relatively higher yields. But to buy them, you'll pay a price higher than the $1,000 face value.)

The market for interest rates moves up or down every day based on traders' and investors' views of the likelihood of future inflation, future Federal Reserve actions to raise interest rates, and myriad other economic factors. The market value of your bond may rise or fall every day as well. Of course, you can hold your bond until maturity, when you'll receive the promised return of your initial $1,000 investment. But if interest rates rise in the interim, you'll suffer by accepting a lower rate of return while you hold your bond.

A special note about bond prices: Unlike stock prices, which are easily found throughout the day and after the daily closing, bond prices have always been more opaque. If you are buying corporate or municipal bonds in amounts less than $100,000, you run the risk that the dealer will make extra money by selling them to you at a higher purchase price, or buying them from you at a price slightly less than the market price.

How can you as the individual investor find real-time current bond prices? At **www.FINRA.org** (the agency that protects small investors) there is a section called "Market Data." Click on that link and you will find prices of all government, corporate, and municipal securities. Or you can make your corporate or municipal bond purchases through a mutual fund, as described later, letting the professional fund manager handle the pricing issues.

The Longer the Maturity, the Greater the Market Price Risk

Think about this intuitively. You lend someone money for two years at a fixed interest rate. In the meantime, inflation returns with a vengeance. When you get your money back in two years, its buying power has dropped dramatically. Thank goodness you loaned your money out for only two years. What if you had made a 30-year loan? If inflation really raged, by the time your money was repaid it would be worth a lot less.

The bond trading market factors in the length of time of the loan as well as the quality of the borrower in assessing changes in price. If you purchase a 30-year bond and interest rates subsequently rise 1 percent, the market price of your bond loan will drop a lot more than the market price of a two-year bond or note.

It's like playing "crack the whip." The momentum is greater the farther out you get. That's why there's greater risk in lending your money (buying a bond) that has a long-term maturity.

Event Risk

Interest rates usually move in tandem. That is, all top-rated bonds, no matter what the issuer, will either increase or decrease in price at the same rate and at the same time. Even differently rated bonds of similar maturities usually maintain a certain price differential. But special factors sometimes enter the marketplace. We saw that kind of risk develop on several occasions over the past few years. For example, in the summer of 2008, the relationship between different types of bonds moved to an extreme.

Seeking safety, global capital rushed into U.S. Treasury securities, pushing prices higher and yields lower, despite the well-publicized financial risk taking place in the United States. It seemed to investors that the United States was the *least risky* place in a world beset with the risk of default.

Since then, despite fears of inflation caused by Federal Reserve *quantitative easing* (a euphemism for "money printing"), investors have continued to seek relative safety in the United States, pushing bond prices higher and interest rates lower. The price spreads between dollar-denominated bonds and euro-denominated bonds increased dramatically. After all, the euro bonds included debt of countries like Greece, Portugal, and Italy.

Similarly, while foreign buyers rushed into the U.S. Treasury market seeking safety, very few of them purchased tax-free municipal bonds and shorter-term notes, since they didn't need the tax benefits. The result was that municipal bond yields stayed relatively high, while Treasury yields dropped as buyers rushed into that market.

But municipal bonds—IOUs of cities and states—carry their own level of default risk in debt-burdened times. That's a risk that should be considered before buying municipal debt. Late in 2010, fears of state defaults became widespread, causing a huge wave of muni-bond selling.

When purchasing bonds, you need to be aware of credit quality, time to maturity, and event risk, which could impact one category of bonds more than another. Since many bond mutual funds are structured to invest in only one type of bond, you also need to understand the investment strategy of your bond funds.

Total Return Is Not Current Yield

It's worth noting here that the yield on a bond is not necessarily the same as its total return or value to an investor. One example is a tax-free municipal bond, which offers a lower interest rate coupon, because most individual investors can receive the interest totally free from federal income taxes and, in some cases, free from state and local taxes as well. So the lower-yielding muni bond might offer a higher after-tax return than a higher-yielding Treasury or corporate bond. It's the after-tax return that counts.

But the concept of total return typically has more to do with price than with tax considerations. Total return includes both the interest you receive and the change in price. Suppose, for example, that you purchase an older, lower-yielding bond at a discount to its face value of $1,000. Perhaps you paid only $950. Then your *total return* would be a combination of that low interest you earn for the remaining term of the bond, *plus* the gain of $50 when the bond is redeemed for the full face value of $1,000.

Traders frequently buy bonds simply to make money on the swings in price, based on the changes in interest rates. So you can have a combination of factors resulting in a short-term trading profit, or loss. But if you're a long-term bond investor, you're probably most interested in the concept of *total return to maturity*, which takes into account purchase price and the interest coupon you'll receive until the bond is redeemed.

(*Special note:* Some bond issuers reserve the right to "call" the bonds and refinance them with lower-priced debt. In that case, your plans to lock in long-term high yields would be disrupted. Be sure to check on this call feature before buying a bond.)

Measuring both aspects of bond ownership to get total return is especially useful when considering the purchase of bond mutual funds. You could look at a bond fund that had a large total return last year because of falling interest rates. Buying that fund today, when rates have stabilized, would not give you anything like the return the shareholders earned last year when rates dropped and bond prices rose. It's important to note the difference between current yield and total return.

Reinvestment Risk

When you've been smart enough to buy higher-yielding bonds and are tempted to sell them at a profit, you're faced with a choice. You can sell the bond and lock in a very tidy profit even after taxes. But then, what would you do with the cash—reinvest it at today's lower rates? Or you can hang onto the bond and keep collecting your annual interest, but run the risk that bond prices will fall because interest rates move higher!

As you can see, even bondholders face risks and decisions about how to manage the rewards. Once you sell a bond, you have to figure out what to do with the cash. And there's another reinvestment risk. What do you do with the interest you earn on those bonds over the years if you're not planning to spend it? When rates have fallen, you can't reinvest and earn the same yield.

Today's bond investors do have a choice: zero-coupon bonds or TIPS (Treasury Inflation Protected Securities). These zero-coupon bonds, issued by the U.S. Treasury and many corporations, are stripped of their coupons by investment bankers. Thus, they are sold at a discounted fixed price that represents the current value of future interest payments.

Instead of making regular interest payments, the value of the bond increases each year by the amount of the interest rate until the zero matures and is worth its face value. However, if a zero is sold before maturity, there could be a gain or a loss, depending on the purchase price and the amount of interest that has accrued. Think of zeros working the same way old-fashioned Series E savings bonds did—purchased at a discount and building up to a certain face value by way of a fixed (or in some cases, variable) interest-rate addition every year.

Notice that the investor in zero-coupon bonds doesn't have the problem of reinvesting the interest check every six months. That reinvestment is built into the appreciation in the bond's value every year. But zero-coupon bonds don't solve the problem of market price risk. In fact, they're even more volatile because their owners don't have the cushion of a semiannual interest payment to offset changes in market interest rates.

That's where TIPS come in. They are zero-coupon bonds, but the amount that accrues each year is not fixed. Instead, it is based on a fixed rate plus an inflation adjustment to the principal value of the bonds. That inflation adjustment is based on the consumer price index (which may or may not correctly measure inflation). At the maturity of a Treasury Inflation Protected Security, you receive the adjusted principal or the original principal, whichever is greater. This provision protects you against deflation.

TIPS can be purchased through TreasuryDirect.gov in minimum denominations of $100. TIPS with maturities of 5, 10, and 30 years are auctioned regularly and can be purchased electronically through your TreasuryDirect account. Or major mutual fund companies such as Vanguard, Fidelity, and American Century offer mutual funds that purchase TIPS.

Zero-coupon bonds may be thinly traded and hard to price accurately. If you're interested, I suggest you buy a zero-coupon bond fund such as American Century Funds' zero-coupon series, with set maturities ranging from 5 to 25 years. Check for information at **AmericanCentury.com** or call 800-345-2021.

Two key reminders: First, as with all bonds, when interest rates rise, your bond or bond fund will lose value. But since interest rates typically rise because of fear of inflation, at least a TIPS fund will lose relatively less in market value.

Second, it's important to keep taxes in mind when buying zero-coupon bonds or TIPS: *Even though you don't receive the semiannual interest payment, you'll owe taxes on that amount.* You'll receive a 1099 form every year for the interest that was accrued to the value of your account but was not actually paid out. That's why you're better off buying these funds in a tax-deferred retirement account.

Why Buy Bond *Funds*

The price risks of bonds may be offset by purchasing a bond fund, with professional management to adjust the types of bonds held by the fund. These bond funds are offered by the major mutual fund companies with no commission cost to purchase and very low annual management fees.

A *managed bond fund* is different from a bond trust or unit investment trust, which is a fixed package of bonds that will be held to maturity. Typically, those trusts are traded on exchanges, and their price is determined by market perceptions of the future value of the trust, based on interest rate and inflation expectations.

The price of a managed bond fund is determined daily by a valuation of the bonds held by the fund. It is the job of the fund manager to adjust the holdings in the fund based on changes in quality of the issuers, or based on an assessment of the future direction of interest rates. When the bond fund manager thinks interest rates will rise (and bond prices will fall) he or she will sell bonds and hold shorter-term securities, hoping to reinvest when rates are higher.

Each bond fund prospectus clearly states the quality and maturity range of bonds it will buy. Thus, you could find a short-term bond fund, an intermediate-term bond fund, or even a long-term bond fund. And the prospectus will tell you whether the fund managers must stick to either Treasuries, high-quality corporate bonds, or even high-risk bonds. Obviously, the yield on the riskier bond fund is higher, a way to attract investors. But could you sleep at night, knowing that even though the portfolio manager is watching, there is a greater risk of default?

Here's a reminder about the one Truth you must keep in mind when buying individual bonds or a bond mutual fund:

When interest rates rise, bond prices fall.

That rule applies to all bonds and all bond funds in differing degrees, depending on the quality of the bonds and the maturity of the bonds. But don't make the mistake of thinking that you can't lose money in good bonds. If inflation returns, bringing with it higher interest rates, all the money you have in bonds is at risk of lower prices.

It works the other way, too. When inflation drops and interest rates fall, bond prices rise. That is, older bonds with higher yields than you could get in a low-inflation climate become more valuable. From 1981 through 2010, we were in a bond bull market. That is, despite ups and downs in interest rates, the overall trend in rates was down.

It's a Savage Truth: *We always invest based on our most recent experiences.*

Today's bond investors have only distant memories of the huge bond losses that took place the last time inflation soared in the late 1970s. If inflation returns, there will be many expensive lessons to be learned by those who are now locking up money in 10-year Treasury bonds earning 3.5 percent, which looks relatively attractive compared to less than one-half of 1 percent in Treasury bills.

Bonds versus Stocks

Although many investors seek out what they perceive to be the relative safety of bonds, there is a certain price to pay for this peace of mind. Over the long run, stocks have always offered superior returns. From 1945 through 2010, the S&P 500 stock index generated a compound annual total return of 11 percent, versus a return of just 5.8 percent for intermediate-term U.S. Treasury securities, according to an Ibbotson Associates study. Of course, for those with a shorter time horizon, a mixture of bonds and stocks can dampen volatility and provide income.

The assumption in building a portfolio that includes both stocks and bonds is that they tend to move in opposite directions. But famed Wharton School of Business professor Jeremy Siegel has demonstrated that stocks and bonds move together much more frequently than they diverge.

The psychological effect, however, of having less-volatile bonds as a portion of your asset allocation cannot be underestimated. It may be easier to ride out downturns and stick with a stock portfolio over the much-vaunted long run of 20 years or more if an investor also has a component of bond holdings.

The real answer to the question of stocks versus bonds depends on the relative valuation of these alternatives. In fall of 2010, with the Dow Jones Industrial Average trading around 12,000, Professor Siegel remarked that the valuation of stocks trading at low price/earnings multiples was cheaper compared to bonds than at any time since the 1950s. Thus, while many investors were searching for higher yields by purchasing riskier bonds, the real advantage based on valuation would be to purchase high-quality dividend-paying stocks.

It's a Savage Truth: *Everything in investing is relative.* Once you understand how bonds and stocks are priced to reflect risk, then you can make an informed decision on how to balance them in your own investment portfolio.

GETTING STARTED

HOW TO BUY U.S. TREASURY BILLS

Go to www.TreasuryDirect.gov and click on "Individual." When you get to that list, click on "Learn More about Treasury Bills" and look for the link to "Open an Account." You'll need one of your paper checks, which has your checking account and bank's routing numbers on it. You can make a one-time purchase, or set up an automatic monthly deduction to schedule repeat purchases of Treasury bills. The interest you earn will be automatically deposited in that checking account. The minimum amount is $100 for each purchase.

It's easy to get started, and you'll get the current rates set by major buyers. That's the way to save chicken money like a pro!

TERRY'S TO-DO LIST

1. Examine your own risk tolerance in light of investment alternatives.

2. Sort out your chicken money and put it in chicken money investments so that you can sleep at night. Let the rest of your money work harder for you in riskier investments.

3. Respect the value of compound interest.

4. Understand the market value price risks in bonds and the concept of total return.

5. Balance your investments between stocks and bonds— and the alternatives that will be explained in Chapters 6 and 7.

6. When buying bonds, either use a mutual fund or check the prices to make sure you are not paying a price that is too high or selling below the true market price.

CHAPTER

5

THE SAVAGE TRUTH ON THE STOCK MARKET

It's Less Risky
Than You Think

The first edition of *The Savage Truth* was published shortly before the stock market crash of 2001, and this chapter originally revolved around a warning that stocks don't go straight up! Well, we've all learned the truth of that warning in the intervening decade. Today, many people have gone to the opposite extreme—swearing off stocks after watching their hard-earned contributions to a retirement plan go down the drain in a bear market.

I intend to make the argument that if you believe in the future of America—the country where you intend to live, work, retire, and hope to watch your children and grandchildren grow up—then you *must* invest sensibly in the stock market for the long run. Even in the face of your current skepticism, the case for stock market investing is persuasive.

But one basic question has arisen in recent years that must be addressed first. It's the issue of whether the stock market is "fair." There's a growing feeling on the part of individual investors that the deck is stacked against them. Headline scams like Madoff, the revelations about Wall Street firms acting against the interests of their clients, and the investigations into insider trading on the part of hedge fund managers have combined to cast strong doubt on the fairness of the markets.

No one wants to play a game that is rigged against you. When even the top government investigators fail to find the scams that are going on in front of them, there's reason to doubt. The financial reform legislation, with its thousands of rules to be written by lobbyists and politicians, doesn't remove the cloud of suspicion. Promises of consumer protection are viewed with skepticism.

In the face of all that, all I can cite is history. We came through a similar period of mistrust in the 1930s, and the stock market recovered not only from its losses but from widespread revelations of impropriety on the part of Wall Street. So I do have strong hope that our government will recognize the importance of free and fair markets, regulated just enough to make sure that people are willing to risk their capital in exchange for getting a chance at a fair return on their investments.

The free enterprise system has created a higher standard of living for more people than any other system ever tried. As a great trader once reminded me: "Yes, capitalism results in the unequal distribution of wealth. But socialism results in the equal distribution of *poverty!*"

If you believe that America will once again restrain its excesses, and use its considerable entrepreneurial talent to grow out of our economic weakness, then you must consider a plan of long-term investing in the stock market. It won't be easy to convince yourself of the ultimate benefits. But then, everyone who vowed in the 1930s to never buy another share of stock surely missed out on some great wealth-building opportunities.

Although it may seem dangerous to put your capital at risk in the stock market, it is equally dangerous to be ruled by emotion. In early March 2009, at the very week the stock market made an important bottom, I wrote a syndicated column headlined: "A Dose of Optimism Required." I urged people not to give up on the stock market or the economic system that it represents.

That column wasn't an attempt to call the market's turn, but the timing was fortuitous. It just seemed to me at the time that there was way too much pessimism—in the midst of the financial collapse, TARP bailout, General Motors bankruptcy, and rising unemployment. The market staged quite a comeback in the ensuing months.

I have always advised investors that even full-time market professionals cannot consistently call market tops and bottoms. A regular program of disciplined monthly investments is likely to prove far more rewarding in the long run than trying to time market entrances and exits. So the advice that follows, so important at the time, has the same ring of truth today. The basic Truths of investing remain the same, despite the ups and downs of the market in recent years. Only the numbers and market statistics have changed.

Still skeptical? Let me lead off with a new and hopefully convincing story about the benefits of regular disciplined investing to create a retirement portfolio. I hope that if you are encouraged, or even tempted, by this example, you will read on in this chapter to learn the Savage Truths about stock market investing.

THE GRASSHOPPER AND THE ANT INVEST

This is the parable of the grasshopper and the ant put into investment action. But neither ants nor grasshoppers have the ability to anticipate or fear the future. Perhaps that is why it is so much more difficult for nature to teach us the lessons of persistence. This story is the result of research done by T. Rowe Price, the well-known mutual fund management company, on the investment results of those who started in both bull and bear markets:

The Moral of the Story: Those who start investing during a severe bear market gain a substantial advantage by investing regularly over those decades until retirement. That's because they have two powerful forces in their favor: the cyclicality of markets, and the ability to accumulate more shares earlier in their investing career.

The Lesson for Today: If you have the discipline to maintain a program of regular investing, even as the market remains discouraging, you will reap greater rewards over the long run.

Compare the results of four investors who each contributed $500 per month (15 percent of a $40,000 annual salary) into a retirement account invested in the S&P 500 index, regularly over a 30-year period. Two of those investors started out just before two of the worst bear markets in history: 1929 and 1970. The others started in 1950 and 1979, just before two great bull markets. (See Figure 5.1.)

The Surprising Result: The ending account balances of the two investors who started in bear markets were more than *double* those of the two investors who began contributing at the start of decades with strong bull markets!

Then, as now, it was discouraging to keep investing monthly in a market that showed poor returns. The S&P 500 had a negative

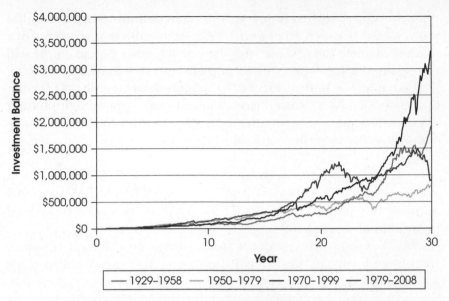

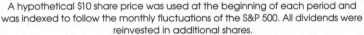

A hypothetical $10 share price was used at the beginning of each period and was indexed to follow the monthly fluctuations of the S&P 500. All dividends were reinvested in additional shares.

Figure 5.1 Advantages of Bear Marketing Investing
Source: T. Rowe Price.

(−0.9%) return from 1929 to 1938, and only a 5.9 percent return in the stagflation of the 1970s, as these investors were starting out. Yet the bear market investors stuck to their plan—and that provided a huge benefit: At the end of 30 years, the portfolios ·of those who started out in the bear markets were worth more than double the value of the two investors who started out in bull markets! All those years of buying shares at low prices put them in a better position to gain from *future* bull markets, after the initial bear market.

The Proof as It Applies to You: Are you thinking that's ancient history? Well, let's project the retirement portfolio results for today's investor, taking a starting date of 1999 and continued regular investments through 2008. Suppose today's investor *never makes any more investments*, but simply maintains her account for the remaining 20 years from 2009 until retirement. We'll project that she earns only the same, relatively low 8.5 percent annualized return that was realized between 1929 and 1958, a very subpar period in stock market history. Even so, at the end of 30 years her account will have gained a 1,208 percent return on her contributions!

Take another look at Figure 5.1, which shows the results for the four investors. As T. Rowe Price demonstrates: A poor start doesn't necessarily equate to a smaller nest egg. History, indeed, demonstrates just the opposite—assuming they maintain their investment program.

(The T. Rowe Price study used a hypothetical $10 share price at the beginning of each period, and it was indexed to follow the actual monthly fluctuations of the S&P 500. All dividends were reinvested in additional shares.)

Sure, it's scary to invest in the stock market, especially after you've seen huge losses, money "down the drain." But can you afford *not* to save and invest for the future? The most obvious way to invest is in the stock market, because it gives you the opportunity to choose a consistent and regular pattern of investing, often on a tax-favored basis.

The stock market reflects the opportunities in America, and around the world, for global growth that will solve today's problems, whether in energy, medicine, finance, housing, transportation, industrial production, or services. But you must still make choices about your investments. This doesn't have to be a full-time passion, but it does require understanding the basic Savage Truths about investing. If you've made mistakes in the past, that's no reason to give up on doing it better in the future.

Remember that old Savage Truth: *The lessons that cost the most teach the most!*

Now that you've "paid your tuition" it's time to go at it again—with better results. Even if you've moved closer to what you hoped would be your retirement age, you'll still need some opportunity for growth in your assets. While you may invest less in the stock market, you'll still want to invest wisely. For that you need to start with some Savage Truths about creating stock market wealth.

THE STOCK MARKET BUILDS WEALTH

What is the real purpose of the stock market? The stock market exists for building wealth—but not necessarily *your* wealth!

Initially, the role of the stock market is to raise capital for companies that issue shares. Here's an example: XYZ company goes public and sells one million shares. Let's say that 20 percent of that stock is sold for the accounts of the founders, and the remaining 80 percent of the money goes to the company itself.

The company founders, who have invested their time and personal wealth to grow the business, are suddenly well rewarded. Not only do they have cash to spend on houses, cars, and other investments, but the market value of their remaining holdings has increased tremendously. The company can use its share of the proceeds to pay off debt, to build new factories, or to pursue other business purposes that will earn more money for shareholders in the future.

To the extent that the company is successful, the stock price will rise and all shareholders will be rewarded. This capital-raising function of the stock market allows businesses to grow and expand. The fact that shareholders' wallets also expand, thereby also boosting the economy, is merely a byproduct of the capital-raising function of the market.

As the stock continues to rise, the only real benefit to the company is that the higher market valuation allows the company to sell more stock in the future to raise more capital. But all the shareholders now feel wealthier as the stock moves higher. When the stock falls, the converse is true. Plans for buying houses, cars, and even putting children through college may have to change.

Stock prices rise in expectation that the company's earnings will grow. Investors look forward to future earnings growth and are willing to pay higher prices for companies whose prospects are good. When both the real economy and expectations for the future are expanding, people are willing to buy stocks at ever-higher prices.

Then you get the kind of bull market of the 1990s. But when the real economy slows down, earnings expectations decline. When real earnings decline, expectations of future earnings start to shrink, and people are less willing to pay higher prices for stocks. In fact, they start to sell. That's what pulls markets down. We've seen that several times in the past decade, starting in 2000.

If the relationship between stock prices, current earnings, and expected future earnings always remained the same, it would be easy to predict the direction of stock prices. But because individual decisions to buy or sell are made out of emotion as well as fact, the market tends to move to extremes. It's not easy to anticipate how far the extremes of sentiment will move the market in either direction.

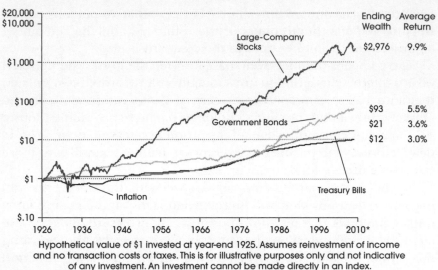

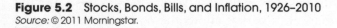

Hypothetical value of $1 invested at year-end 1925. Assumes reinvestment of income and no transaction costs or taxes. This is for illustrative purposes only and not indicative of any investment. An investment cannot be made directly in an index.
Past performance in no guarantee of future results.

Figure 5.2 Stocks, Bonds, Bills, and Inflation, 1926–2010
Source: © 2011 Morningstar.

Stocks Build Wealth Over the Long Run

If you have any doubt about the long-term potential of the stock market to create wealth, just look at Figure 5.2. This chart has appeared in every book I have written over the past 20 years, and is the cornerstone not only of my belief in the future of stock market investing, but of my faith in this country.

Using the landmark Ibbotson research into past stock market performance from 1926 through 2010, you can clearly see how much wealth was created by taking the risks inherent in stock market investing as compared to leaving your money in the bank.

If you had invested $1 in risk-free Treasury bills in 1926, it would have grown to $21 by the end of 2010; the same $1 invested in stocks of major companies (the Standard & Poor's 500 stock index) would have grown to $2,776, including dividends. On an inflation-adjusted basis, the stock investment today would be worth $243.63—still far ahead of the T-bills, which would be worth $1.68 in inflation-adjusted dollars.

But think of the scary times you would have encountered along the way, including the market crash of 1929, the Great Depression, the 50 percent market decline of 1973 to 1974, and the crash of 1987. Like the Othmers and Gladys Holm (whose stories are described in

Chapter 1), you would have needed tremendous self-discipline to stick to your investment plan.

For those without historic perspective, the volatile performance of stocks during the first decade of this century has been especially difficult to withstand. Many investors during this period were new to the market, suddenly watching their 40l(k) dollars virtually disappear. Professional pension fund managers were more equipped to deal with the emotions and the opportunities created by the market decline. But amateur investors were scared out of the markets just at the wrong time.

At the end of 2010, the overall return of the market for the decade was slightly negative. But as seen in the story at the start of this chapter, those who continued to accumulate shares by investing a regular dollar amount throughout the period are now well-positioned to take advantage of future stock price increases. Those eventual higher stock prices may come as a result of economic growth, as well as a reflection of future inflation.

The Stock Market Barometer of Wealth

The stock market is both a barometer of the economy and a factor in economic growth. A rising stock market gives confidence and an improved financial position to investors. Even non-investors feel better when the stock market rises because a bull market encourages business to expand and create jobs. This synergy between the economy and the stock market has been called the *virtuous circle*. That's the opposite of the *vicious circle* we saw in 2008, and in the 1930s, when a declining stock market reinforced fear and resulted in a spiraling economic decline.

There's general agreement that a rising stock market is good for everyone and a falling market that wipes out wealth is bad for everyone and for the economy in general. So everyone is cheering for the winners—as long as everyone gets to share in the benefits of a rising stock market through retirement accounts and mutual funds.

History shows that stock market optimism has always paid off, with equities far outdistancing safer, risk-free investments over the long run. But sometimes that's a longer run than most people expect. And sometimes there are relatively long periods of stock market declines. If you decide to sell, or need to sell, when the stock market is in a downtrend, you'll take a loss. But where does that lost money *go*? It's a question on the minds of many investors.

Market Losses Go to Money Heaven

It's commonly accepted that the stock market can create wealth. But did you ever wonder what happens to the money that is lost when the stock market goes down?

Suppose, for example, that Microsoft, IBM, or Google had 10 million shares outstanding. (They actually have many more shares outstanding, but let's keep the math simple.) The market has a very bad week, and the share price of one of these companies drops by $20. Our easy math shows that the shareholders have lost a collective $200 million worth of market value. Multiply that by all the other companies whose stocks dropped during the week. Individually the losses are painful; collectively they are huge. In fact, at year-end 2008, the broad-based Wilshire 5000 stock index had lost 37.23 percent, which translated into a loss of $6.9 trillion!

Where did all that wealth go?

Only the futures markets are truly a zero-sum game, with a winner for every loser. In the stock market, the only ones who profit from a decline are the very few speculators who sold shares short—shares they didn't own but expect to buy back at lower prices, generating a profit. No one gets the money stockholders lose when prices fall; it's just gone. It's the same thing when stock prices rise, and wealth is created—but fewer people question the sudden appearance of wealth in bull markets.

When stock prices fall day after day, money simply disappears. Or as one wise old trader explained to me years ago when I asked where all the wealth had gone: "My dear, it went to Money Heaven!"

That leads us to the question of *risk* in the stock market—and some Truths that might surprise you.

THE SAVAGE TRUTH ON STOCKS AND RISK

Your most recent experience with investing in your 401(k)—or just following the newspaper headlines—has probably convinced you that the stock market is a very risky place to put your money. Certainly, you know people who "lost" a lot of money in the market. Perhaps that's because they sold out at the wrong time. I'm sure you know people who tell you they *always* sell at just the wrong time. That's because they're ruled by emotion—not by long-term perspective.

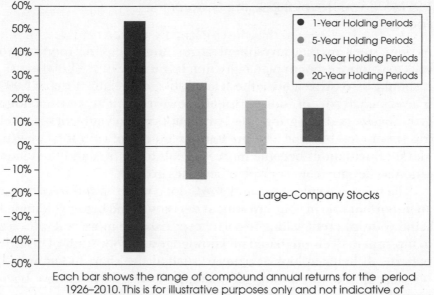

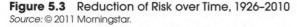

Each bar shows the range of compound annual returns for the period
1926–2010. This is for illustrative purposes only and not indicative of
any investment. Past performance is no guarantee of future results.

Figure 5.3   Reduction of Risk over Time, 1926–2010
Source: © 2011 Morningstar.

Stock Market Risk Diminishes over Time

Figure 5.3 gives a different perspective on stock market risk. It's
statistical proof that risk actually diminishes over time. Looking at
the chart, you can see that if you invest in the stock market for only
one year, there is substantial risk of loss. In fact, if you look at only one-
year investment periods, according to the Ibbotson data, you'd have
a one-in-three chance of sustaining a loss. If you remain invested for
five years, then that risk of loss diminishes.

And if you stick with your stock market investment for 20 years,
modern market history, dating back to 1926, shows *that there has never
been a 20-year period when you would have lost money in a diverse portfolio of large company stocks with dividends reinvested—even adjusted for
inflation.*

Even if you take into account the declining purchasing power
of money caused by inflation, the longest period to break even was
20 years—from January 1973 to July 1993. Overall, it's easy to see
that time diminishes risk—*if* you can discipline yourself to ignore
the shorter-term fluctuations, which are sometimes quite large.

The More You Have at Risk, the Greater the Fear Factor

As your stock market investment grows, the discipline required to stick to your investment plan is greater. If you have only $1,000 at risk, it should be easy to ignore the fear of loss, especially if that $1,000 is a very small part of your personal net worth. But as your portfolio grows in size and you grow older, you'll notice that your stock market investment has become a far greater percentage of your total wealth. Market fluctuations become more difficult to ignore, and the temptation to deviate from your plan becomes greater.

The twin concepts of *fear* and *greed*, along with *risk* and *reward*, play an important role in your investment decisions. The better you understand your inherent willingness to accept risk, the more you will stick to investment decisions based on knowledge and your study of historic patterns. It helps to look at patterns such as the chart in Figure 5.3. It's clear that even the most devastating market declines have been part of long-term economic and investment growth. But when that investment represents your entire future lifestyle (i.e., your ability to retire and live in comfort), it's harder to remain detached.

Your Time Horizon Determines Your Risk Perception

Do you know your real time horizon? You may tell yourself—or your stockbroker or financial planner—that your time horizon is a long one. You may announce that you're saving for retirement or your toddler's college education. You make your stock market investment decision armed with the knowledge that over a 15- or 20-year period you're likely to be far ahead if you stick to your plan.

Then you check the price of your stock or mutual fund every day or every week. When you receive your quarterly statement, you tote up your gains or losses. If you hear that the stock market has fallen a record amount, or a number of days in a row, you get slightly queasy. Never mind that you planned to hold onto this investment for 15 years. Your real time horizon is your internal tolerance for loss, and that can be played out over a very short time period. Inevitably, you'll feel an irresistible urge to sell at just the wrong moment.

There is a way to mitigate this aspect of human nature. If you divide your assets into short-, medium-, and long-term investments, it's easier to close your eyes to the short-term fluctuations of the stock market. This is not mental accounting, but a real process of designation. You may even create separate IRA accounts to help you compartmentalize your thinking. Or simply announce to yourself (as I have) that this particular well-chosen growth mutual fund investment is the last you will spend in your old age—or will be left to your heirs. You will not touch it under any other circumstances, and until that time you'll just forget it. Now that's a long time horizon!

One more thing to keep in mind: Your time horizon isn't necessarily the market's time horizon. You may have your investment horizon pretty well planned out—planning to take money out for college for your children, or for your retirement. But, the stock market isn't paying attention to your personal cash flow needs, so you can't expect the market to be at its peak levels just when you need to make some withdrawals. We'll deal with that issue in Chapter 13 on retirement planning.

THE SAVAGE TRUTH ON MAKING MONEY IN STOCKS

What's more important to your ultimate investment success—picking the right stocks and mutual funds, or just being invested in the stock market? Some investors are paralyzed by the vast choices available in mutual funds. They're like the guest at a buffet who sees so many desserts he loses his appetite. (Not my problem!) Well, you can't make money if you don't invest—and the most important choices are surprisingly simple.

Being There Is the Key to Profits

If you're overwhelmed by the necessity to choose your investments, you will be heartened by an important study that was done by Gary Brinson in 1986 and reconfirmed in 1991. In 2000, respected market historian Roger Ibbotson replicated the study, using slightly different parameters, and came to the same conclusion: The choice of asset categories—U.S. large-company stocks, U.S. small-company stocks, non-U.S. stocks, U.S. bonds, cash—was the major determinant of investment returns. The simple point of these landmark studies is that *asset allocation*, not stock picking or market timing, is the most important aspect of successful investing.

That is, the most important decision is the decision to *be there*. The choice *of* stocks is not as important as the decision to invest *in* stocks. The choice of mutual funds is not as important as the decision to invest in equity (stock) funds. Of course, if you choose only one stock, and that one is a loser, this theory won't hold true.

The solution is to choose *index funds*—those funds that represent a broad cross-section of the market segment. Those are the kind of funds readily available in your 401(k) plan, or through major mutual fund companies such as Vanguard, Fidelity, American Century, and T. Rowe Price for your IRA account. You can even buy indexes through exchange-traded funds (see Chapter 6), in the form of stocks traded on the major exchanges that trade on the basis of an underlying index.

Bottom line: Just open that IRA, choose index funds representing these asset classes, and invest consistently. You can *weight*, that is, add extra contributions to those different sectors based on your expectations if you want to try to beat the market. But as demonstrated earlier, over the long run you'll do well just matching the performance of the market through these index funds.

So if you're staying awake reading the latest reports on best-performing mutual funds, or scouring the Internet for the latest research recommendations on hot stocks, you can rest a little easier. The first and most important decision you must make is simply to invest in the market.

Beating the Market Requires Defining the Market

If you're a competitive person or a typical investor, you figure your investment should do at least as well as the market. You might even spend a lot of time trying to beat the market (more on that later). But the first step is to *define* the market.

Ask 9 out of 10 people who are interested in stocks how the market is doing, and they'll make reference to the Dow Jones Industrial Average. But as popular as this 30-stock average is with the general public and the nightly news reports, it no longer represents either the mainstream of the U.S. economy or the stock market as a whole. Yet, while most investors can tell you the level of the Dow within about 50 points, very few could quote you the current level of the Standard & Poor's (S&P) 500, the National Association of Securities Dealers Automated Quotation (Nasdaq), or the Russell 2000 indexes.

Each index has its own characteristics and performance record. For example, 1998 was a classic year for divergences. The Dow Jones Industrial Average was up nearly 17 percent, the broader-based S&P 500 index was up about 27 percent, and the tech-weighted Nasdaq composite index gained 37 percent. But in that same time frame, the Russell 2000 index of small-cap stocks was up a mere 2 percent. At the other extreme, in 2010, the Dow Jones Industrial Average gained 14.06 percent while the Russell 2000 index of small-cap stocks nearly doubled that return, gaining 26.85 percent.

Here is the lesson: Different sectors of the market can have significantly different gains and can even move in opposite directions.

And popular beliefs about the direction of "the market" are not always correct. Here's a fact that might surprise you: As of year-end 2010, the S&P 500's total return has been positive in 17 of the past 20 years. The S&P 500 lost 2 percent in 1996, 5.9 percent in 2002, and less than 1 percent in 2007.

Yet from all those negative headlines about the stock market in recent years, most people would assume the stock market was a terrible investment. Surely, there were huge *swings* in the market during those years. Many people got scared and sold out at just the wrong moment, in hindsight.

The overall return of the S&P 500 index for the first decade of this century was actually slightly negative, even with dividends included. But that's just one decade. And as noted earlier, one decade—whether the boom years of the 1990s or the bust years of the opening decade of the twenty-first century—does not make a retirement portfolio that covers 30 or more years of investing.

If you're a long-term investor who reads the daily headlines, you need some long-term perspective to temper your expectations. The decade of the 1990s produced an average annual total return (stock prices and dividends) of more than 19 percent. So the subpar performance of the past ten years balances out the fabulous gains of the previous decade—if you stayed invested.

Taking a longer perspective is essential. The average annual total return of large-company stocks between 1926 and 2010 was 9.9 percent, according to Ibbotson market historians.

But the averages are meaningless, except as a *benchmark*, unless you've invested in the averages by using an index fund (see next chapter). If instead you've decided to invest in certain stocks or sectors of the market, your returns will differ from the broad averages.

But averages don't tell the whole story, even if you're invested in the averages through the use of index funds. During that sub-par decade from 2000 to 2010, the Dow Jones Industrial Average advanced to a peak of 14,164 on October 9, 2007. But the global financial collapse of 2008 brought the Dow to a low of 6875 on March 4, 2009. The subsequent quick 50 percent rebound caught many investors by surprise. They had sold out in panic early in the year and so could not recoup their losses. Thus, the average return for that year had little meaning for them.

There are a few lessons to be learned from these historic refer-ences. First, be aware that unless you are invested in the market averages (see the next chapter on index mutual funds), your invest-ment returns are not likely to match the averages. Second, long-term average returns apply to your investment returns only if you stick around for the long run.

If you can take that long-term perspective, the Savage Truth is clear: *You don't have to beat the market to prosper.* You only have to match the market over the long run to get reasonable investment returns. And when it comes to averages, beware of the extremes that averages may mask. Remember the old Savage Truth: *The man who is standing with one foot in a bucket of ice water and one foot in a bucket of boiling water will tell you that, on average, he feels fine!*

Most Investment Pros Don't Beat the Market, but They Keep Trying

In a November 2010 Fidelity poll of active investors (those who trade 36 times a year), 66 percent said they expected to beat the market in the coming year. That is, whether the market went up or down, they thought they could do better than the indexes. Well, that's why markets exist—to offer a benchmark to those who want to make a serious effort at doing even better than those indexes.

Investment professionals are paid to beat their benchmark averages—or at least to outperform other managers with similar styles. But in spite of all the advertising dollars fund companies spend to convince investors that one fund is "top-rated" and in spite of all the research dollars management companies spend to pick the best-performing stocks, in many years the market (or the index that represents the market or market segment) has continually managed to beat the majority of investment professionals.

Hedge funds are run by professionals using complex strategies designed to beat the market. They may be both long and *short* (betting on market declines) and they can use futures, options, and other tools and strategies that might be a mystery to the ordinary investor. Hedge funds were very popular in 2007, yet in the ensuing financial crisis more than 2,000 of the 11,000 hedge funds shut down—most showing big losses for the period.

Of course, some hedge funds posted stellar results. But even most professionals don't manage that task over the long run. One of those exceptions might be hedge fund manager John Paulson, who made billions in the mortgage market collapse in 2007, and then reportedly made another $5 billion in 2010, betting on the rise of commodities. Stories like that inspire people to try to "beat the market"—and provide the opposite side of the trade for those who win.

The point of all of this discussion is to support the argument that most investors are better off in index funds than in managed mutual funds. Not only are costs lower, but performance—in recent years, anyway—has been better. But whether you choose to invest through index funds or to devote more time to trying to beat the market, it's important to remember that—over the long run—a well-chosen portfolio of stocks has, on average, provided far better returns than sitting with all your assets in cash.

THE SAVAGE TRUTH ON SELECTING STOCKS

If you want to pick winning stock investments—those that beat the market—you have to answer this question: What moves stock prices? You'll get a lot of debate on that subject. Some analysts say the best way to pick stocks that will go higher is to find companies with good fundamental valuations. That is, they look at a company's balance sheet, cash on hand, and business basics and compare this intrinsic value to the company's current stock price in order to determine a stock that is undervalued. These *value* investors avoid companies whose stock *prices* are high relative to their *earnings* per share; they search out *low P/E* stocks.

Other analysts pick stocks and manage mutual funds based on a *growth* outlook. They look for companies with rising earnings prospects and a regular string of past earnings that they can predict into the future. These analysts are not so concerned about how much debt a company has, or other fundamentals. High price-earnings ratios do not keep them from buying a stock if they believe that growth in earnings will continue.

Some analysts try to combine the two disciplines by purchasing stocks that will exhibit *growth at a reasonable price* (GARP). It's easy to get confused by these investment methodologies. After all, when a growth company posts disappointing earnings, many of its followers will sell. That pushes down the stock price to where it appears to be a value company with a relatively low stock price compared to where it once was. (But value investors will tell you that a low price is certainly not the only indicator of value.) Conversely, rising stock prices attract attention, creating their own momentum for future price increases.

In fact, the concept of *momentum* has its own disciples, who want to purchase only stocks whose prices are already moving in the right direction. Momentum investing is based on the law of inertia—the belief that a stock in motion will continue in motion in the same direction.

This momentum theory directly contradicts the *efficient market* theory, which postulates that stock market movements are random. In an efficient market, all new information is immediately available to all market participants. Thus, news is immediately reflected in stock prices. No one should be able to get an edge.

While all of these investment disciplines have advocates and critics, one simple Savage Truth rises above the argument: *Money moves markets.*

If buyers are not more aggressive than sellers, the stock price won't go higher. When there's plenty of money around to buy stocks, prices of most stocks will move higher, regardless of the popular investment style. And in light of the Federal Reserve's recent attempts to flood the economy with new credit and money, it might be wise to add that the overall supply of money does matter very much to the stock market.

The Fed is very powerful—and all that new money has to go somewhere. If businesses don't choose to build facilities and inventory, and if banks are slow to make loans, then it's not surprising that some of that money finds its way into the stock market. Perhaps that's why stocks have beaten inflation over every 20-year period going back to 1926.

Value Is in the Eye of the Buyer (and Seller)

The greatest debate in the stock market is the measurement of *valuations*. The bull market of the 1990s far exceeded many historic stock market measurements, and the bear market of more recent years caused share prices to fall to levels that many analysts considered highly undervalued. What is "fair value" for the stock market—and how do you measure it? One traditional measure of valuing companies is the price-earnings (P/E) ratio of the entire market. To calculate it, you need to understand

- *Earnings per share*—a basis for comparing the profitability of companies of differing sizes. Simply divide the total after-tax profits of the company by the number of shares outstanding.

- *Stock P/E ratio*—a comparison of the current stock price to the most recent (or expected future year's) per-share earnings. For example, a company selling at $10 per share and expected to earn $1 per share, is selling at 10 times earnings. If a company has very small earnings and a very high stock price, the ratio will be very high. To get the P/E ratio of the market, analysts take current prices and earnings expectations for all the stocks in a broad index, such as the S&P 500. The traditional analysis of price-earnings ratios says that the higher the ratio, the higher the risk.

The P/E ratio of the S&P 500 stock index has averaged about 14.6 times earnings. When a group of stocks or an entire market has high P/E ratios, traditional value analysts worry that the market is overvalued, or overpriced. At year-end 2010, the P/E ratio of the S&P 500 was just over 14 percent. In 2001, at the bull market peak, the P/E ratio reached 29 times earnings, its highest level ever.

Another traditional measure of value for the entire market as well as individual stocks is the *dividend yield*—the ratio of stock price to the money paid to shareholders in dividends. For example, if a stock is trading at $50 a share and pays a $1 annual dividend, the dividend yield is 2 percent.

Certainly some stocks pay very low or even no dividend, believing they can make better use of their cash in expanding their business. Or company executives may choose to use excess cash to buy back shares, boosting the earnings-per-share ratio (EPS), and typically leading to higher stock prices.

As an investor, you might choose to buy a stock with no dividend, assuming that management will make good use of their profits to grow the company, resulting in a higher stock price. Or you may chose high-dividend-paying stocks, to have a stream of income from well-run companies.

Figure 5.4 S&P Dividend Yield
Source: Bianco Research.

(I highly recommend *The Little Book of Big Dividends* by Charles Carlson [John Wiley & Sons, 2010]. In it he explains how to choose stocks based on dividend yields, for creating wealth and income.)

Over the years the dividend yield of the S&P 500 index has been considered an indicator of valuation, since historically dividends have been responsible for 44 percent of the total return of the index over the past 80 years.

The dividend yield of the S&P 500 has ranged from a high of 6.5 percent at the market bottom in the early 1980s to a low of 1.3 percent in 1999. At year-end 2010, the dividend yield of the S&P 500 was 1.83 percent. (See Figure 5.4.)

THE SAVAGE TRUTH ON STOCK MARKET TIMING VERSUS BUY-AND-HOLD

There's an entire world of trading based on signals sent by the market. Those who follow these signals are called *market technicians* and they use a variety of techniques to predict future stock market trends. *Technical analysis* involves charting systems, which primarily track prices and volumes, and their interactions. It's a respected art form for some investors, but it also requires patience and diligence as well as the willingness to follow the signals to buy and sell no matter what your mind or heart tell you.

If this approach intrigues you, there are plenty of books and newsletters on technical analysis. Be sure that you don't spend more on the tuition than you make in trading profits. There are numerous online charting websites that will draw not only price charts, but *moving averages* of prices, and help you understand trendlines and all sorts of formations from "double tops" to "flags." One of the easiest places to start, with plenty of free content, is **BigCharts.com**, a part of the Marketwatch website.

But with all due respect to market technicians, I am still waiting to see the *Wall Street Journal or Barron's* profile a strict market technician who *consistently* beats the averages—over a long period of time.

Market Timing Works Best in Hindsight

If being in the market is a key ingredient in financial success, wouldn't it be better to be there when the market is going up and not be there when the market is going down? Of course it would. But is it possible to continually time the market correctly? Consider this quiz based on the Ibbotson research mentioned earlier:

- If you had invested $1 in stocks in January 1926, by the end of 1998 that investment would be worth $2,351.

- If you had invested that same $1 in Treasury bills in January 1926, at the end of 1998 your investment would be worth only $15.

  Question: If you were able to guess (or make a timing decision) for each of the 864 consecutive months between 1926 and 1998 whether to be invested in T-bills or stocks, what would your $1 be worth?

  Answer: $2.314 billion.

Obviously, correct timing can add incredible value to your investment account. But can you figure out a system—or find someone else's system—that has a consistent track record? Why would anyone sell such a great system if it really worked?

Certainly, some investors say they can detect market patterns and predict direction by using charts of price and volume. And many can substantiate a track record of success using market timing. However, you should be aware of an inherent mathematical edge that works against market timing techniques. Instead of being right just once, in order to succeed at market timing you must be correct twice, or even three times. You must know when to buy, when to sell, and when to get back in again. That's quite a chore, involving both timing and self-discipline.

THE SAVAGE TRUTH ON MARKET ADVICE

Market gurus come and go, and sometimes live to forecast again. Today, CNBC's Jim Cramer is always making headlines, and deservedly, because he's had some great calls. And the very existence of a daily, all-day financial television channel means that other market commentators become stars. That's not a new phenomenon.

The 1970s and 1980s featured Joseph Granville and Robert Prechter. Their pronouncements about market direction proved self-fulfilling, at least for a while. Then, when markets fell sharply after their predictions, they were blamed for causing the losses. In the early 1990s, Elaine Garzarelli won acclaim for correctly getting her followers out of the market before the 1987 market crash, but she faded from popularity in the mid-nineties after her newsletter incorrectly predicted a market decline. By the end of the decade, Goldman Sachs's Abby Joseph Cohen had taken center stage.

Bert Dohmen of the *Wellington Letter* made headlines and even wrote a book in 2007 predicting a "global market meltdown," well before it actually happened. Commodities guru Jim Rogers correctly predicted the rising price of gold and other global commodities over the past few years, based on global economic growth and demand from China. Dennis Gartman is widely followed by professional traders for his broad insight into both domestic and global markets, and for his on-target trading advice.

Give these market forecasters credit for being willing to state their views publicly and for being correct as often as they are, but remember that no person or system is infallible. Placing all your bets on one guru's forecast may look like a winning strategy, but it works only if your prophet makes an equally good call in getting you out at the right time.

It's a basic Savage Truth: *The best lesson the markets teach is humility!*

Long-Term Track Records Matter

Whenever you are given a prospectus—an official notice explaining a stock or mutual fund share offering—you'll see these words highlighted: "Past performance is no guarantee of future results." It's considered fair warning. But somewhere between "guaranteed" and "shot-in-the-dark" it does make sense to check out any forecaster's long-term track record. A novice might be right a few times, and you can chalk it up to intuition, luck, or brains. But when a forecaster is correct more often than not, on balance, it's worth taking a closer look.

Baseball players get huge salaries for batting .300. That's getting a hit about one of every three times at bat. Weather forecasters rarely get it right, or else we wouldn't carry an umbrella just in case. Still, they make big money on television. Even economists have a dismal record of correct forecasts. The *Wall Street Journal* polls economists every six months for their forecasts on interest rates, economic growth, and stock market performance. The results are often far off the mark.

If a stock market forecaster has been more often right than wrong, on balance, it may be worth the price of a subscription. But you can't always believe the advertisements or direct-mail solicitations. That's why many investors turn to the *Hulbert Financial Digest*—a newsletter that tracks the recommendations of other financial newsletters. The *Hulbert* ratings are eagerly awaited—and hotly debated—by the investment newsletter industry. It's now part of **Marketwatch.com**, where you can find more information. An e-mail subscription costs $59 per year, with a money-back guarantee.

Hulbert tracks investment performance for more than 180 newsletters, some with performance data going back 20 years. The rankings are based on the returns the typical investor would have obtained if he or she had followed a particular newsletter's advice on the day it arrived. It rates newsletter performance in both up and down markets, under the theory that huge gains in bull markets are easier to come by than defensive advice that minimizes losses amid general market declines.

Interestingly, *Hulbert*'s tracking shows that 80 percent of those newsletters fail to beat the market averages. But those that do beat the averages are worth the cost. For example, for newsletters tracked for more than 25 years, *The Prudent Speculator* comes out on top with an 18 percent average annual gain, compared to a 12 percent return for the Wilshire 5000.

Again, time parameters are important. The current top-five newsletters *Hulbert* follows had gains averaging 20 percent or more for the past five years. But choosing a newsletter, or investment advisor, on less than a five-year track record is very risky, since many are "one-hit wonders" that lose money in subsequent years.

THE SAVAGE TRUTH ON MARKET BEHAVIOR—AND YOURS!

Here's a basic Savage Truth: *The market is always right!*

If you're determined to trade the markets with a portion of your capital, you must always respect the power of the market. Most investors suffer big losses out of stubbornness, because they are unwilling to listen to what the market is telling them. They become convinced that eventually the market will see it their way!

The market may turn eventually, but that typically comes long after they have run out of money. Everybody is wrong in the markets at some time. The problem is compounded if you *stay* wrong in an attempt to prove you're right. There's an old stock trader's adage: "The market can stay 'wrong' longer than you can stay long."

Not only is the market always right, but it's always bigger than any individual or group. As long as a market is run fairly, with prompt dissemination of all relevant information, the market will be king. Speculators may attempt to corner a market, as Bunker Hunt did with the silver market in 1980. Human emotion may combine to extend a market past logical reason, as in the housing bull market of the past decade. But the fundamentals will eventually prevail if a market is allowed to continue functioning freely, and fairly.

Don't Fight the Fed

As with so many of my Savage Truths, this one is common wisdom on Wall Street, though often forgotten. Although individual speculators and hedge funds can't change the intrinsic direction of the stock market, there is one power that can turn markets. In this economic era, that power belongs to the Federal Reserve Bank. The Fed is a quasi-independent body charged with making monetary policy that affects both the supply of available credit and the price of money (interest rates).

Remember the simple truth that "money moves markets." If the Federal Reserve is making money available at a low cost (low interest rates), a good portion of that money should flow into the stock market. The only exceptions in modern memory were the deflationary Great Depression in the United States in the 1930s and the deflationary period in Japan in the 1990s. Then, money was too scared to move into investment markets.

In 2011, the Fed under Chairman Ben Bernanke is determined to keep creating money and keep interest rates low, so it's a reasonable bet that stocks will react to the upside. There's still a great inflation–deflation debate, and the Fed is using every tool to make sure the economy doesn't sink into deflationary mode.

When investing, it's best to be aware of Federal Reserve policy and remember that Savage Truth: *Never fight the Fed.*

Leverage Cuts Both Ways

Leverage is the art of getting a lot of movement out of a little pressure, or getting a lot of profit out of a small investment. When leverage is used in an investment sense, it implies the use of borrowed money to maximize returns on the amount invested. When you purchase stocks on margin, putting down 50 percent in cash and borrowing the rest of the purchase price, you're using leverage.

For example, if you purchase 100 shares of a $20 stock, you'd ordinarily need to pay the $2,000 purchase price in cash. If you use margin, you could put up only $1,000 to control $2,000 worth of stock. Every one-point increase in the price becomes a 10 percent return on the $1,000 you have invested, a far better percentage return than you would get if you put up the entire purchase price. That same leverage works against you very powerfully on the downside.

Futures markets operate on the principles of leverage. A *margin,* or good faith deposit, of only 5 percent of the contract value is often all that's needed to control a sizeable amount of corn, soybeans, bonds, oil, gold, or currencies. Thus, a very small move in price can either double your initial investment or wipe it out completely.

When leverage is carried to an extreme, it can produce fantastic, or disastrous, results. One good example is the collapse of the Long-Term Capital Management (LTCM) hedge fund in the fall of 1998. Its investment techniques were masterminded by two Nobel Prize–winning economists who calculated that the risks of their extreme leverage were mitigated by the strategies they had chosen to hedge against risk. At the peak, LTCM owned securities totaling more than $100 billion, although it had only $2.3 billion in capital.

Its leverage was compounded through the use of derivatives and forward contracts with a face value of approximately $1.25 trillion.

The resulting disaster, which nearly brought down the entire U.S. and, perhaps, global financial structure, was a classic example of the brightest minds being caught up in the accepted belief that markets would continue to function in the same way they always had.

You would have thought the financial world had learned a lesson about the dangers of leverage through the LTCM debacle. Instead, what the financial institutions learned was that government would bail out those entities deemed "too big to fail." That belief ultimately resulted in the mortgage market meltdown in 2008. Once again a bubble based on leveraged bets almost brought down the global financial system. And once again, it resulted in a government bailout that was much larger this time around.

It seems you can't legislate against human nature, even with "reform" on the minds of both political parties. And so the next section on the psychology of investing should serve as a warning for the future debacles that are certainly incubating somewhere around the world.

THE SAVAGE TRUTH ON THE PSYCHOLOGY OF INVESTING

While our stock market returns are measured in gains and losses, there is an additional dimension of investing that impacts your results. It is the psychological component that makes all the difference as we make investing and trading decisions.

At **TraderPsyches.com**, Denise Shull researches the subject of "neuro-economics"—a combination of twenty-first century psychoanalysis with her years of experience in the trading markets. To vastly oversimplify some of her work, Shull postulates that human emotions travel faster to the brain decision centers than rational thought. Thus, many investment decisions are made because the brain is overwhelmed by an emotional reaction that outweighs rational decision making.

The best investors and traders have instinctive, or learned, behavior to overcome that physical difference in the neurons in our brains. They react differently than most people—and their trading results show it.

While you might not want to enter psychoanalysis to determine whether you have the makings of a good trader, you certainly should be aware that the more emotional a situation (that is, the more of your money at risk), the less likely you will act rationally. That's why you might want to enter a stop order to sell when the market declines to a certain level—so you won't be paralyzed by fear. Or why you might set up an automatic monthly investment program so you won't hesitate to follow your plan in a down market.

It's Less Painful to Be *Out* and Wishing You Were *In*, Than *In* and Wishing You Were *Out*

Investing provides both positive and negative rewards: pleasure and pain. People react differently to those stimuli. There is a frequently cited psychological study that illustrates this principle. A group of people is asked how they would react to the following situation: They have purchased $100 worth of theater tickets, but upon arriving at the theater they discover they have lost them. Most people say they would not spend more money to replace the tickets at the box office.

When the question is phrased differently, it elicits a different reaction. Suppose, they are asked, you arrive at the theater to find that you're missing $100 out of your wallet. Assuming you still have more cash, would you spend it to buy tickets anyway? In this case, the majority say they would.

Each scenario involves the loss of $100 in value, but the loss is perceived differently.

In the same way, if you "knew" you should have purchased Apple or Microsoft, it would be very painful to watch the stock move higher while you sat on the sidelines. You'd be thinking of the profits you could have made, "if only. . . ." However, suppose you had indeed purchased shares in a company that went bankrupt, like General Motors. You would have watched your very real money melt away.

Now, which would be more painful: to be on the outside wishing you were in, or invested and wishing you were out? That's a very personal reaction, and when you can answer that question honestly you'll have a better idea of your own tolerance for risk.

THE SAVAGE TRUTH ON BEAR MARKETS, BUBBLES, AND NEW-ERA INVESTING

This section on bear markets was written just before the market peaked at the height of the dot-com boom. But it was equally applicable to the market decline that started in August 2007. And it will apply to the next bear market—whenever that starts. The Savage Truth is that *few are ever prepared for a bear market, because bear markets only start when everybody is feeling bullish and there is no one left to buy!*

I have left this section unchanged except for some of the statistics at the end of this chapter. Also updated are the charts on "Bear Market Duration" (see Figure 5.5) and the explanation, to reflect the most recent market declines.

Bubbles Eventually Burst

Sometimes the market defies logic or all the historic rules of valuation. Historians call these periods *bubbles,* or *manias.* One well-known mania occurred in seventeenth-century Holland when prices of tulip bulbs were pushed to incredible valuations. A contemporary history describes how one man traded "his silver drinking cup, his oxen, a carriage, and two gray horses" for one rare black Viceroy tulip bulb. History is rife with examples of financial hysteria pushed to extremes: from the South Seas Bubble of 1720, in which investors bought shares of a company formed to explore the riches of the New World, to the speculative investment pools of the U.S. stock market in 1929. Manias typically end when there is no one else left to buy.

Manias unleash the basic human emotion of greed, and the belief that you really can get a lot of something for nothing. Manias are different from scams in that there's no mastermind organizing the scheme. Instead, at the heart of every speculative mania, there is a widely accepted, intellectually justified belief that the ordinary rules do not apply in this situation: a belief that "this time it's different." In every mania, there are many people who are completely ruled by emotion, and a few who claim to understand that they are in the midst of a whirlwind but plan to get out before it's too late. Very few do.

Bear Markets Eventually Occur

Bear markets deserve a section of their own, perhaps because they are so rare in recent history. Yet, in spite of all the studies and reports showing that the stock market has been a fantastic investment over the long run, there are always bear markets. By definition, a *bear market* is a price decline of 20 percent or more, generally over at least two months. A smaller decline is sometimes called a *correction*—a brief dip in stock prices that lasts just days or weeks. No one really knows whether a correction will develop into a full-fledged bear market.

The average bear market of the twentieth century took 1.5 years from market peak to bottom and required an average of 4.5 years to fully recover. There have been nine bear markets since 1956, representing an average decline in the Dow Jones Industrial Average of about 29 percent. These bear markets lasted, on average, 16 months. (See Figure 5.5.)

By contrast, the first downwave of the 1929 market lasted two years and nine months from top to bottom. And the bear market that started in 1938 lasted 3.5 years—until the onset of World War II. Perhaps the most memorable bear market in modern history started on January 11, 1973, and took the Dow Jones Industrial Average down a staggering 45.1 percent in 23 months. It took 9.8 years for the market to reach its previous highs, but during that time, inflation destroyed a significant portion of the dollar's value. In real terms, it took investors who held onto their Dow stocks nearly 20 years to break even.

The decade from 2000 to 2010 gave us two bear markets, reflected in the updated charts in Figure 5.5. The bear market that started in 2000 was the third-longest on record. The bear market that started in 2007 was associated with the near-collapse of the global financial system, engendering more fear than even its longer predecessor. Yet, put in perspective, this latest bear market is less chilling than it seemed while living through it.

Bear Market Choices

Eventually—which is long after current investors lose their fear based on recent experience—there will be a significant market decline that inspires fear and challenges your well-planned, long-term investment strategy. It is better to contemplate your reaction in advance than to

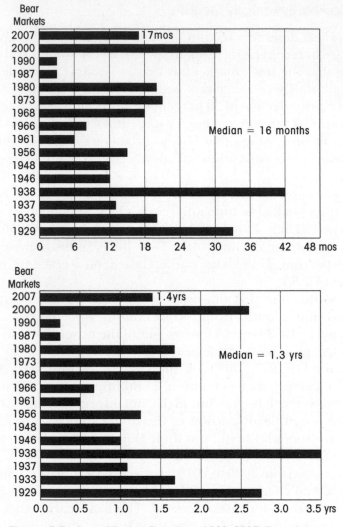

Figure 5.5 Bear Market Duration, 1929–2007: Time from Market Peak to Bottom (S&P 500)
Source: InvesTech Research.

panic and be overcome with emotion. Of course, no one will know at the time whether the decline is merely a market correction or a full-fledged bear. In either case, as prices fall, your wealth will melt away.

You have basically three choices: ride it out, sell down to the sleeping point (an old Wall Street sentiment), or attempt to hedge against losses.

If you're truly a long-term investor, it will be easier to ride out any size market decline if you are not expecting to use your stock market investments for short-term purposes. That means having a cushion of cash or available credit, as well as a secure income. In that case, you can afford to ignore the bear's growls.

Selling a portion of your assets under pressure is the most dangerous way to take on a bear market. In fact, this type of panic selling creates bear market bottoms. Determine in advance which is your trading money and which is your long-term investment fund. You might even place limit orders to sell at fixed prices below the market in your trading account, to eliminate emotional decisions.

Or you could choose to take out some "insurance" against bear market losses. For example, you could seek profits from a market decline by purchasing put options on the Dow Jones Industrial Average or on the S&P 500 stock index in order to offset losses in stocks or mutual funds you don't want to sell.

Even if your long-term investments are held inside a company retirement plan, which likely doesn't allow you to trade options, you could purchase put options in a regular investment account. Your mental and emotional account ledger will let you calculate the gains on your puts as an offset against the losses in your long-term retirement accounts. Consult your broker for advice on this type of hedging and its costs.

Another bear market hedge is the purchase of shares in a mutual fund designed to profit in market declines. For example, the Prudent Bear Fund (**PrudentBear.com**) or the Rydex Ursa Fund (**Rydex-SGI .com**) both take short positions and buy put options in an attempt to profit from market declines. Read the prospectus to understand the risks and costs.

While a bear market can devastate stock prices, not all stocks will be crushed forever. Look at the historic charts of companies that weathered the tech crash, including Microsoft. Amazon, and Apple. Good companies survive. You just don't want to be left holding the Pets.com sock puppet—although lately that sad loser is appearing in commercials for a financing company that proclaims: "Everybody deserves a second chance!"

Perhaps the most significant aspect of this section on bear markets is a Savage Truth that most were unable or unwilling to recognize at the time: *Markets don't grow to the sky; then again, neither do they disappear forever into a black hole.*

THE SAVAGE TRUTH ON THE ART OF INVESTING

The art of investing is to exchange overvalued assets for ones that are undervalued. That simple principle related to me years ago by investment historian Donald Hoppe puts the entire concept of investing in perspective. Stepping back and taking the historic overview, it's easy to see that all markets reach extremes. Figure 5.6 gives you a long-term perspective on extremes, by comparing the total market value of all stocks to the annual gross domestic product (GDP). From this chart, it's clear that sometimes the stock market is wildly overvalued—and that at some times, it's undervalued. In the first edition of *The Savage Truth*, written in 1999, I showed this chart—which had just peaked—and warned against the market's overvaluation. The bear market decline of 2000 started within months.

The same principle applies to the bond market. When no one wants to hold bonds, they trade at low prices and high yields. Back in 1981, you could have locked in 30-year yields on U.S. government bonds at more than 14 percent. But there were few takers because so many people worried that inflation would continue to

Figure 5.6   Stock Market Capitalization as a Percentage of Nominal GDP
Source: Bianco Research.

make bonds less valuable. Who wanted to be "stuck" with 30-year bonds yielding *only* 14 percent, if inflation would rise to over 20 percent as many then feared? At that time, cash (money market) accounts were returning 15 percent. In retrospect, it was the perfect time to switch from overvalued assets (cash) to undervalued assets (bonds).

Similarly, everyone wanted to purchase real estate in the early 2000s because it was assumed that prices would always go higher. When that enthusiasm peaked, it would have been a good time to sell. Instead, people took on more debt, more leverage, and actually spent more on their credit cards, based on the illusion of wealth created by rising real estate prices.

There's a simple Savage Truth: *The "right" thing to do is the most difficult thing to do.*

If everybody is rushing into a "sure thing," then it's a good time to sell. But you need both perspective and discipline to take action. And those major turning points are few and far between—and easily identified only in hindsight.

So, you may ask, what's overvalued now? We can't invest in hindsight, so how do the visionaries manage to get out on top and get in early? Ah, that's the true art of investing. One way to figure it out is to stand back and watch the crowd. If people will do anything to earn higher yields instead of the very low rates paid on safe bank deposits, the risk in getting those yields might be greater than percceived.

Only liars catch tops and bottoms. For the rest of us, the task is to sort out long-term probabilities and stick with them, maintaining flexibility to adjust our commitment at the edges.

THE SAVAGE TRUTH ON EASY INVESTING

One of the best-kept secrets of investing is the fact that you can buy stocks without going through any brokerage firm—discount, online, or traditional. Most large companies, and some foreign companies, offer direct stock purchase plans where you can make your initial investment directly through the company. Learn more about these companies at Charles Carlson's website, **www.DripInvestor.com**. Or, as you'll see in the "Getting Started" box at the end of this chapter, you can buy just one or a few shares of a stock very easily without even opening a traditional brokerage account.

When buying shares of stock directly from a company, the minimum investment requirements are usually low, and you pay no commissions when you purchase stock directly from a company. But you will not be able to set price limits, and your purchase is likely to be made only at the close of business on a specific day of the week. Smaller purchases result in fractional shares, and most companies insist that your shares be kept in record form on their books, instead of issuing certificates. These programs are best for regular investment plans that start with small initial purchases—a great gift for children or grandchildren.

It's Worth Paying for Good Advice

It's always worth paying for good advice, and brokers are typically paid through commissions. But it's also important to remember that unless you make a trade, most brokers receive no compensation. That's why many brokerage firms use the concept of "managed" or "wrap" accounts. You pay a set fee for the advice, typically based on a percentage of the assets managed by the broker. Any commissions are additional and should be at minimum rates.

It's important to understand the full impact of the costs of these managed accounts. If you simply wanted to invest in a broad cross-section of the stock market, you could buy a no-load index fund at a far lower initial and ongoing cost. But there comes a time when you want to diversify your holdings, or purchase individual stocks, or perhaps do some trading. That's where a good brokerage firm—and a good broker—become useful. It's always worth paying for good advice.

There's also a significant difference between *stockbrokers*—no matter what they may be called—and *registered investment advisors* (RIAs). Brokers have the duty to "know their customer" when making investment recommendations. But registered investment advisors have a higher duty requirement. They must fully disclose all conflicts of interest (such as the firm having a position in the stock they are recommending) and they must fully disclose all fees and commissions.

The SEC has recommended that all brokers be required to abide by this "fiduciary standard" required of investment advisors, and by the time you read this it will, hopefully, have been enacted. However, in one way this is a moot point. If you have a stockbroker whom you trust and respect, then the designation is not important. All the laws on the books can't legislate morality, which is at the heart of the issue.

Nonetheless, you really should ask questions about compensation, commissions, and all fees. And you should check the disciplinary history of the broker. As mentioned earlier in this book, you can use the "BrokerCheck" tool at **www.FINRA.org**, the industry regulatory arm. To check the disciplinary history of an investment advisor, go to **www.AdviserInfo.sec.gov**.

Your account is guaranteed up to $500,000 by the SIPC (Securities Investor Protection Corporation). But it is not guaranteed against market losses—only against brokerage firm malfeasance, such as lost or stolen securities. The Securities and Exchange Commission (SEC) is charged with regulating broker-dealers, but in the wake of the Madoff scam it is a reminder to investors that they always need to be on guard.

It's an old market truth, and a definite Savage Truth: *Anything too good to be true, is not true!*

Record Keeping Is Your Responsibility

One of the most important things you can do, whether you're a frequent trader or a long-term investor, is to set up a record-keeping system that will give you current information and track historical data regarding cost of purchases and subsequent investments. Computer money management programs like Quicken have good built-in tracking and updating systems, but be sure to keep your paper records in order in case you ever have to justify taking a taxable gain or loss. And, of course, you should check your statement online, or be sure to open and scan your paper monthly statements to make sure no one is trading in your account without authorization.

Handling Disputes

One day a dispute might arise over the way your brokerage account has been handled. The first step in any such disagreement is to limit the exposure to market losses. You can insist over the phone that the position be liquidated, and follow up with a certified or overnight letter that requires a signature. Then, at least, you'll be disputing a finite amount of damages. That letter or e-mail should be sent to the office or branch manager who is responsible for supervising the broker.

You'll find that when you opened the account you gave up your rights to file a lawsuit, and instead agreed to arbitration. The arbitration process is designed to resolve conflicts between brokers and customers with a sensible financial result. You do not need an attorney to participate in an arbitration proceeding, but be aware that the brokerage firm will be well represented.

You cannot appeal the results of an arbitration, so it is important to present your best case. Ignorance is not a defense; you must prove that you were deliberately and maliciously harmed. If the claim is $25,000 or less, the dispute is likely to be settled by written arguments. Otherwise, there will be a hearing set at which both parties can present their case.

To learn more about your rights under arbitration, and to find an attorney to represent you, search under "Arbitration" at www.FINRA.org.

A Final Thought: Take Stock

It's easy to be overwhelmed by the world of the stock market. There are many ways to analyze the market and choose stocks. No one has the perfect answer to creating wealth in the stock market. But, in spite of all the ups and downs, the stock market has a terrific record for creating wealth if you give it a sensible chance.

Instead of trying for perfection, accept the fact that you'll make mistakes, and recognize that those mistakes are measured in dollars and cents, just as your success in the stock market will be measured in tangible terms. If you can overcome the emotional reaction to loss, you improve your chances of creating gains. Remember that the stock market is a reflection of America—its growth in the past and the opportunities for the future. No one has gone wrong—over the long run—in being bullish on America!

GETTING STARTED

Here's your task: Pick a stock you'd like to buy and purchase just a few shares with whatever small amount of money you have to invest. It's easy. Here's how to do it:

Go to **www.ShareBuilder.com**, which is owned by ING Direct. You can purchase any number of shares in almost every listed company, and there *is no minimum dollar amount.* The fee for the purchase is $4.00 if you are willing to wait for your stock to be purchased on Tuesdays, or $9.95 if you want to purchase the shares immediately on a real-time basis.

You won't get a stock certificate, but you will get an online confirmation of your purchase, and you can check back at any time to see the value of your account. And, of course, you can purchase more shares at any time, or set up an automatic monthly investment program to buy a certain dollar amount of a specific stock on a regular basis through an automatic deduction from your checking account.

If you have questions, representatives will help you through the process if you call 800-747-3537.

TERRY'S TO-DO LIST

1. Learn and understand the concept of stock market risk.

2. Determine your *real* time horizon.

3. Decide whether you want to be a market timer or a long-term investor.

4. Examine your current stock market investments to see how they match your goals.

5. Allocate your investment dollars to a plan that fits your own needs and personality.

6. Create—and stick to—a plan of regular investments.

7. Have reasonable expectations based on historic results over the same time frame.

CHAPTER 6

THE SAVAGE TRUTH ON INVESTMENT CHOICES

Balancing Made Easy

BALANCING RISK AND REWARD

When you move beyond the basics of credit and debt, and have your "chicken money" set aside, you'll be faced with quite an array of investment choices. The whole idea of investing is to make your money work for you as hard as you work for your money. But the Savage Truth is that *every investment choice you make is impacted by your own perception of risk and reward*. While your goal is to make your money grow, there is always a downside to investments—a possibility of loss, or illiquidity, or misunderstood costs.

Although you cannot be absolutely sure that your investment decisions will be correct, at the very least you should understand all the risks and invest when the balance is in your favor. Having the knowledge of risks and costs tilts the odds in your favor—and helps you avoid emotional responses that lead you astray.

It's always wise to get professional advice when it comes to your investments, but how will you know the advice is good if you don't understand the basics? This section is intended to give you that basic knowledge you need to ask the right questions—and sources to give you more in-depth answers—about the investment choices that the financial services industry has created for you.

Whether you are considering mutual funds or ETFs (exchange-traded funds), whether you are wondering about annuities or options, whether you are considering futures or gold coins, you need to understand how these investments work, how much they should cost, and how risky they can be.

Mutual Funds

Mutual funds are the easiest way for you to build a diversified portfolio of stocks with professional management. But if that's all you needed to know, there wouldn't be an entire industry devoted to managing and advertising a wide variety of mutual funds. You don't have to become an expert to make mutual fund choices, but you do need to understand some of the basic differences between all those funds, and the costs and risks involved.

There is more than $11.8 trillion invested in nearly 8,000 mutual funds. About $2.5 trillion of that total is invested in money market mutual funds (see Chapter 4), leaving the balance invested in some combination of stocks and bonds. That leaves you—or your advisor—with important choices to make about which fund or combination of funds will best meet your investment objectives and risk tolerance.

FUND FEES AND COSTS

Before you even consider those choices, you need to understand how you make money in mutual funds—and how mutual funds charge you for their services. Every mutual fund has an *annual management fee* (known as the 12b-1 fee), which is taken right out of the fund assets. It covers the costs of running the fund, including administrative and marketing costs. The amount can range from less than one-tenth of one percent (on index funds, for example) to as much as 1.5 percent, or even more. Those annual fees can make a significant dent on your investment returns, so you should ask about them before investing, or search them out in the fund prospectus (that small-print booklet that describes all the legalities of the fund investment).

The other type of fee you might pay is a *commission* or *load* paid to the salesperson who guides you to this purchase. It can be as high as 8.5 percent, so it's definitely an important issue. You can buy mutual funds directly from fund management companies such as Vanguard, Fidelity, T. Rowe Price, American Century, and many others without paying a commission. If your advisor helps you make these decisions to create a balanced fund portfolio, this advice may be well worth the fees you pay, but you should ask about this cost. (*Note:* Some advisor-sold funds charge fees up front, while others charge a *back-end* commission, which you pay when you redeem shares later.)

Those aren't the only cost considerations. In a typical managed mutual fund, the portfolio managers will make buy-and-sell decisions about the securities they own within the fund. That generates *transaction costs.* The buying power of a large fund means that commissions paid to brokers are minimal, but they can add up if the fund does a lot of trading. To figure out whether the managers are very active traders, you'll want to ask about the *portfolio turnover*—how frequently the investments inside the fund change. This is not necessarily a negative, because some aggressive funds trade frequently and make more money by doing so.

Another cost you bear is *capital gains* (or losses). You know you will be required to report a capital gain or loss when you sell your mutual fund shares unless they are held in a retirement account (where all your ultimate withdrawals will be taxed as ordinary income). But even if you don't sell your fund shares, you'll receive a notice of capital gains each year based on the gains (or losses) taken by the fund managers as they buy and sell. (If your fund is held inside a retirement account, you can ignore these notices.) Otherwise, you must add them to your taxable income or subtract them under the tax-loss rules.

Did your eyes just glaze over? Your first inclination is probably to choose a fund based on its performance. But I have put this cost section first because, no matter what the performance, these costs will come out of your net returns. So you might want to start your search by limiting it to low-cost choices that give value for the fees you do pay.

MUTUAL FUND BUYING AND PRICING

If you're willing to do some homework, it's very easy and inexpensive to buy mutual funds. If you want advice about mutual funds, you should consider discussing your needs with an investment advisor or financial planner. Ask how the advisor is compensated for your fund purchases. Again, good advice (and hand-holding) is worth paying for.

You can buy funds on your own directly through the website of the mutual fund company. Many major fund companies now also have local offices. You can also buy through a "fund supermarket" such as those offered by Charles Schwab Mutual Fund OneSource or Fidelity Funds Network, both of which offer advice on selecting funds and creating a diversified portfolio of funds. And most discount brokerage firms will also offer access to *no-load* (no commission) mutual funds, most without paying any transaction fee.

Whether you purchase your traditional *open-end* mutual fund directly from the company, through a financial advisor, or through one of these fund supermarkets, the price per share will be the same. It is set after the close of business each day, based on the value of all the investments within the fund, divided by the number of shares that have been purchased by investors. That is the per-share price you will pay, and it is set only once daily. You can track the ups and downs of the price of your mutual fund every day.

Most mutual fund companies will let you set up a regular, automatic investment through electronic deductions from your checking or savings account. If you set up these regular monthly contributions, your fixed dollar amount will buy a different number of shares (or fractional shares) in the fund.

That's a process called *dollar cost averaging*. When share prices are low, your contribution will buy more shares, giving you more profits when the markets rise. And it removes the temptations of trying to time the market with your purchases. In fact, if you're new to fund investing, you might want to put some of your investment into a money market fund, with instructions to transfer a regular dollar amount into a stock fund on a certain day each month. That way you'll never pick exactly the low point, but you won't put all your money in at the top, either!

BEFORE YOU BUY, CONSIDER CREATING AN IRA

I know you're anxious to get started investing in mutual funds, but before you open an account, there's one more thing you should consider: how you will *title* your account. You're probably thinking you should just open an account in your name. Or you might want to open a *joint account* with a spouse or relative. It's simply a matter of creating ownership as part of the title of the account. But you may have another, better alternative, which you should consider when you open your mutual fund account.

If this is money you're trying to save and grow for your retirement, you might be wise to open the account as an *individual retirement account* (IRA). You're eligible to open a traditional, tax-deductible IRA if you are under age 70½ and have earned income, or if you're a nonworking spouse filing a joint return. If you're covered by a company plan, you can contribute to an IRA, but you cannot fully deduct the contribution if your joint income is above $90,000.

Remember: You'll have to leave the money growing in this traditional IRA at least until you're age 59½ or face penalties for early withdrawal in addition to ordinary income taxes on the money you take out.

You can make a full contribution to an after-tax Roth IRA if you qualify with income under $107,000 (single) or $169,000 (married) in 2011. All the money in a Roth IRA grows tax-free for retirement, although you do not get a tax deduction when you make the contribution.

You can contribute up to $5,000 a year to either type of IRA, or $6,000 if you are age 50 and over. You must have at least as much *earned income*—from wages or salary—as the amount you contribute. (The exception is for nonworking spouses, who may contribute to their own accounts based on the spouse's income.) You have until the date your tax return is due (usually April 15) to make your contribution to an IRA for the previous year. (See Chapter 13 for details.)

I mention this at the start of this section on mutual funds because so many people seem to believe that an individual retirement account requires different investment decisions. That's simply not the case. It's just a matter of deciding whether you qualify for an IRA and whether you're willing to follow the rules to keep your money growing inside your IRA. Remember, you can always switch funds *within* your IRA, or even move them to a different *custodian* such as a bank or another fund or financial services company. But by titling your mutual fund investment account as an IRA, you can get the benefits of tax deferral, or tax-free growth (in a Roth). So the title on your account is something to consider *first*.

CHOOSING MUTUAL FUNDS

This chapter couldn't begin to give you advice about all your mutual fund choices. Fortunately, there is one place you can go to get all the information you need, as well as advice, and to track your mutual fund portfolio. So this is the moment to go to **Morningstar.com**—the online "bible" of the mutual fund world—and a great source for all kinds of market information and education. It is well worth the $185 annual membership fee, because it's likely to save you that much in costs, not to mention helping pick the best funds!

When you get to Morningstar.com, I'd suggest you begin with the tab marked "Real Life Finance" and then click on "Start Investing" to learn all the basics of mutual fund investing. Whether you're a complete novice at investing or just want some help diversifying into the best funds in different categories, you'll find explanations and helpful advice. But to help you understand the possibilities, here's an overview of the mutual fund landscape.

Index Funds: You've heard of the popular market indexes such as the Standard and Poor's 500 stock index of large companies, or the Dow Jones Industrial Average of 30 companies, or perhaps the Russell 2000 index, which includes much smaller companies. These are the *benchmarks* for performance, watched by every mutual fund manager since managers typically get bonuses if they beat their benchmark. But what if you were content to do just as well as the index, and not pay extra for the manager's judgment?

That's where index funds come in. These are mutual funds that own the same shares, in the same percentages, as the most popular market averages. They don't buy and sell stocks in the fund based on a belief that some shares will outperform the index; their job is to *match* the index. Of course, if a new stock is added to the index, then there will be some adjustments. But, basically, when an investor opens an account and adds new money to the fund, it is distributed among all the stocks in the index.

Before you seek the presumed safety of an index fund, you must understand how the index is constructed. The S&P 500, for example, is not an equally weighted ownership of the 500 largest companies in the market. The index is weighted by market capitalization—company size—so that the largest and most popular stocks account for a greater percentage of the index. Thus, when new money is invested in an S&P 500 index fund, a larger proportion goes to buy shares of companies that are already top-performing and may have the highest price-earnings ratios. It's a self-reinforcing cycle, pushing the hottest big company stocks even higher in a bull market.

The costs are lower in an index fund, because there are fewer transactions. The fund management company doesn't have to pay salaries for securities analysts or fund managers. Most of the work is done by computer. In fact, index funds are sometimes called *passive* funds, as compared to *actively managed* funds. As noted in Chapter 5, doing just as well as "the market" by purchasing an index fund is not a bad choice for obtaining long-term profits.

According to Standard & Poor's year-end 2010 scorecard, more than 65 percent of large-cap mutual funds failed to beat their benchmarks for a one-year period, and nearly 62 percent failed to beat their benchmark index over a five-year period. Matching benchmark performance was even more challenging for mid-cap funds. In 2010, nearly 75 percent of mid-cap mutual funds underperformed their benchmark index, and 78 percent fell behind their benchmark over a five-year period.

That means many managed funds failed to do as well as their market sector. For you, the ordinary investor, it means you don't have to devote a lot of time to picking funds that *beat* the market. Instead, you can do just fine matching the overall performance of the market over the long run.

There are probably index funds as a prominent choice inside your 401(k) plan. And you can easily choose index funds for your IRA because every major fund management company offers them. Plus, the annual fees are minimal.

Stock or "Equity" Funds: There are thousands of mutual fund companies that try to beat the popular market averages, by picking stocks (also known as equities) or by concentrating on one particular category of stocks, such as smaller companies, or dividend-paying companies, or funds that specialize in technology, or financial institutions, or the energy sector, to name just a few categories.

That's where Morningstar comes in handy. Their "style box" shows you where each fund is categorized, from large companies to small, and from aggressive to conservative. That helps you create a portfolio that is not overly concentrated in one sector, unless that's your goal. Then the Morningstar Portfolio X-Ray tool (part of premium membership) helps you analyze where the specific investments inside your different funds intersect and overlap. That keeps you from being overweighted in specific stocks or types of stocks.

Equity Income or Balanced Funds: Perhaps you'd like some sort of balance between stocks and bonds, or at least more conservative stocks that have a track record of paying dividends. Search on Morningstar among funds in these categories, paying careful attention to the investments within each fund. Typically, when the stock market is rising, they won't beat the funds that are fully exposed to stocks purchased for their future growth prospects. However, the cushion of dividends or interest income should keep fund share prices from falling quite as much in a bear market.

Sector Funds: There are also very narrowly focused funds, called *sector funds.* You pick a segment of the economy, from technology to energy to health care or financial services, or any of dozens of other sectors, and there's bound to be a mutual fund designed to own stocks of just this one market sector. The big advantage, of course, is diversification of companies and yet focus on a segment of the market that you think will outperform the others. The downside is that when one major stock in a category declines, it tends to draw others in that sector down with it. It may be easier to invest in market sectors through exchange-traded funds (ETFs) described later in this chapter.

Target-Date Funds: If you just gave up on the idea of researching and choosing mutual funds, the fund management companies have created a product designed especially for you. They're called *target-date* funds and they're designed for people investing for retirement. You pick the date of your hoped-for retirement, and they'll adjust the investments inside the fund to become more conservative as you approach that date. It takes away your responsibility for making adjustments to your portfolio as you grow older.

Again, these funds are offered by the major mutual fund companies such as Fidelity, Vanguard, T. Rowe Price, American Century, and others. Each has its own name and its own strategy. For example, Fidelity calls these target-date funds Fidelity Freedom Funds, while American Century calls this category its "Livestrong" funds. You can search for "target-date" fund reports and comparisons on Morningstar.com.

Be sure to read the fund information carefully, especially the explanation of their investment allocation process. You might think that you'd like to be all in "chicken money," safe investments, the day you retire. These funds take into consideration the fact that you're likely to live 20 years or longer in retirement and that you'll need the growth provided by stocks. So make sure you understand exactly how conservative the portfolio will be when you reach retirement age.

Fund of Funds: Here's another way to get help in diversifying your investment portfolio. Many fund management companies create a sort of "superfund" that invests in other funds they manage at no extra cost.

For example, the T. Rowe Price Spectrum Income Fund can invest in as many as nine different bond funds to gain exposure to various quality bonds as well as geographical diversification. The Spectrum Income Fund's holdings are designed to increase income but balance risk. Similarly, the T. Rowe Price Spectrum Growth Fund invests in other T. Rowe Price–managed stock funds, ranging from small to large cap, value to growth, and domestic to international.

Vanguard offers its Star Fund, which invests in 11 underlying Vanguard funds, aiming to keep a mix of stocks and bonds that is 60/40. This balanced fund will easily give you broad diversification at low cost—a sort of one-stop-shopping choice for mutual funds. It is the only Vanguard fund that has a minimum of only $1,000 to invest.

Financial Planning Funds: Mutual fund companies realize that there's a huge universe to choose from and that you can easily be overwhelmed. So they've created funds designed to do the decision making for you when it comes to balancing stocks, bonds, and cash.

Vanguard offers its LifeStrategy funds, which range from an income fund, a conservative growth fund, and a moderate growth fund, to a more aggressive growth fund. Each has a different proportion of stocks and bonds and is set up for a different time perspective. The fund maintains the balance of investments, so that you do not have to make decisions about rebalancing your investments.

Fidelity takes a slightly different approach. It offers seven Asset Manager Funds, each with a different asset allocation mix among stocks, bonds, and short-term instruments that range from a more conservative and lower-equity allocation mix to a more aggressive and higher-equity allocation mix.

Socially Responsible Investing: You can even design your fund investment portfolio to reflect your social conscience—without impacting your investment returns. At the website of the Social Investment Forum, **www.SocialInvest.org**, you can compare the investment performance of hundreds of mutual funds that have been screened for categories such as climate, pollution, human rights, labor, alcohol, tobacco, animal testing, and many other similar features. This site features research showing that returns from socially responsible investments are competitive with non-screened investments. In other words, you don't have to sacrifice performance for conscience.

HOW *NOT* TO CHOOSE A FUND

Unfortunately, most people choose funds based on past performance. That is certainly no good guide to the future. In fact, according to an analysis done by Standard & Poor's, very few funds repeat a top-quartile performance, and it is likely that a majority of next year's top-quartile funds will come from this year's second and third quartiles! There are some good reasons for this lack of follow-up.

Funds that receive a lot of publicity for outstanding performance sometimes receive a flood of new cash, making it difficult for the fund manager to find appropriate new investments. Popularity itself can be a detriment to future fund performance. On occasion, the fund management will close the fund to new investments except from existing shareholders just to avoid that kind of problem. And sometimes the fund changes managers, which could yield different results.

So, yes, you want to know the overall track record of a mutual fund, but also you need to consider whether the managers have been changed, whether the economic conditions that may have favored this type of fund have changed, or simply whether this is the type of fund to do well in the kinds of markets you expect. Of course, if you're investing for the long run and not looking to get in and out of funds, then your considerations are quite different. You'll want to choose a fund you can stick with through ups and downs, and keep investing in on a regular basis.

The Savage Truth is that *using mutual funds doesn't take away your own responsibility to investigate and choose wisely*, either on your own or with the help of an advisor. Remember, fund managers are paid to be fully invested in stocks or bonds that are described in the fund's prospectus. It is your responsibility to raise cash, if you want to be more liquid, by selling fund shares.

Exchange-Traded Funds (ETFs)

You're probably familiar with traditional open-end mutual funds that allow you to invest more money at any time, with fund share prices determined at the close of the day by valuing the individual securities owned by the fund. *Exchange-traded funds* (ETFs) don't work that way.

ETFs are fixed baskets of securities that are generally designed to track an index or hold stocks from a specific, narrow market sector. Like individual stocks, ETFs are traded on major exchanges (NYSE, Amex, or Nasdaq). They must be purchased through a broker (or discount brokerage firm), instead of being purchased directly from a mutual fund company.

Investors and traders buy and sell shares in these funds throughout the day, with prices being set by bid and offer, as with all listed securities. Depending on demand, the shares in the ETF might be worth more than the securities in the basket, or they might trade at a discount to the underlying value of the securities in the basket.

ETF shares can be bought on margin and even sold short. If the basket of securities represents a major segment of the market, you have a convenient way to own that segment or, if you're hoping to profit from falling prices, to sell it short. Because most ETFs are passively managed, fixed portfolios of stocks, expenses within the funds are very low. You will, however, have to pay a commission to buy and sell the shares through your broker.

Exchange-traded funds allow a focused, yet diversified, exposure to various market segments in a cost-efficient format. They allow you to invest in targeted sectors of the market or in broad market indexes with one purchase. For example, you could purchase the equivalent of the Standard & Poor's (S&P) 500 index in the form of an ETF called the *SPDR*, popularly known as *Spiders*. It is traded on the NYSE under the symbol SPY.

QQQQ (*Cubes*) is the symbol for an ETF that represents the Nasdaq 100 index of stocks, which is dominated by the tech sector. Another ETF with the symbol DIA, called *Diamonds*, replicates the Dow Jones Industrial Average. There are also ETFs for major market sectors, from health care to real estate to financial services to natural resources. And there are ETFs that hold the representative stocks from individual foreign countries.

There are many fixed-income (bond) ETFs, including corporate bonds and Treasuries, as well as ETFs that replicate foreign stock and bond indexes. These bond ETFs have quite a range, from short-term maturities to longer term, and represent different risk characteristics, depending on the bond ratings of the assets they hold. As a result, they will perform differently when interest rates rise or fall.

There are also ETFs that either hold physical commodities or track commodity indexes using futures and swaps. There are even ETFs that track commodity subsectors, such as agriculture or energy or metals, and include several commodities in the underlying basket.

An example of a broad-based commodity index ETF is the GSCI commodity indexed trust (symbol: GSG), which replicates a basket of 24 commodity components, representing everything from energy to industrial metals, agricultural commodities to precious metals. However, energy represents about three-quarters of the fund's exposure. The fund owns five-year futures contracts, which minimizes trading costs and exposure. The Rogers International Commodity Index (NYSE symbol RJI) is an ETF that represents a much more broadly diversifed group of commodities.

Other ETFs are designed to track the price of a specific commodity, and represent an actual share of ownership in that commodity. For example, the SPDR Gold Shares ETF (symbol: GLD) buys gold bars for every share issued. The bars are stored in vaults in London. So this ETF tracks the price for immediate delivery of gold, the *spot* price. Similarly, you can invest in ETFs that track natural gas, or oil, or platinum, as well as oil or currencies.

You have to do your homework when investing in commodity ETFs, since some are backed by the physical commodity, and others are backed by futures contracts, which require a potentially expensive "roll" into future-months contracts.

There are even *leveraged* ETFs and *inverse* ETFs, which are daily trading vehicles that can be very volatile and expensive. The leveraged ETFs are designed to give you more return (or losses) for your small investment. And the inverse ETFs are designed to let you profit from a move to the downside in an index or group of stocks or commodities. But, by design, the returns are amplified far more than you might expect.

These ETF portfolios of stocks are prepackaged, or put together by a sponsor or *provider*. For example, Barclays Global Investors created iShares ETFs (which are now owned by Black Rock), which can be found at **iShares.com**. Vanguard sponsors a series of ETFs, most of which are considered a separate share class of a Vanguard mutual fund; these can be found at **Vanguard.com**. State Street Global Advisors sponsors the *Spiders* group of ETFs, which track not only the well-known S&P 500 index, but many sectors of the market (**www.StateStreetspdrs.com**). And Merrill Lynch sponsors HOLDRs (*holding company depositary receipts*), a series of stock-sector ETFs (**www.holdrs.com**).

For tax purposes, ETFs are treated just like other securities. You pay capital gains taxes on the sale of your ETF shares based on your profit or loss and on the length of your holding period, just as you would with any other security. Because these portfolios are fixed, there are rarely capital gains distributions to shareholders unless the manager has to sell a security inside the portfolio, as in the case of a merger. But when large shareholders of an ETF want to get out, they can take securities instead of cash, meaning there is less likelihood of securities being sold for a profit (or loss) inside the ETF.

(*Special note:* Not all ETFs are "tax-efficient." Some do have a high turnover rate. Some that hold underlying physical commodities, such as precious metals, are taxed as *collectibles* rather than securities—at a current 28 percent rate, compared to the current 15 percent for long-term capital gains on securities.)

The low expense of ETFs makes them attractive to long-term investors. But if you're planning to invest a fixed amount every month, you'd probably want to avoid paying a commission on each transaction and send your monthly check to a low-cost traditional mutual fund, if there is one that represents a similar portfolio as the ETF.

Although I have listed the websites of the major ETF providers/ sponsors, the very best place to learn about ETFs, and to compare and contrast their content and performance, is under the "ETF" tab at Morningstar.com.

Hedge Funds

I'll be brief: If you're just learning about hedge funds here, you don't want to invest in them! Hedge funds are unregistered funds designed for high-net-worth, sophisticated investors. They can use a variety of strategies to help them bet on future directions of the market or subsectors of the market. That is, they could be *long* (own) some stocks or *short* (betting on a price decline) other stocks. Some use futures or options to magnify the leverage of their directional bets. And, believe it or not, sophisticated investors often feel there is so much opportunity for profit that they agree to give the hedge fund manager a 20 percent cut of the profits—on top of steep management fees and commission costs.

For more insight into the industry you can go to **www.HedgeFund .net,** and pay for premium access to data. Or check out the hedge fund ratings at Morningstar.com.

Near year-end 2010, every one of the 36 hedge fund categories tracked by Morningstar had failed to beat the total return of the S&P 500 for the year, and fewer than half the hedge fund indexes had captured even half the return of the S&P 500. Sure, there are some hedge funds that make billions—and headlines. I don't think those are the ones that are being offered to you. Enough said.

Options

Options are both one of the most useful and one of the least understood aspects of the stock market. Though some see them as a low-priced way to speculate on future stock prices, they are actually better suited to ordinary investors as a way to increase portfolio income and protect your existing stock portfolio from losses.

An option on a stock gives you the right to buy a specific number of shares in a company at a specific price for a specific period of time. The option gains in value if the price of the underlying stock rises before the time runs out (expiration). You can buy options on a single stock, or on a major market index, or on most ETFs.

If you believe a stock will rise, you can buy a *call* option instead of paying for the full 100 shares or paying the 50 percent margin required to buy 100 shares of stock. If you believe the stock will fall, you can buy a *put* option. With a far smaller investment, you get all the benefits of owning the stock, or selling short, but only for a limited amount of time. If you guess right about the direction of the stock but your timing is off, you can lose all the money you spent on the option.

Basically, options allow you to diversify your portfolio for a relatively small amount of money. The trade-off is that you own the option for only a limited amount of time. When it comes to investing in options, truly timing is everything!

There's another use for options. As an investor, you can use them to protect your portfolio. You can sell (*write*) options on a stock you already own, and you can pocket the amount (the *premium*) you are paid. But by selling the option, you are granting the buyer of the option the right to purchase your stock at a specific price during a specific period of time. So you have to be ready to give up your stock to the owner of the option during the period of time the option is outstanding.

For example, if you own a stock that is trading at 50, someone might pay you $5 for a six-month option. (Price is determined by the market.) If the stock rises, the option holder will call the stock away from you, paying you $50 a share. But since you collected the option premium, it is as if you sold the stock at $55. You'll have to decide in advance if that's enough profit for you.

If you change your mind and don't want to sell the stock at 55, then you can buy the option back. Again, the price of the option will be determined by the market, which weighs the time left until the expiration of the option against the likelihood that the stock will move higher. If the stock has moved up, and there is time left on the option when you buy it back, then you will suffer a loss on your option trade—but you will still have the stock.

And if you sold the call at $50 a share, but the stock falls instead of rising, you have some protection on the downside. Until the stock falls below 45 (offsetting the $5/share you collected in premium), you're not actually losing money on your position.

Selling options on stocks you own can increase your income in retirement and cushion the impact of a declining market. You can set up a regular program of call-writing, and if the market stays at about the same level, you can substantially increase your return on investment by taking in option premiums.

The main drawback to this strategy is that until the option expires, you are obligated to deliver those shares. If the market declines, you are free to sell your underlying stock to cut your losses—but the obligation remains. So if there's a subsequent rally, you could be forced to buy back the stock at higher prices to deliver to the call buyer at any time until the expiration date!

For more information on options, go to **www.CBOE.com**, and click on "Education." You'll find resources from beginner to advanced, and might particularly be interested in the courses and seminars offered by the CBOE Options Institute.

Real Estate Investment Trusts

This book won't go into direct real estate investing for the simple reason that every property is different and it's hard to give general rules for investors who simply want to diversify their portfolios. That is not to say that investing in real estate couldn't play an important role in your investment strategy. The Great Recession has certainly made some bargains available, presuming you have the cash or credit to qualify for a purchase.

But if you just want to give your investment portfolio some exposure to real estate, there is a certain category of stocks designed to do just that. They are *real estate investment trusts* (REITs), and they invest directly in real estate. Their shares are traded on the major exchanges, and when you buy shares, you own a piece of those real estate assets.

There are nearly 153 publicly traded REITs, with nearly $400 billion in market capitalization—the price of the shares multiplied by the number of shares the companies have outstanding. REITs are simply a form of holding company for real estate properties and services. Typically, equity REITs have concentrated ownership in one type of property: apartments, offices, shopping malls, hotels, or even storage units. Other REITs offer mortgages to existing properties. If you can't decide which REIT to buy, there are dozens of mutual funds that invest primarily in the shares of REITs.

The attraction for investors is twofold. First, REITs offer a chance to own a diversified piece of choice properties that could appreciate in value, especially if inflation returns. Second, these companies are required by law to pay out 90 percent of the rents they collect in the form of dividends to shareholders. So REIT shares offer a tempting regular dividend payment that is higher than most other equity investments.

A portion of that dividend may be ordinary income, capital gains, or even return of invested principal. That creates some beneficial tax opportunities as well as a stream of income. This payout of dividends is based on the *flow of funds from operations* (FFO), which is the traditional measure of REIT earnings.

REITs add balance to a portfolio. In times of inflation, REIT shares may become more valuable, reflecting the increase in value of underlying properties. And in a slowing or deflationary economy, the dividends—secured by rents—make REIT shares relatively more attractive than many other companies.

Of course, there are risks in REITs. In a deep recession, vacancies increase and tenants may be evicted or go bankrupt. During the most recent recession, the sharp decline in consumer spending impacted REITs that specialize in shopping malls. Business travel slowdowns caused problems for hotel REITs. But although income may decline, the REITs still own the properties. That's the attraction of REITs and the mutual funds that specialize in them.

At the National Association of REITs (NAREIT) website (**www .REIT.com**), you can get a list of all publicly traded REITs and a quick link to their websites. You can search by category. There's also a list of mutual funds that specialize in REITs. You can also research REIT funds at Morningstar.com.

Futures

These days, *commodities* are making more news headlines amid worries about inflation, and worries about China's growing demand for raw materials. It's an overgeneralization, but prices of commodities tend to rise in a growing global economy because of the demand for raw materials. Oil, copper, aluminum, fertilizer, and other basic materials prices reflect this increased demand. But they are also considered a way to hedge your exposure to inflation—the declining value of paper currencies.

Futures markets exist to allow producers and users of products to hedge against risk. Many of the products traded in these markets are tangible commodities, such as oil, natural gas, corn, wheat, cattle, coffee, and pork bellies (bacon). But there is also risk in the future value of intangibles, such as interest rates, currencies, stock prices, and the relationships among these vital parts of the financial system. So there are futures contracts to hedge against financial risk as well as commodity risk.

Futures markets exist to transfer that risk at a price decided on by global market participants. Your mental picture of futures trading might be one of wild shouting and hand-waving on a physical trading floor, but most futures trading today takes place electronically. But wherever a transaction is made, there are two sides—a buyer and a seller. Only when they come together is a contract made. Thus, it could be said that futures trading is a zero-sum situation: For every side of the contract that wins, there is an opposite side that posts a loss.

Among the futures market participants are users of that commodity who need to hedge prices for the future. A U.S. manufacturer who is selling products in Europe needs to know what the dollar value of the euro will be when he is paid for his product in a few months. And there are speculators who participate merely to make a profit if they are correct in forecasting the direction of prices.

Since futures are traded with a very small cash margin, there is a lot of leverage to the money invested. Leverage works both ways: You can easily double your money, but you can also lose all of your initial investment, or even more. The major futures exchanges have websites with educational features that explain how futures work. Check out the Chicago Mercantile Exchange Group's site at **www.CMEgroup.com**. (Full disclosure: I am a public director of CME Group Inc.)

Although you may never be a speculator, you might want to use futures to hedge against the stocks and mutual funds in your retirement portfolio. If you believe that the market will decline but don't want to sell your stock funds, you could easily sell a futures contract that roughly represents the stocks in your portfolio or buy a put option on a stock futures contract.

If you're interested in commodity futures, you will have to do your homework and deal with a reputable brokerage firm. The first place to start is at the website of the National Futures Association, **www.nfa.futures.org**. There you can research individual brokers, firms, and money managers that specialize in futures.

Or you may choose to add commodities exposure to your portfolio through an index fund that does not speculate but simply tracks an index of physical commodities. Several funds provide this service: The PIMCO Commodity Real Return Strategy Fund (PCRAX) uses a portfolio of derivatives to simulate the performance of an index. The Oppenheimer Real Asset Fund (QRAAX) uses the Goldman Sachs commodity index as its benchmark. And the Rogers International Raw Materials Fund, LP, created by global investment guru Jim Rogers, uses a proprietary index to track more than 35 commodities used in global trade. Go to **www.RogersRawMaterials.com** for more information.

Another way for sophisticated investors to gain exposures to futures is through *managed futures accounts*. Most of these accounts are within hedge funds open only to clients with substantial risk capital. And here's a word of caution if you are approached by a broker to open a managed futures account: There is tremendous leverage, volatility, and potential to lose more than your initial investment in these accounts. Beware.

There is one mutual fund that tracks a broad array of commodities and financial futures. It is the Rydex Managed Futures Strategy Fund (RYMTX) and it is open to investors with a minimum $2,500 investment. The fund takes both long and short positions in commodity, currency, and financial instruments, seeking to benchmark its performance against the S&P Diversified Trends Indicator. Investors pay a 4.75 percent sales charge (or alternatively a back-end sales charge) to gain access to this fund, in addition to more than two percentage points in annual management fees.

Hedging the Dollar with Foreign Currencies

We live in dollars, shop in dollars, invest using dollars, and plan our retirement in dollars. But what will the dollar be worth in a few years? If you buy only "made in America" goods, you're less exposed to the changing global value of the dollar. But because we are all dependent on imported oil, and might want to drive imported cars, or wear imported clothes, we are all better off when the world respects the dollar and it can buy more of anything made outside the United States.

But the dollar itself is a commodity dependent on others' perceptions of its future value. When the Federal Reserve announces it is creating more dollars to get the economy growing, those who hold substantial amounts of dollars suddenly realize that this printing process will cause their dollars to lose value. That's the simple definition of *inflation*.

In recent years we've all become far more aware of the value of the dollar versus other currencies, such as the yen or Canadian dollar or euro. It's not just a matter of what things cost in a foreign currency when we are shopping, or of what things cost to foreigners when they are shopping here. We've learned that when the dollar loses value, foreigners take the dollars we've sent to their countries and come back to buy bargains—from real estate to luxuries—made cheaper to them because as the dollar falls in value, their currencies buy more.

Americans have always felt the world revolved around the dollar. But in recent years the countries that have collected the dollars we spent as we shopped globally are now starting to get worried about holding so many dollars. With nearly a trillion U.S. dollars in its reserves, China is one of our largest creditors.

China has publicly commented that maybe the world needs a different reserve currency, or basket of currencies, on which to price global transactions. They feel there are just too many dollars floating around out there, and the United States owes too much money, to maintain confidence in the dollar. But since China owns so many dollars, they are somewhat restricted in the actions they can take, lest they cause a decline in the value of their own dollar holdings!

It's worth remembering that when the global financial markets were on the verge of collapse, there was a giant rush to the presumed safety of the U.S. dollar. Perhaps the lesson is that the world doesn't trust the dollar, but it trusts other currencies even less!

Although most of us will always make financial transactions in dollars, there is a good reason to watch the value of the U.S. dollar against foreign currencies. The value of the dollar not only impacts the cost of imported goods, but the price we pay to "import" capital. That price is interest rates. If our global creditors demand higher interest rates as an offset to feared inflation, it will impact the entire U.S. economy, from mortgage loans to credit card rates.

As long as the world is willing to hold those dollars and reinvest them in U.S. Treasury bills or other government securities, at low rates based on confidence in the future value of the dollar, there's no problem. But if you have a global business, you need to hedge against the possibility of a falling dollar. Similarly, if you have an investment portfolio, you'll want to protect against that same risk.

To hedge your need for foreign currencies or simply to speculate on the value of the dollar (and indirectly on global interest rates), you can use futures and options contracts traded on the Chicago Mercantile Exchange.

Or you can actually trade cash currencies at Fidelity, which has an international currency trading program that gives you direct access to trading international stocks in 12 countries and to trading dollars for eight different currencies. Access is limited to investors with substantial assets.

There's another easy way to speculate on the future value of the dollar. At **www.EverBank.com**, you can buy certificates of deposit (CDs) that are denominated in a wide variety of foreign currencies or baskets of currencies. The CDs are insured by the Federal Deposit Insurance Corporation (FDIC). Your dollars are converted to the currency when you purchase the CD. The interest rate is set based on competitive rates in that currency. When the CD matures, you will have earned the promised rate of interest plus or minus changes in the value of the currency if you choose to convert back to dollars.

Gold

The ultimate hedge against currency inflation is gold. It has kept its value throughout history against paper currencies that ultimately became worthless. While any government can create paper currency, no one has ever been able to create gold! Even medieval alchemists tried to no avail, and you remember the story of Rumplestiltskin, who tried to spin straw into gold!

Gold is virtually indestructible, and in all of history, only 161,000 tons of gold have been mined, barely enough to fill two Olympic-size swimming pools. More than half of that was extracted in the past 50 years, and there have been few recent discoveries. That's part of what makes gold unique—and so special.

A BRIEF HISTORY OF GOLD

America has an interesting historic relationship with gold. A century ago, our country (along with England, France, and Germany) backed its paper currency with gold, meaning the paper money was interchangeable with gold at an official price. Then in 1933, during the depths of the Depression, the United States went off the gold standard. The government demanded that its citizens turn in all their gold bullion coins in exchange for paper currency. President Roosevelt's Executive Order in 1933 proclaimed a national emergency and called for the "requisition of all privately held gold in America," with a penalty of "up to 10 years in prison and/or up to a $10,000 fine." Some numismatic, *collector* coins were exempted, but gold bullion coins and bars were confiscated.

In 1946, after World War II, global powers created a fixed international exchange rate based on the ability of major central banks to exchange gold with the U.S. Treasury for a fixed price of $35 an ounce. It was called the *Bretton Woods Agreement*. The dollar, implicitly backed by the gold held in Fort Knox, became the world's medium of exchange.

This system of fixed exchange rates lasted until August 15, 1971, when President Nixon "closed the gold window" just as France, under Charles de Gaulle, decided that it would rather have bullion than the paper dollars that the United States was starting to print excessively. At the same time, Nixon imposed wage and price controls in a fruitless attempt to control inflation, then running at around 4 percent annually.

It wasn't until January 1, 1975, that Americans were again allowed to own gold bullion coins and bars. At the time, gold was trading in global markets at around $170 an ounce. Just five years later, in 1980, amid growing inflation fears, the price of gold rose to more than $800 an ounce. When the Fed, under Chairman Paul Volcker, regained control over inflation and inflation expectations, gold prices dropped back to below $300 an ounce, where it traded for years before the most recent rally.

Since August 1971, there has been no official link between the dollar and gold. Gold owned by the government was officially priced at $38 an ounce in 1972, although no foreign central bank or individual could access that gold. In February 1973, the official price was raised to $42.22 an ounce, where it remains today. The U.S. Mint says there are currently 143.7 million ounces of gold in Fort Knox.

It is possible that if the world were to completely lose faith in the value of the U.S. dollar, our government could be forced once again make the dollar convertible into gold—at much higher prices!

HOW TO BUY GOLD

There are several ways to invest in gold, and each has its own advantages and drawbacks. If you decide to purchase gold, you might want to choose several of these alternatives:

Gold-Mining Stocks or Mutual Funds: The advantage of buying shares of gold mining companies is that they pay dividends. That gives you a stream of income that you don't get when you buy bullion or coins. In addition, these gold-mining companies are leveraged, in the nicest sense of the word. Their mining costs are fixed; if the price of gold bullion rises, they make more profits without much additional cost. You don't have to become a gold stock expert, since there are many gold mutual funds listed at Morningstar.com.

Gold Exchange-Traded Funds (ETFs): The NYSE-listed stocks SPDR Gold Trust (GLD) and Central Gold Trust (GTU) reflect daily price changes in gold. You are in effect buying a share of their bullion holdings. There are ETFs that purchase shares of gold-mining companies, such as the Market Vectors Gold Miners ETF (symbol: GDX).

Gold Bullion Coins: Many countries issue gold bullion coins, including the United States, which currently issues U.S. Gold Eagle coins containing one ounce of gold, and also smaller gold coins, as well as gold "Buffalo" coins. As well, you can purchase Canadian Maple

Leaf coins, Australian Kangaroos, and the Austrian Philharmonic gold bullion coin. All are priced based on gold bullion, with a slight premium for minting and distribution costs.

Numismatic (Collector) Coins: Older gold coins may have collector's value and a more limited marketplace. Their value is based on rarity and the condition of the coin. Some investors remember that in 1933, most numismatic coins were exempted from confiscation, so they are willing to pay a premium over the gold value to hold these coins.

Always make sure you are dealing with a reputable company, take possession of your coins, and store them in a safe place. Check the registry of American Numismatic Association dealers at their website, **www.Money.org**.

Gold Bars: You can purchase gold bullion bars in various sizes. One ounce is standard, but there are smaller *wafers*, and bars as large as 450 ounces. The problem with larger gold bars is that they should be kept in custody to ascertain they have not been tampered with in any way. Thus, there are storage charges. And the storage provision opens the way for fraud. In the early 1980s, there were revelations of warehouses filled with bricks painted gold to look like gold bars!

Futures: You also can trade futures contracts on gold, and options on futures contracts, but this is the riskiest way to participate in the market because so much leverage is used.

Why is it important to understand the historic role of gold in a world of paper currencies? It's because few governments have resisted the temptation to "print" their way out of economic problems. The lessons of Germany in the 1930s have been forgotten—except for many older Germans who would rightly choose austerity on the part of government instead of the secret tax of inflation, which destroys buying power. Always remember that a little bit of inflation (creation of too much money) can easily turn into a conflagration when everyone runs to exit the currency.

When you buy gold in one of the forms previously described, you are buying "insurance," so this should be done only with a portion of your total investment portfolio. Sadly, if gold were to soar, it would reflect a breakdown in this country's financial system—a situation that would be far more costly in other aspects of your life.

Just Get Started!

The choices presented in this chapter range from the very basic—mutual funds and ETFs—to the more sophisticated ways to deal with the market and the economy, ranging from the use of options and futures and hedges to the dollar.

Each of these choices has its own costs and risks. Always ask, and always get specific answers, about these issues. Your investment advisor can guide you to the balance that is appropriate for your personal situation.

Don't be overwhelmed by all the choices. You can open an account—or better yet, an individual retirement account (IRA)—in any of the mutual funds listed in the "Getting Started" box following. Or you can choose from the huge universe of funds at Morningstar.com.

And don't be put off by the thought that you need a lot of money to get started. Most major mutual fund companies make exceptions to their minimums for those who start a regular contribution program. See the "Getting Started" sidebar coming up.

Now, let me overcome your second excuse—that you don't have "extra" money to invest or that you "can't afford it." It's always difficult to save and invest for the future. But take a look at your paycheck, with all its deductions for income tax withholding and Social Security. You can't afford that, either! At least when you invest in a well-diversified mutual fund you have a better chance of seeing something of value for your future.

Don't wait until it's the "right time" in the market. There's never a right time. Just get started. With an ongoing program of regular investing, you might never get the lowest price, but you'll never pay the top price, either. Over the years, as you build up shares in your mutual fund, you'll find that your money is starting to work for you.

Yes, there may be temporary setbacks. But look at the long-term stock market investment chart in Chapter 5 (Figure 5.2). Think of all the people who gave up investing during the Depression, or during the sad seventies, or even after the 2008 global financial crisis. Look at what they missed out on in subsequent years. Remember, *no one ever got rich betting against America!* And that's The Savage Truth.

GETTING STARTED

Here are four ways to get started on mutual fund investing—
even if you have only a small amount of money.

1. T. Rowe Price (**www.TRowePrice.com**) allows you to open
   an account in most of its funds with an initial deposit of
   only $50—if you agree to an automatic monthly contri-
   bution of at least $50 per month, deducted from your
   checking or savings account.

2. At Fidelity (**www.Fidelity.com**), the SimpleStart program
   allows you to open an account with as little as $200, if
   you agree to contribute an automatic $200 per month
   to your account in any of their funds.

3. At Vanguard, you can open an account in the Star Fund
   (described earlier) with $1,000 and no regular invest-
   ments required. (All other Vanguard funds require a
   minimum initial investment of $3,000.)

4. At U.S. Global Investors (**www.USFunds.com**), you can
   open an account in the well-diversified All American
   Fund with $1,000 and a required automatic minimum
   contribution of $100 per month.

These choices remove your natural first objection—that it's
"too difficult" to invest. You can simply go to their websites or
call the toll-free number to easily open your account.

TERRY'S TO-DO LIST

1. Sign up for Morningstar.com's "premium service."

2. Use the Morningstar Portfolio X-Ray service to evaluate your mutual fund holdings.

3. Use exchange-traded funds to get sector exposure.

4. Go to **www.CBOE.com**, click on "Education" and then
   on the free Option Tutorials.

5. Start to hedge your dollar exposure by purchasing one
   gold coin or a few shares of a gold stock mutual fund.

CHAPTER

7

THE SAVAGE TRUTH ON ANNUITIES

Risks and Rewards

Insurance companies have a special tax deal, authorized by Congress, that other financial companies simply can't match: Any extra money inside a life insurance policy can grow tax-deferred, thus building up a huge pool of cash. Then this money can be borrowed out of the life policy tax-free, usually reducing the death benefit by the amount of the loan plus any accrued loan interest over time.

What if you don't need the life insurance and just want the tax-deferred buildup of cash? The insurance companies and Congress created *tax-deferred annuities*, which are investment accounts that also allow a buildup of cash inside a policy. The only insurance connected with these annuities is typically a guarantee that at death your account will be worth at least what you originally invested.

Tax-deferred annuities are *not* life insurance policies; they are tax-deferred investment opportunities—at either a fixed or variable rate of return—inside an insurance company contract. In recent years, insurance companies have become very creative about offering investment opportunities, and guarantees, within these products.

As a result, tax-deferred annuities have become increasingly popular for retirement savings for people who have maximized their use of 401(k) or 403(b) plans or individual retirement accounts. In fact, some of the guarantees are so attractive that these products are actually being used *inside* retirement accounts that are already tax-deferred.

But behind the enticing guarantees are a number of caveats that you should understand before you invest in these annuity products. They come with costs, penalties, and restrictions that may offset the benefits of tax-deferred growth, depending on your personal situation. But, first you need to understand the differences between *immediate* annuities and tax-*deferred* annuities.

UNDERSTANDING
IMMEDIATE ANNUITIES

When you think of the word *annuity*, it probably brings to mind the traditional concept of a monthly check for life. Indeed, that is the definition of an *immediate annuity*.

You give the insurance company a lump sum of money, and it promises to pay you a fixed monthly amount for as long as you live, or you and your spouse live, or for a fixed period of years —as little as five years to as long as 20 or 30 years. The size of that monthly check is based on the amount of money you put into the annuity contract, your age (and presumed life expectancy), the type of contract chosen, and the current level of interest rates (which determines how the insurance company can invest your money).

With an immediate lifetime annuity you can never outlive your cash flow. Even if you beat the actuarial statistics and live past 100, the insurance company must keep paying you a check. On the other hand, if you die shortly after starting the annuity payout, the insurance company gets to keep the balance of your investment. So it makes sense to start a life-only immediate annuity only if you believe your health will let you live at least as long as the insurance company is betting you will, and if you don't care about leaving the balance of your money to your heirs.

If you do want to have an immediate annuity and make sure your heirs receive the balance of your account after you die, you should take an immediate annuity that guarantees payment for a *certain term*, or a single or joint life payout with a term certain. If you're in your seventies, a 25- or 30-year term-certain payout should give you a stream of income that will cover your life expectancy. If you die before the end of that term certain, your spouse or other heir will continue to receive the same monthly check. If you outlive the term certain annuity, the checks will stop at the end of the chosen term, so choose the length of that term wisely.

Immediate Annuities and Taxes

The taxation of the money that comes out of an immediate annuity depends on the status of the money that went into it. For example, if you rolled your retirement account into an immediate annuity that pays out a guaranteed monthly check for life, then all of the money coming out of the annuity would be taxable as ordinary income because neither the money going into the contract nor the earnings had been previously taxed.

If, however, you invest a lump sum of after-tax cash into an immediate annuity, then part of your monthly check will be considered a tax-free return of your own capital, and part will be considered a taxable payment of interest earned on the cash inside your annuity. The contract will specify the percentage of your monthly check that is taxable and the portion that is tax-free. If your heir receives the monthly check after your death, the same proportion will be taxed at his or her marginal tax rate.

Immediate Annuity Risks

When considering an immediate annuity, most people focus on the gamble that they might die "too soon," leaving the insurance company with a windfall of cash from the balance of the investment. But the real risk is accepting an insurance company deal that promises too small a check. People don't know they can compare the monthly check amounts promised by different insurance companies. Even though all insurance companies use the same mortality tables, they may use different investment assumptions or other calculations to determine the amount of the monthly check they promise to you.

To find out what amount you could get for life, go to **www .ImmediateAnnuities.com** and you can compare the monthly payment promises you could receive from various top-rated insurance companies. All fees and costs are included in these numbers, so you can simply compare monthly payments.

This can also be a useful strategy if your company retirement fund offers an option of a fixed, immediate annuity. You're not locked into what the company plan offers. If you want that fixed monthly check, you can always roll over a lump-sum payout from your company plan into another insurance company's immediate annuity that offers a higher monthly check.

A final warning: Just remember that you'll be paying for this promise of lifetime payments. You can never break out of this annuity deal, or renegotiate. Once you sign up for an immediate annuity, you're stuck with that regular monthly check for life. Even if interest rates rise, your life circumstances change, or the insurance company has some bad publicity, you must stick with your ongoing plan. That's why it's so important to consider all aspects of the deal before you sign up for the plan—especially the insurance company's safety rating.

If you die tomorrow, the insurance company keeps the balance of your account, unless you've chosen that term certain feature, or life with term certain, or even one of the annuities that offers a refund feature (which substantially reduces your monthly payment). And even more significantly, that fixed monthly payment might look good today, but could seem small if inflation returns. As a general principle, it is extremely unwise to tie up more than a portion of your money in this type of fixed payment.

Best of Both

There is such a thing as an immediate *variable* annuity, where the money is invested in a mutual fund–like subaccount and your monthly check varies, depending on how your investments perform. These annuities do provide a minimum or floor payment amount, but this is usually lower than the investment amounts generated from the same amount deposited in a fixed immediate annuity. But that uncertainty belies the real reason most people opt for an immediate annuity: the peace of mind that comes from knowing that a regular monthly check will arrive in your mailbox or be deposited into your checking account.

There is one other type of immediate annuity that offers some protection against inflation: an *immediate annuity with inflation protection*. Through Vanguard Annuity Access (800-523-0830), you can choose from immediate annuities that adjust payments over time to reflect changes in the consumer price index for urban consumers (CPI-U). You are guaranteed a minimum payment that will never decline relative to inflation. Every year on January 1 (or on the contract anniversary date), payments are adjusted upward. If the index were to decline, reflecting deflation, your monthly check could not be made smaller than your initial monthly payment amount, although it might drop below the previous year's payment level.

The cost of this protection is embedded in the monthly payment, which is initially smaller than you would otherwise get in an immediate annuity. For example, at current rates as of this writing, a 65-year-old male depositing $100,000 could choose a standard immediate annuity with a lifetime check of about $628 per month. The inflation protection program would reduce the monthly check to an initial $453 per month, although the amount would increase with inflation.

Remember, without inflation protection, the traditional immediate annuity would keep paying $628 a month—better in the initial years, or if there is no inflation. There's a big difference in your check when you pay for inflation protection. That should make you aware of the potential impact of inflation on a fixed monthly check.

UNDERSTANDING TAX-DEFERRED ANNUITIES

Insurance companies offer a different type of annuity, which is designed not for immediate income, but to give you a place to let your money grow tax-deferred. The company may guarantee you a fixed interest rate that will be credited to your investment deposit. Or you may be given a choice of investment accounts that work much like mutual funds. Either way, the money grows inside your annuity account and is not taxed until you withdraw it.

Tax deferral is a powerful attraction. But there are so many variations on these tax-deferred annuities that you need to understand all the wrinkles and costs before you invest. Still, if you've made the maximum contribution to your employer's 401(k) or 403(b) retirement plan, and perhaps contributed to an IRA, you should consider tax-deferred annuities. You'll pay for the privilege of tax deferral, and you'll lose the benefit of lower capital gains taxes made outside a tax-deferred plan. But in return you'll get some interesting benefits and guarantees with some tax-deferred annuities.

Taxes on Tax-Deferred Annuities

Tax deferral is not tax avoidance. So right up front you should be aware of the tax considerations upon withdrawal from tax-deferred annuities. With a tax-deferred annuity, you give the insurance company a check now and the insurer invests it, with all the growth-compounding tax deferred inside the contract. Eventually, you can take the money out, either in one withdrawal or in any amount you choose at any time. Or, you can take a monthly check for life.

If you take money in one or more withdrawals, you'll pay ordinary income taxes *on the gains.* That's assuming that there *is* a gain. The first withdrawals are always considered ordinary income, and ultimately you can withdraw your original investment tax free. If you annuitize and take a check a month for life, a portion is taxed as ordinary income and a portion is not taxed because it is considered a return of principal.

Surrender Charges

There are two more considerations with tax-deferred annuities that might make you think twice before buying. The first is *surrender charges.* Although these charges can be as high as 20 percent and last as long as 15 years, they generally start at 8 percent and decline over the years.

Surrender charges are levied if you cash out early to offset the marketing expenses and sales commissions that are paid to the insurance agents. The sales agent is paid an immediate commission by the insurance company of approximately 2 to 7 percent of your annuity investment, even though all of your money is invested in your account. If you leave early, the company recoups the commission it paid out through the surrender charge. Many companies allow a withdrawal of 10 percent of your initial investment every year, free from surrender charges.

Surrender charges aren't the only fees and expenses charged to your account, but until they expire at the end of a set period, they are the most burdensome.

Federal Early Withdrawal Penalties

The second concern is the federal rule that says withdrawals of earnings from tax-deferred annuities before age 59½ face a 10 percent *federal tax penalty.* (There are certain penalty exceptions for annuity withdrawals under age 59½, if the payments are taken in equal payments over your life expectancy, under Rules 72T and 72Q.)

So tax-deferred annuities are usually best for people who don't need their principal for a number of years, and certainly not until they are older than 60. Some annuities do allow withdrawals of up to 10 percent of the account value each year without surrender charges. There are other hardship considerations such as waivers if the money is needed for a nursing home or terminal illness. These make the annuity more liquid, but you'll have to read the fine print!

Basically, if you're considering a tax-deferred annuity, you'll want to be sure you have no immediate need for the money you're investing, unless you're using a *guaranteed minimum income rider* to start the flow of retirement income.

Fixed-Rate Tax-Deferred Annuities

A *fixed tax-deferred annuity* pays you a promised interest rate for a specified period of time. The rate may be guaranteed for one year or several years. There may even be a bonus crediting of extra interest for the first year or two. At the end of the promised rate period, the rate will be reset, based on prevailing interest rates. The growth in value of the account depends on the rate at which interest is paid. There are no additional fees, since the costs are built into the rate you are being paid.

Remember to check those surrender charges, and look for an annuity in which the surrender charge doesn't last longer than the fixed-rate guarantee. For example, you may be promised a 5 percent annual yield on principal invested for five years, with surrender charges that end after five years. That way you won't be trapped in an annuity that doesn't keep up with rising interest rates.

Fixed-rate annuities seem so simple that it's easy to overlook the hidden language and to fall for marketing techniques that may make you think you're going to earn more than the true, guaranteed rate of return. Watch out for these hidden traps:

- Many advertisements promise a very high bonus rate for the first year but don't display the minimum guaranteed rate for the remaining years. Since each annuity deal is slightly different, it's often difficult to figure out which is better. You can compare by asking how much your initial deposit is guaranteed to become at the end of a specific period, typically six or seven years. If the advertised rates are not guaranteed for that long, ask the agent to calculate using the minimum guaranteed rate the annuity must promise to pay. If the market rate isn't guaranteed for the entire period, in the later years the company might pay only slightly more than the guaranteed minimum.

- Beware of *market value adjustment* (MVA). This deceptively simple statement masks the fact that the insurance company reserves the right not only to levy surrender charges if you opt out of your account before the end of the term, but also to adjust the cash value of your account to reflect changing market conditions such as higher rates. You're likely to want out of your account early if interest rates rise and you're stuck with a low promised rate. You may even be willing to pay the surrender charges if they are low. The insurance company reserves the right to subtract some cash from your investment to offset its losses when it sells some of its matching investments at a loss to give you your cash. How much can it nick your account? It's up to the insurer at the time you withdraw. When the surrender period is over, there is no market value adjustment.

■ Watch for the *window.* Your policy may have a short period of perhaps 30 days when you are allowed to withdraw all your cash without any charges against your account. This is not the initial period immediately after purchase, which is called a *free look* and complies with state laws allowing you to back out of your initial purchase. The window will typically occur several years into your policy holding period. It usually coincides with the end of the guaranteed-rate period and gives you a chance to take your money out if you don't like the newly posted rates. The window is not the same as the surrender period, and if you miss this window of opportunity to move your annuity, surrender charges may go back into effect.

One more word of advice when it comes to getting out of your fixed-rate annuity, either during the window or when the surrender period expires: Don't simply take the money into your own checking account. That will trigger taxes, and possibly penalties. Treat it much as you would an *IRA rollover*—except that for insurance contracts it's called a *1035 exchange.* This provision of the tax law allows you to move directly into another insurance contact, even with a different carrier, and preserve your tax-deferred status on existing gains.

Variable-Rate Tax-Deferred Annuities

A *variable tax-deferred annuity* allows you to choose among a variety of mutual fund subaccounts or separate accounts. The growth of your money depends on the choice of funds and the performance of the stock market. A variable annuity typically offers many choices of funds, often named and managed by and in the same style as well-known mutual funds.

Depending on the terms of the variable annuity contract, the investor may make unlimited switches among fund subaccounts or may be limited in the number and timing of changes. Because these moves are made inside the annuity contract, there is no capital gains tax, or loss benefit, when you switch between funds. The growth in value of a variable annuity depends on the performance of the fund separate accounts chosen for investment.

These variable annuities carry penalties and surrender charges similar to those that impact fixed-rate tax-deferred annuities. But there are some additional costs that aren't always easy to measure.

- Tax-deferred variable annuities convert capital gains to ordinary income, the reverse of most investment goals. All of the gains in your investment accounts are taxed on withdrawal as ordinary income instead of at the much lower capital gains tax rates. If you cash out your annuity at a loss, the amount of the loss (not including surrender charges) may be deductible against ordinary income if the loss exceeds 2 percent of your adjusted gross income. Check with your accountant.

- Many tax-deferred variable annuities charge costly annual fees. First there is the management fee, paid to the advisor of the mutual fund subaccount, which could rise to more than 1 percent unless you are using an annuity with a low-cost fund manager, such as Vanguard. Then there is the mortality charge for the small bit of insurance that promises your account can be worth no less than your original investment at the time of your death, or not less than some "stepped-up" value that reflects your investment gains each year. That insurance benefit is supposed to offset the risk of investing in the variable subaccounts.

It's reassuring for your heirs to know they'll never inherit less than your original investment, but if you were planning to withdraw cash to pay for retirement expenses, that insurance provision won't help you while you're alive. If you lose money in your investments, you'll have a smaller pool of cash to draw on during your lifetime.

The average mortality charge and insurance fees total 1.26 percent per year. Additional annual contract fees of $25 to $50 per year may be charged against your account. All in all, you may be paying as much as 2.1 percent in annual fees for the benefit of tax deferral inside your variable annuity. That may not seem like much in a year when your funds register double-digit gains, but the costs will really stand out in a year when the market declines. Even over the long run, those high costs are a drag on investment returns.

THE LATEST ANNUITY PRODUCTS

Insurance companies have recognized that investors are looking for security but don't want to lock themselves into fixed-rate annuities, so they developed new products that combine certain income guarantees, either now or at a future date, if your annuity investment account does not perform well. But you have a chance at larger streams of income if the market goes up—even after you start receiving income.

Each of these products has its costs and limitations; but, depending on your willingness to pay the price and give up some of the upside, they may appeal to investors nearing or in retirement and seeking tax-deferred growth as well as guaranteed current income. In fact, some of the guarantees are so attractive that investors buy these products inside individual retirement accounts, which are already tax-deferred. It's a question of whether the benefits and guarantees outweigh the costs.

Guaranteed Minimum Income Benefits

Annuities with *guaranteed minimum income benefits* (GMIB) are designed to grow your money on a tax-deferred basis with a guaranteed protected withdrawal value, from which you can take income regardless of the market performance of the funds inside your annuity. On the upside, you get the benefit of stock market gains, but your future income stream is protected if the stock market falls. The ultimate goal is to create a predictable lifetime stream of income along with growth of principal.

With these guaranteed minimum income benefits annuities, the insurance company offers a fixed, guaranteed rate of return (today around 5 percent) on an amount usually called the *protected withdrawal value*, or the *guaranteed income base*. It is important to note that your actual cash value can be lower than this amount. If the investment subaccount values are lower, and you cashed out your annuity, the insurance company would send you that lower amount.

When you are ready to start receiving income, these income riders will pay you the withdrawal benefit's stated rate of return on the protected value amount, or the cash value amount, whichever is *higher*. The amount you can get in that monthly check is based on the protected withdrawal value or the value of your account, whichever is greater.

When you decide you want to turn on that lifetime income stream, the promised compounding on the income base will stop. You will continue to get your monthly check, based on the greater of your initial investment, compounded at 5 percent a year (or whatever your rider has promised), or the current cash value based on your investment growth, whichever is higher.

You'll get that same monthly check as long as you live, even if your investment account goes to zero. If the investment account were to increase because of a bull market, and your account grew more than the amount of your locked-in protected withdrawal value, you might even get a larger check. Many riders allow for *spousal protection* (at an additional cost), which will preserve this *income benefit* for your spouse as well, so that both of you would receive lifetime income.

If you need more money than the monthly check that is guaranteed by the income benefit, you can draw your cash value out, once you are beyond the surrender charges. (And you can usually access up to 10 percent annually without penalty during the surrender charge period.)

If at that point your protected withdrawal value (the initial deposit compounding at the promised rate) is higher than the cash value (because of poor market performance), you might think twice about withdrawing cash versus taking the monthly check based on the higher protected value.

When you die, your heirs will receive the amount you invested (less any withdrawals) or current cash value, whichever is greater. However, you can purchase a *death benefit rider* in addition to the *income benefit rider* (at an additional cost), which guarantees your heirs will receive the promised compounding on the initial investment at your death—unless the cash value goes to zero as a result of your withdrawals. When purchasing a death benefit rider, it is important to know how your death benefit is affected by withdrawals, and at what rate, if any, it can grow.

Consider this example: At age 60, you invest $100,000 into a 5 percent GMIB annuity, and also purchase a death benefit rider, also at 5 percent providing dollar-for-dollar withdrawal treatment. Here's what could happen 10 years from now:

■ There's been a bull market and your investment account has grown by 10 percent annually and in 10 years is worth $269,000.

At that point you could start to take 5 percent withdrawals, based on that $269,000 value.

■ There's been a bear market and your investment account has fallen to only $75,000. You need the income, so you start taking withdrawals based on your original investment of $100,000, which has been compounding at the promised rate of 5 percent per year. Thus that protected withdrawal value is now $162,889. At age 70, you're going to get a check for about $8,144 a year. And you will never receive *less* than that amount as long as you live. (You could receive more if the market turns upward sharply, though.)

■ Ten years from now, you might die without taking any withdrawals. If there has been a bull market, your heirs will receive the $269,000 cash value of your account (assuming a 10 percent annual rate of return). If there has been a bear market, your heirs will receive the initial $100,000 investment (if you did not purchase that death benefit rider). But if you *did* buy the death benefit rider, even with the bear market they will get the $162,889, which was the promised value based on the 5 percent compounding. And, as long as you stayed within the 5 percent dollar-for-dollar withdrawal guidelines, even if you've been receiving income, and your cash value is less than $162,889, your beneficiaries will receive no less than $162,889 as long as the account still has cash value.

■ Ten years from now you might need a hunk of cash. Since you are beyond the surrender charge period, you can take out the entire cash value. That cash value would be determined by the market value of your investment account.

When you buy one of these annuities, you should give careful thought to the costs of both the income and death benefit riders. The cost will be roughly 1 percent for the guaranteed withdrawal benefit, and half a percent for the death benefit rider, all taken out of the cash value of your investment account. Those seem a reasonable price to pay for the guarantees, but some annuities charge even more, so you must ask.

These annuities have another challenge. You must decide *when* to start making withdrawals. (Remember, your account stops compounding at the promised rate when you start making withdrawals.) And some of these income riders stop growing at the promised minimum rate of return after the tenth year, while others promise minimum growth for as long as you live.

So you want to take withdrawals early enough to get the maximum value withdrawn before you die! Adding a death benefit rider can help you deal with that challenge, potentially giving you the best of both worlds: income for as long as you live, plus providing a legacy for your beneficiaries.

In spite of this annual rate promise, this is really a variable annuity. You'll have a choice of mutual fund—type subaccounts that are invested in the stock market. If the market falls, the insurance company is promising that you'll at least get your principal, plus that 5 percent annual interest added to your *protected withdrawal income base* if you decide to take a check a month for life.

If the market rises, of course, you'll have gains that you can withdraw at any time after the surrender period expires, paying ordinary income taxes on the gains. This would also be your *locked-in income base* once you begin income under the terms of the rider.

If your investments perform poorly, your monthly check will be based on the original investment plus the promised interest. And after you begin taking income, if your investment choices perform well, your monthly check could even increase. But it will never fall below that initial check amount.

As I noted at the start, annuities are a complicated investment, with many variables and costs that are not obvious. Please avoid seminars geared toward convincing novice investors that they can get higher returns and guarantees. Frequently they don't mention costs and inaccessibility of your money.

For independent advice you can trust, contact my annuity expert, Jeffrey Oster, at **www.JeffreyOster.com**. You do not have to mention my name, and I get nothing out of this but the confidence that you will be treated with intelligence and integrity.

Equity-Indexed Annuities: A Warning

Equity-indexed annuities offer tax deferral with features that take some of the attractiveness of fixed-rate annuities, which guarantee a certain amount of interest each year, and variable annuities, which have a return that depends on your investment decisions. In my opinion, equity-indexed annuities contain the worst features of both—typically at a high cost—and should usually be avoided.

Here's how they work. The interest you earn on the money you invest in this annuity is based on the performance of some stock market index—typically the Standard & Poor's 500 stock index—without the dividends, which can provide as much as 40 percent of the total index return over the long run! So you have a guaranteed base interest rate, combined with a chance to earn a bit extra based on the return of a stock market index. It sounds good if that's all you know, but in this case the devil is in the details.

On the downside, there is typically a floor. If the index falls, you don't lose principal. But, depending on the contract, you may not be credited with any interest. Or you may be guaranteed a low minimum rate of interest on at least 90 percent of your original investment, even if the index falls. There are a variety of combinations, which makes it difficult to compare these products.

But it's not the downside protection that makes most of these annuities a bad deal. It's the restrictions on what you can earn on the upside to pay for that protection. You get some of the benefit of the stock market's gains, but definitely not all of the upside.

There are several ways the upside can be limited. The insurance company may set a *participation rate*, giving you perhaps only 70 percent (or even as low as 50 percent) of the total return of the index. That percentage factor might change every year, it might be guaranteed for as long as you keep your money in the annuity, or it might have a certain minimum. In any case, you're losing out on the upside potential of the stock market.

Other equity-indexed annuities provide for a *rate cap*, an upper limit on what you can earn. Even in a bull-market year, your return may be capped at 6 percent. That cap offsets the protection the insurance company offers in guaranteeing a floor—the promise that you won't earn a negative rate of interest even if the market falls. In my opinion, you're always paying too much for the protection. Of course, many insurance salespeople will disagree. These products pay some of the highest commissions offered on annuity sales.

The bottom line is that you might be better off with two separate annuities: (1) a fixed-rate annuity that will give you guaranteed positive interest and (2) a variable annuity that lets you capture all the upside gains on your investment subaccounts. Remember, much of the stock market's historic long-term return of around 10 percent per year is made up of some very big years of gains that offset down years. Why limit your upside potential just because you're seeking security?

If that argument hasn't convinced you to stay away from equity-indexed annuities, you'll want to consider the additional costs that can be packed into these products. For example, there may be an administrative fee, or margin, subtracted from your return. That could be 2 percent or more, again cutting into your upside potential. And the way the value of the index is calculated could, again, limit your participation.

Even worse, many of these contracts have extended periods for surrender charges with extremely high amounts, some as high as 20 percent, effectively locking up your money for an extended period of time, some for as long as 15 years! Others restrict you from withdrawal at any time, insisting you, or you and your heirs, *annuitize*—take a monthly check for life—to get your money out without a penalty.

In Most States, Annuities Are Protected from Creditors

In most states, but not all, assets held inside an annuity (similar to assets held in retirement accounts) are protected from creditors—in bankruptcy or as a result of legal judgments. Physicians who might be liable in malpractice suits often put money into annuities, well before a judgment is upon them. Check with an attorney about the legal status of annuities in your state to see whether this might be a reason for funding a tax-deferred annuity.

Some planners use annuities to protect assets from seizure by Medicaid when the owner enters a nursing home. Those strategies use an annuity to convert cash to a stream of current income that may be used for the care of a spouse remaining outside the nursing home. Annuitization must take place before applying for Medicaid, and the income stream must meet the Social Security mortality standards. There is no guarantee that this strategy will remove the asset from the patient's estate if your state's Medicaid program challenges the purchase.

Again, state laws govern the protection of annuities from creditors, lawsuits, bankruptcy, and state Medicaid programs, so be sure to check with a qualified attorney, *in your state,* about changing laws, before you assume that an annuity will protect your assets in all eventualities. You can be sure that, in any case, a fraudulent transfer of assets into an annuity to avoid seizure will be challenged in court.

Consider the Impact of Annuities on Your Estate Planning

Here's one final estate planning issue to consider before you purchase a variable annuity to defer taxes on your investments: Unless you plan to take the money out in your lifetime and pay taxes on the gains at ordinary income tax rates, you may be doing your estate a disservice. Heirs to a tax-deferred annuity pay ordinary income taxes on all of the gains, so they don't get the "step-up" benefit of investments held outside an insurance contract.

Almost all annuities do allow for a stretch payout to beneficiaries, only requiring life expectancy payouts to occur, even to heirs other than the spouse. Spouses have special treatment under the tax laws: They are allowed to continue deferral as long as they live, or cash out and pay taxes on gains, if any. Also, many annuities will pay the death benefit on the death of either spouse, even if the surviving spouse is the owner.

It's important to consider these estate tax implications, which may change as estate tax laws change. You might want to set up a conversation between your annuity advisor and your estate planning attorney.

Here's When Tax-Deferred Annuities Work Best

After reading all these caveats about costs, terms, taxes, and penalties involved in tax-deferred annuities, you might be tempted to give up. But these tax-deferred annuities can serve a good purpose in some cases if:

- You buy a low-cost annuity with low fees and surrender charges.
- You plan to spend the money that accumulates inside the annuity while you're alive.
- You expect to be in a far lower tax bracket when you withdraw the gains in your annuity.
- You don't need any more life insurance (and are willing to pass up the ability to withdraw premiums you paid into a life policy and borrow additional cash tax-free).
- You can't qualify for life insurance but still want to build up a tax-deferred investment.
- At some point you will want to take advantage of a guaranteed income benefit or annuitize—take a check a month for life—to make sure you never run out of retirement income because you expect to live a very long time, or you can pick a guaranteed period certain of 10 to 30 years.

The bottom line on annuities is that insurance companies have created some complex but enticing products to help guarantee retirement income while giving you the opportunity for investment growth. In an era of uncertainty about outliving retirement savings, these tax-deferred variable annuities have a certain appeal. But the costs and benefit trade-offs are not always apparent, so it requires the services of an expert who holds your interests above his or her own juicy sales commissions on these products.

GETTING STARTED

If someone suggests that you purchase an annuity, do the following things:

- Ask whether it is an immediate or tax-deferred annuity.
- If an immediate annuity, compare payment amounts from other insurers at www.ImmediateAnnuities.com.
- If tax-deferred, ask whether it is fixed or variable.
- If fixed rate, ask how long the surrender charges last and how long the guaranteed rate lasts.
- Ask what happens to the remainder of your money when you die.
- Ask how long before you can take money out without penalty.
- If it's a variable annuity, do what I do: Contact Jeffrey Oster (Jeffrey.Oster@RaymondJames.com) and ask for a free analysis!

CHAPTER

8

THE SAVAGE TRUTH ON LIFE INSURANCE . . . AND MORE

Don't Wait Until It's Too Late

What's your life worth? Can you measure in terms of dollars and cents what the impact would be on your family and loved ones if you suddenly lost your life? Yes, you are priceless to those who love you. But if there would be financial consequences to those loved ones, you must consider life insurance.

And then think of the financial burden if you were disabled, or were diagnosed with a life-threatening disease or condition. No one wants to think about that—especially in monetary terms. But the bills will keep coming, adding even more stress to your situation.

It's understandable that you don't want to think about these terrible possibilities. Insurance on your life is a bet you won't be around to collect! But it can protect those for whom you care, and for whom you have a responsibility to provide. And a cash payment if you are unable to work or face a medical challenge would certainly be welcomed.

So here's a brief look at insurance basics. If you skip this chapter and these products, you're tempting fate. And that's the Savage Truth.

LIFE INSURANCE: A BET AGAINST THE ODDS

Life insurance is an intimidating topic, perhaps because for many years insurance salespeople convinced us that the subject was so complicated we needed their help to buy a policy. These days it's easy and relatively inexpensive to buy simple insurance policies via the Internet. Websites like **AccuQuote.com**, **SelectQuote.com**, and **TermQuote.com** will give you instant access to price comparison and easy access to the applications.

The Savage Truth is that the basics of life insurance are actually pretty simple and logical. Yes, there are more complex policies that include savings and investment features. And yes, there are important discussions over how the policy should be owned, and who should be the beneficiary, and how to deal with estate tax issues. But don't get buried in the details (pun intended). The very first step is to determine whether you need coverage, how much coverage you require, and for how long you'll need it. Let's start there.

Do You Need Life Insurance?

The first decision is whether you need life insurance at all. Life insurance is merely a way of leaving money behind to take care of those you love—or to pay estate taxes to the federal government. If you do not have a financial responsibility to someone else (children, spouse, aging parents), you may not need life insurance. Typically, your health insurance plan at work will have a small life insurance component to pay for funeral costs. Any creditors will file claims against your estate to be repaid from your assets, and unpaid balances will be written off.

If you're single and unencumbered, you might be better off buying *critical illness insurance,* which pays you a lump sum upon diagnosis of serious illness. You can use that cash to cover daily living needs (see the section on specialty insurance policies later in this chapter). Or *disability insurance* could provide salary continuation. If you fear being seriously disabled, *long-term care insurance* might be a better solution than life insurance for those who have no obvious beneficiary for life insurance.

(At the end of this chapter, I show you how to cover most of those needs with one simple product if you're just starting out.)

Some singles prefer to buy life insurance even though they have no immediate heirs because they figure they're more insurable at reasonable rates when they're young. That presumes that there will be a future need for insurance to meet loved ones' financial needs. Even worse, some parents buy life insurance on young children, wasting their premium dollars on unnecessary mortality charges when they could be saving for college in a tax-deferred 529 college savings plan.

There's no amount of life insurance that can replace the loss of a young child.

However, you definitely *should* have life insurance if you have children who will need to be educated or a mortgage that needs to be paid so your family can continue to live in the home, or people who are dependent on your income or services. That group includes mothers who are not primary breadwinners but handle the tough job of raising children and running a household. Your services are priceless and would be very expensive to duplicate in your absence.

That's the basis for determining how much life insurance you need. Just ask yourself how much it would cost, and how long that cost would last, to replace the value of your income and services to those who are dependent upon you. That will give you a more realistic idea of the magnitude of the financial hole your absence would leave.

Once you've calculated the amount of coverage that would be required, you can examine the alternatives to find the type of policy that best suits your needs and your budget.

First Decide How Much

Many people look at the cost of life insurance to determine how much they can afford. That's a backward approach. Your first consideration should be how much insurance coverage you *need*, based on the ages of your dependents, your desired lifestyle for your family, and your spouse's ability to make up for your lost income. If you need insurance only for a specific purpose, such as paying off a mortgage, it will be easier to estimate the amount of coverage to purchase. It's far more subjective to evaluate how much cash—wisely invested, of course—it will take to protect and educate a young family in your absence.

Some experts advise leaving an amount equal to six times your annual gross salary, or 10 times your net income. Since life insurance will pass income tax-free to your beneficiaries, this may be an adequate amount. Then again, it might not be enough, depending on special circumstances. The "experts" won't be around to help your family if you're underinsured!

One big mistake that many people make when it comes to buying life insurance is assuming that the need for insurance will go away on a certain date: when the children finish college or when the mortgage is paid off. So they purchase less expensive level-term insurance, which will stay in effect for only 20 or 30 years.

There is one need for life insurance that may last beyond the need to house or educate your family. As your wealth grows—including the value of your home, investments, and retirement account—you may need life insurance proceeds to help defray the cost of estate taxes. If you purchase a policy that has a fixed term and fixed annual payments, you might find yourself unable to qualify for more insurance just at the time you need it to cover estate tax issues. But term life is certainly the way to get started.

THE SAVAGE TRUTH ON TERM LIFE INSURANCE

If you're looking for the most insurance at the least cost, simple term life insurance is certainly the place to start. Term life insurance covers the cost of insuring against your death for one year at a time. You pay only to cover that cost—no additional amount goes into savings or investment within the policy. The annual premium you pay is based on the likelihood that you'll die that year. Since that possibility of death increases a bit every year as you age, the cost of this type of term life insurance rises every year.

Insurance companies long ago recognized that people want to be able to plan ahead for their annual insurance costs, so they invented 10-, 20-, and 30-year *level-term* policies. That is, the insurance company establishes a flat premium that remains the same for every year of the policy, no matter what happens to your health. But these level-term policies still do not build up any cash value.

As long as you pay the premium every year, your insurance policy stays in force. If you miss paying the premium, your insurance will expire after a short grace period of about one month. There is no cash value to these term insurance policies. That is, there is no money to borrow out of the policy. And your death benefit will never grow to be more than the face amount you originally purchased.

When the term expires, you have no more life insurance. So if you purchase 30-year level term at age 25, when you're worried about covering college costs for your young children in the event of your untimely death, you might find that at age 55 you have no insurance to protect your spouse—even though your children are grown and out the door. And at age 55, your health might make insurance very expensive.

It's important to think long term about the amount of the insurance you need and the length of time you will need this coverage.

Many term policies guarantee you the right to convert your term plan into a permanent policy without evidence of insurability. Some policies will let you convert from term at any time; others allow conversion only within a certain number of years. And others allow conversion only into less competitive cash value policies. So if you think you might have a longer term need for coverage, consider "permanent" cash value insurance now.

If you're young, you're probably not considering the need for longer-term, affordable coverage. But family and health situations can change, and you don't want to find yourself uninsurable just when your family might need the benefits most. So, when purchasing term, make sure you have the right to convert at any time. Of course, the premiums on a conversion policy will be substantially higher the longer you wait to convert.

Term Insurance Prices Are Competitive

Term insurance is the least expensive type of life insurance you can buy. The annual cost is based on your age, current health, gender, and the amount of coverage you purchase. With the advent of comparison shopping on the Internet, prices have become more competitive—and lower. In fact, by 2010, prices for term life insurance were nearly 50 percent lower than they were 15 years ago.

For example, in 2011, a 40-year-old male in the preferred, nonsmoker category could buy $500,000 of coverage for $355 a year. Even if you don't qualify for the very top rating, you could get the same coverage for $460 a year. Women pay lower rates, so a 40-year-old woman could buy a half-million dollars in coverage for $310 in preferred plus, or $400 a year in the preferred health category.

Premiums are also relatively inexpensive even if you're in your sixties. The same 20-year level-term policy for a 60-year-old man would cost $2,555 annually if he is in the top (preferred) health category, or $2,990 in a health category that is a step down. A 60-year-old woman pays $1,735 per year in preferred, or $2,075 if her health isn't in the top rating.

Note: When it comes to buying life insurance, your health is a critical aspect. Preferred rates can easily be 30 percent lower than standard rates. So if you haven't ever smoked and maintain a healthy weight, you're about to get your reward. Of course, not all health conditions are under our control, and the need for insurance may be greater for those who have less-than-perfect health. The price of your coverage will reflect that—and insurance companies are very sophisticated about pricing risk.

Those premium levels can change, of course, because they reflect not only lengthening life expectancies, but the fact that many owners drop their policies in tough economic times. The premiums they've already paid thus subsidize lower prices for other buyers. But insurers also need to earn money on their investments to subsidize low premiums. So locking in 20 or 30 years of level premiums when prices are low is a very good idea.

To find the least expensive term policy, consult the term insurance quotation services on the Internet. These websites are perfect for making price comparisons, but you'll also want to deal with competent representatives at the websites through their toll-free numbers. Their insurance advisors help you get through the application process, and any physical exams that might be required if you apply for a large amount of insurance.

Check Insurance Company Ratings

Just as individuals have different risk profiles, so do insurance companies. Some have stronger financial reserves than others. Before purchasing a policy, check the insurance company's rating from an independent agency. It's easy to search for an insurer's rating at **www .Insure.com** using the "Ratings Lookup" tool on the home page.

Since you hope you won't be using the benefits of your life insurance for a long time, it's only smart business to purchase your policy from a company with assured financial staying power.

THE SAVAGE TRUTH ON CASH VALUE LIFE INSURANCE

While term insurance is the least expensive, and designed to cover your insurance needs for the next 20 or 30 years, there are some instances in which it makes sense to buy more "permanent" life insurance. That type of insurance is variously called *whole life* or *cash value life* insurance. It is not easily purchased online because of its complexities. Some variations of whole life include *universal life* and *variable universal life*.

Each has its own strengths and potential pitfalls, which is why these policies are "sold," not purchased. You'll probably be dealing with a registered insurance agent for this type of insurance. But you definitely need to understand the basics so you can ask the right questions.

Since it's more expensive and more complex, you might be wondering why you should ever consider cash value life insurance. First, you might believe that you will outlive term insurance, but still want to leave insurance proceeds to your loved ones or to a charity. You want a policy that will provide the cash, if you have spent most of your money by the time you die.

Or you might use a whole life policy to provide liquidity for estate taxes, with the policy owned by an irrevocable trust outside your estate. (See Chapter 15.)

And finally, these policies do build some cash value, unlike term insurance. So, they can be a source of "forced savings" should you need to withdraw some of that value in the future. However, you are paying for mortality charges, so there are other, better ways to save if you don't need the insurance coverage.

How Cash Value Works

The advantage of whole life, assuming it is issued by a major quality insurance company, is that it has guaranteed premiums for life along with guaranteed cash values that are almost always enhanced by nonguaranteed dividends. Whole life is designed to *endow*, which means the guaranteed cash value will equal the contractual death benefit, generally at age 100 (although some contracts provide for endowment at other ages).

Most policies allow the owner to borrow out a portion of the cash value at very low rates of interest. If you die with a policy loan outstanding, the amount of the death benefit is typically reduced by the amount of the loan plus any accrued interest.

Other policies allow cash withdrawals, but this defeats the point of having life insurance, because the amount withdrawn reduces the death benefit. And in cases of variable policies, described later, if too much money is withdrawn, the policy value could be destroyed. That would be a shame because you paid huge fees along the way to keep this policy growing.

Of course, this great deal comes with a few minor drawbacks. First, the government realized that wealthy people might dump huge amounts of cash into these policies to grow tax-free, and then borrow it out again, so it set ratios of the amount of insurance coverage versus the cash invested inside the policy to qualify it as a legitimate life insurance deal instead of a modified endowment contract. And, of course, there is the annual cost of the life insurance that goes along with this tax-free buildup. If you need the life insurance anyway, this is a fine place to invest your money, but be aware of the insurance charges, fees, and commissions that you're paying along the way.

Three Basic Choices in Cash Value Life

Let's make this simple. You have three basic types of permanent life insurance, each with its own way of building cash value:

1. *Traditional whole life.* You give the insurance company extra money in premiums every year, above the actual cost of death benefits (the mortality charge). The insurance company promises that the premium will always stay the same and that it will always give you a fixed amount of life insurance. A mutual insurance company credits dividends from its investments to your policy, building up cash value along the way. A stock-owned insurance company pays interest on your cash buildup. You can borrow against this cash value, but if you die before the loan is repaid, the insurance payout is reduced by the amount of the loan.

2. *Universal life.* This policy is similar to whole life, but the extra money you pay in premiums goes into a tax-deferred account. You can decide how much extra money you want to pay in premiums. If you pay enough in the early years, and if your cash account keeps earning the projected interest rate, at some point in the future there will be enough cash in the account to pay future premiums. If the cash account grows at a lower rate than projected, you could lower the death benefit instead of paying more premiums. Universal life gives the policyholder flexibility over premium payments, death benefits, and how long the coverage will last.

3. *Variable universal life.* This policy is similar to universal life, but you have options about how your cash is invested. Instead of accepting the interest rate provided by the insurer, you'll have a choice of stock or bond mutual funds to make your money grow inside the account. If the market moves higher, your account will grow in value, perhaps enough so you never have to pay in another premium dollar. However, if the value of your investments inside the policy declines, you could have

to add more cash to pay the premiums to keep your insurance in force. If you don't have the cash, you can lower the death benefit. And these variable policies typically have the highest fees, because there are management fees for the investment subaccounts, as well as surrender charges that can last as long as 10 to 20 years.

Those are the basics of the three kinds of permanent life insurance being sold today. The risk is that if the market moves against you, your ability to keep the policy going might not be so permanent, after all. Unless you truly need coverage for longer than the longest term policy—30 years—you're probably better off with term.

Illustrations Are Not Promises

When you are considering purchasing a permanent or cash value life insurance policy, the agent will give you some illustrations. These are long lists of numbers that will make your eyes glaze over. Basically, they are projections of how long you will have to keep paying premiums to keep your insurance in force.

In the past, many insurance buyers mistakenly figured these illustrations were guarantees of future premiums. When interest rates declined over the past decade, the actual investment earnings inside these policies lagged far behind the projections. Suddenly, people who figured they had to pay into the policies for only 10 years to create enough cash value to keep them going in their old age were told they'd have to keep paying huge premiums for 20 years or more. Their only choice was to lower the death benefit substantially, and it was a shock for people who believed they had fully paid policies.

There are two ways to avoid this kind of shock. First, when you consider purchasing a universal life policy, ask the agent to project what the premiums would be if the interest earnings dropped to the minimum guaranteed level (typically about 4 percent annually, or even lower) or if the mortality charges were to rise to the maximum allowable level. Some universal life policies offer a *no-lapse guarantee* that so long as the customer continues to pay a specified target premium, the coverage will remain in force to a specific age—regardless of whether there is money in the investment account inside the policy.

The second way to avoid being surprised if your investment account inside the policy falls short of its intended goals is to ask your agent for a policy checkup every year. Request a *current illustration* or *in-force ledger*—a projection of current cash values that shows how much more money you'll have to invest at the current rates to keep the policy in force until the desired age.

You don't want to be surprised to find out later in life, when you can least afford it, that you need to pay increased premiums to keep your insurance in force, because either interest credit rates or market returns were lower than your agent initially projected.

The Hidden Costs

If you think a variable universal life policy is a winning deal because you're an astute investor, take a second look. Yes, this is a way to make your premium dollars grow tax-free fast enough to pay future premiums, or even to increase your death benefit, but that benefit is not without substantial costs.

It's difficult to sort out all the fees inside these policies, but you can be sure the insurance agent and the insurance company are making a small fortune off your premium dollars. First there's a *premium expense load* of as much as 8 percent that is deducted from every premium payment. The agent actually receives far more than that as a commission from the insurance company in the first year or two, as much as 100 percent of the first year's premium when you take into account other benefits to the agent, such as vacation trips or clerical assistance provided by the insurance company.

Next there's the actual cost of life insurance, which is buried inside the premium you pay. It varies by age and by the actual amount of death benefit the insurance company has at risk, compared to the cash value of your account. There are also administrative fees, state premium taxes, and even a fund management fee for the mutual funds inside your variable account. If you cancel your policy in the first 10 years, you'll have to pay a substantial surrender charge unless you have a low-load policy.

You can find lower-cost variable universal life policies, which are offered through fee-only financial planners. At the **AmeritasDirect .com** website, you can take a peek at what these lower-cost plans might cost, without the typical huge up-front fees that most insurance premiums use to cover sales commissions.

With all policies, these ongoing fees must be broken out separately in the prospectus for a variable universal life policy, but few people read the details. That's unfortunate because these costs all affect the ability of your cash to grow inside your policy. It's like trying to run a race with wings on one foot (the tax-free growth) and a lead weight on the other (the fees and charges). Unless you're planning to keep the policy for a very long time, you'll actually be a loser for the first 10 or 15 years of this policy. And remember, if you don't have enough cash in your investment account inside the policy—because of high fees or poor performance—your coverage will lapse.

According to LIMRA International (the insurance industry trade association), 12.7 percent of whole life insurance policyholders will lapse their policies in the first year, 8.1 percent will lapse in the second year and another 5.5 percent will lapse in the third year. That means the insurance company—and its agents—make a lot of money on insurance policies that they will never be required to pay out or for which they will not be required to hold reserves.

The way to figure out the real impact of the charges is to look at the surrender value of the policy as illustrated in a few years, not the cash buildup. If you're not sure about the real cost of these charges, or if you're wondering whether it makes sense to exchange for a new policy that promises lower internal costs, here's how to get an independent appraisal.

If you'd like a professional evaluation of your policy, go to **www .EvaluateLifeInsurance.org**, where noted consumer insurance advocate James Hunt provides individual policy evaluations and comparisons at a very reasonable charge of $85 for the first policy, and $65 for additional comparisons. You can get this independent review and advice either before you purchase a policy, or for an existing policy.

When to Switch

There is no fixed rule about when it pays to transfer policies. But remember: Insurance agents receive a maximum bonus on the first year's premium of a new policy, so they have an incentive to ask customers to switch. The best companies demand to know whether an older policy is being surrendered, and they may limit agents' commissions on such transfers. When you complete an application for a new policy, you can expect to be specifically asked whether it is replacing an existing policy.

Also compare the *surrender values* on the new policy versus the old one. As you'll easily see, the surrender value may even be negative in the early years, reflecting the big commissions and other up-front costs that are paid to the agent. So you need a very compelling reason to move the existing cash value from an older policy into a new one. Use the service mentioned earlier at EvaluateLifeInsurance.org if you're not sure that the switch deal is a good one.

If you do decide on a replacement policy, never simply cash in an old policy, take the cash, and buy a new policy. That could trigger taxes on the gains in the investments inside the policy. Instead, you'll want to examine a *1035 exchange*—named for the section of the tax law that authorizes this tax-free exchange into a new insurance or annuity policy.

"Buy Term and Invest the Difference" Works Only if You Do It

Even with these explanations of life insurance policies that build cash value, you may decide that, for your needs, term insurance is cheap and easy to purchase. If that's all you can afford—and you need life insurance—then purchase a term policy immediately. Leaving your insurance needs uncovered is like tempting fate.

In fact, even some people who could afford to pay more in premiums have decided to go with the cheaper term insurance and invest the difference. That strategy has become a mantra among those who advocate term insurance, but it's a strategy that works only if you *do* invest the difference every month, preferably in a tax-sheltered account such as an IRA. You'll avoid the commissions and fees associated with many life insurance policies that build cash value, although with an IRA you won't be able to withdraw your premiums tax-free or borrow your cash value tax-free. And you'll still have the concern over how to pay the rising costs of term insurance when your flat-rate guarantee expires.

The way to compare the benefits of "buying term, and investing the difference" is to get the *internal rate of return* (IRR) calculation for your cash value policy versus what you might reasonably expect to earn (with or without risk) in an investment account. The IRR on the insurance policy might be negative for the first few years, reflecting those up-front charges. But over the longer run of perhaps 20 years, you might get a higher return on the policy than on your investments. Your agent should be able to illustrate the promised IRR of any policy you purchase.

Those are the trade-offs for the higher-cost universal and variable universal life policies. The insurance industry will continue to try to structure both types to make sure you can afford coverage.

I leave you with this persuasive argument from a very successful insurance agent, Byron Udell, President of AccuQuote.com:

Term insurance works fine for temporary life insurance needs. Today's term products are available with guaranteed level premiums for as long as 30 years. They are very inexpensive, assuming you are in good health. But remember, they are inexpensive for a reason. Odds are, you'll outlive the policy and collect nothing. The only way to win the game on a term policy is to die before your time!

Permanent plans can be structured to last forever, so that they are still around when you die. If you die with your policy in force, you will have won the game. Since everyone dies, and since no one is better off dying *without* life insurance, it would seem that people would be lining up to buy some sort of permanent insurance policy to make sure that they have the coverage in force when they die—whether that's tomorrow or in 40 years.

Owner, Insured, and Beneficiary

Before you make a final purchase decision, give some careful thought to the who's-who of your life insurance policy. Figuring out the *insured* is simple; that's the person whose life is covered by the policy. But there are several choices for the *owner* of the policy, and the wrong decision can make a big impact on the eventual payout. It's also important to consider the *beneficiary*—the person who will eventually receive the proceeds when the insured dies. Remember to update or change the beneficiary when your life circumstances change. (That's a subtle reminder that you don't want your "ex" collecting the payout!)

POLICY OWNER

If you own the policy on your own life, at death it becomes part of your estate—although the actual proceeds of the policy pass tax-free to the designated beneficiary. Even if your children or a charity are the beneficiary and receive the full death benefit, the total amount of that benefit is included in your estate for federal estate tax purposes. When you combine the death benefit with all your other assets, including your home and retirement plan, the federal government could take a huge tax bite, depending on estate tax rates in force that year.

You may choose to make your adult children the owners of the policy on your life and gift them enough money each year to pay the premiums. Or, you may want to set up an irrevocable life insurance trust to own the policy on your life. That gets the death benefit out of your estate. Have the trust purchase a new policy rather than transfer an existing one, because for the first three years after a transfer an existing policy is still considered part of your estate. When the life insurance is owned by an irrevocable trust, the trustees can then lend the proceeds to your estate for tax purposes and distribute the rest to your heirs according to your instructions. The trust must meet several legal requirements, so use a competent estate planning attorney.

POLICY BENEFICIARY

Your estate planning attorney can also help you decide the appropriate beneficiary. Each situation will be different, and you may choose to leave some less liquid business assets to one adult child and cash proceeds of an insurance policy to another. In some cases, it may be best to name a revocable (not irrevocable) trust as beneficiary to safeguard the policy proceeds in case of a subsequent remarriage.

Unfortunately, many young parents make the mistake of naming minor children as beneficiaries of the parents' life insurance policies. Since a minor will not have the authority to handle the money, the state will then name a trustee to act as fiduciary to invest and dole out the funds. You can avoid these problems by setting up a revocable trust (naming a trustee and successor trustees) to be the beneficiary of your life insurance policy, with instructions for how the money is to be used on behalf of your children.

And here's a special note for spouses who might become beneficiaries of a life insurance policy as part of a divorce settlement. The *owner* of the policy always has the right to change the beneficiary—or simply stop paying the premiums. If you want to make sure the coverage stays in force, insist that you become the owner. Request either a fully paid policy or enough cash as part of the settlement to cover the future premiums you will need to pay as owner. You will remain the beneficiary and because it was part of your divorce agreement, you will have what is called an *insurable interest* in the policy.

Specialty Life Insurance: It Costs Less to Insure Two Lives

Second-to-die life insurance policies, sometimes called *survivorship policies*, cover two lives but pay off only on the death of the second insured. They're particularly useful in estate planning situations, where cash will be needed to pay federal estate taxes at the death of the second spouse. That's because unlimited assets can be left to a spouse without being subject to estate taxes, but when the second spouse dies the remaining estate could face a heavy tax burden.

Since survivorship policies insure two lives, but pay off only on the death of one, they can cut premiums by 50 percent or more.

First-to-die life insurance can save premium dollars for a young couple who can't afford to insure both lives but want to make sure there is cash to help a surviving parent care for children. With today's low term rates, this isn't a particularly appealing solution, as both spouses should have individual policies.

But first-to-die policies do make sense for business partners, who often use this type of policy to make sure there is cash available for the surviving partner to buy out the interest of the deceased partner. These policies are costly, and unless coverage is needed for many years, two separate term policies may be a better solution. Fewer companies are offering these policies today, and it is almost always priced too high in comparison to term.

Accelerate Death Benefits without Dying

In the past 20 years, insurance companies recognized the need to allow people who have terminal illnesses or other special needs to access the cash death benefit before they die. This is different from a policy loan, in that no interest is charged on the amount withdrawn. And since it is an advance payment on a death benefit, it is tax-free.

The accelerated death benefit was an insurance industry response to a growing business of *viatical settlements*—cash advances on life insurance policies, offered at a discount by investors to terminally ill people, given impetus by the initial wave of AIDS cases. (In fact, many of those investors were burned in the late 1990s when they gave cash advances to AIDS patients who were presumably terminal but who then recovered as a result of new medicines.)

What subsequently developed was a huge market for these viatical settlements, with incentive payments given to individuals who took out insurance policies, even though the death benefits were not needed. "Investors" then purchased the policies at a discount, expecting a substantial return on the investment if the policyholder died sooner than the actuarial tables on which the premiums were predicated. During the recession, many of these deals collapsed due to lack of funding. Even worse, and to put it simply, if you participate in this kind of deal, you are giving a stranger a strong incentive to see you die sooner rather than later!

Life Insurance—A Final Thought

If all this talk about death and dying makes you queasy, you're not alone. As a man once told me: "Life insurance is a bet against my own life." There's a better way to think of it. Eventually we will all die. One way to "cheat" death in a small way is to make sure that those who depend on you are well taken care of in your absence.

THE SAVAGE TRUTH ON SPECIALTY HEALTH, LIFE, DISABILITY, AND LIABILITY INSURANCE POLICIES

I'm sure you have basic health, homeowners, and auto insurance to cover your most valued possessions, but there are additional insurance needs that may be overlooked because they are not pushed by insurance agents or widely advertised. Read the following discussion to see whether some of these situations apply to you and your family. People often don't find out they could have insured against a risk until it's too late. Be sure to turn to Chapter 14 for a complete discussion of long-term care insurance policies. And then take a look at the end of this chapter for a combination policy that could get you started with affordable coverage for the most unexpected events.

Critical Illness Insurance Provides Immediate Cash

We all understand the importance of life insurance to leave cash for support of those we leave behind. But these days, you have a greater chance of surviving a critical illness, which can deplete all your savings. If you are single and childless, it may be more important to have cash during your illness than to leave an estate for your heirs. Unreimbursed medical expenses are a leading cause of bankruptcy, even when an individual has health insurance. And many cutting-edge treatments are not covered by health insurance plans.

That's where a relatively new concept—*critical illness insurance*—steps in. It's a policy that pays a lump sum in cash if you survive 30 days from the date of diagnosis of the most life-threatening medical conditions.

Imagine buying an insurance policy that would pay off if you were diagnosed with cancer, stroke, heart attack, paralysis, renal failure, multiple sclerosis, Alzheimer's, blindness, deafness, or organ transplantation. It sounds like a litany of your worst health-care nightmares.

Like life insurance, critical illness insurance is purchased in lump-sum amounts from $25,000 to $2 million face value for the policy. But unlike life insurance, you don't have to wait until you die to receive a payout. You'll receive a check a month after your diagnosis. You can use the cash to pay uncovered medical bills, maintain your lifestyle, make mortgage payments, or cover college tuition. The entire payout is tax-free, as long as you (not your employer) paid the policy premiums.

We tend to think more about illness as we age, but this policy is available only to those ages 20 through 64. Critical illness policies appeal to singles who don't need much life insurance but worry about having enough assets to see them through a serious illness. Two-income families who need both paychecks to make monthly mortgage payments might also consider this new type of coverage.

The critical illness policy is *not* a substitute for adequate health-care insurance. And because the proceeds are likely to be used during the patient's lifetime, it is not a substitute for life insurance. It may, however, be considered a substitute for, or work in tandem with, disability insurance—with some differences.

A traditional disability policy would cover a much broader array of situations that keep you from performing your usual occupation, but it would pay benefits only on a monthly basis. And if you have a critical illness, you might not survive long enough to collect much in the way of disability benefits. Also, people without a regular income (including nonworking spouses) can't get disability coverage.

Not everyone qualifies for critical illness insurance—certainly not at a reasonable price. If your family has a history of heart disease, stroke, or breast cancer, then you may be denied coverage or charged a steep premium. As usual, smokers also pay a lot more for a policy.

Critical Illness coverage is offered by most major insurers, including MetLife, AFLAC, Mutual of Omaha, and many others. Compare prices and features. Most exclude skin cancer, and some common procedures such as balloon angioplasty. Some offer a *return of premium* feature if you die without using your policy.

The price you'll pay for this critical illness insurance depends on your age, medical condition, and the amount of coverage you buy. Some employers offer these benefits as part of a workplace health-care plan. This insurance is expensive, but that's the price some people are willing to pay for peace of mind.

For more information, a cost calculator, and links to carriers and brokers, go to the trade association website, **www.CriticalIllness InsuranceInfo.org**.

Disability Insurance Covers a Real Risk

One of the greatest risks to your financial security is the possibility that an illness or injury will keep you from earning current income and from contributing to your retirement plan. If you are between the ages of 35 and 65, your chances of being unable to work for 90 days or more because of disabling illness or injury are about equal to your chances of dying, according to the Health Insurance Association of America. The average disability lasts two to four years, but some people are disabled for life. So it makes sense to insure your ability to earn an income.

Disability insurance may be offered as part of a group benefit provided by your employer or purchased independently. Disability insurance costs less when purchased through a company benefits plan, and premiums are usually paid with pretax dollars. But if you ever have to receive a monthly disability check from a company plan, you'll owe income taxes on the payments. Some companies allow payroll deductions on an after-tax basis, so future benefits would be tax-free. If you purchase a disability policy on your own, you can expect to pay more, and you won't receive any tax deduction for the premiums, but any future payouts will be tax-free. And keep in mind that if you leave your company, your disability insurance may not be portable.

Don't make the mistake of assuming that company-paid sick leave will last long enough to cover all your income needs in case of a disability. Workers' compensation payments cover only injuries or illnesses that are proved to be work-related. Social Security does provide some disability income, but only after an arduous claims process that results in benefits only for the severely disabled. None of these programs comes close to replacing your previous income.

The most important consideration in purchasing a disability policy is the definition of what constitutes a disability. Some policies pay benefits if you are unable to perform the duties of your customary occupation; others pay only if you cannot work at *any* gainful occupation. And some cover only the difference between what you can earn after your disability and what you were earning before the illness or injury, up to the limits of the policy. These days, even *own occupation* policies have some limitations, requiring you to work at some occupation after two years of full benefits, if possible. Then they'll pay residual benefits that reflect the percentage decline in your income as a result of your disability.

You also want to make sure your disability policy is noncancelable (as long as you keep paying the premiums), does not require periodic health examinations, and has a guaranteed annual premium that cannot be increased. Of course, you'll have to take a physical exam before the policy is originally issued.

There are several key considerations in pricing a disability policy:

- *The amount of monthly benefits.* This amount is typically limited to 70 or 80 percent of your current pretax income.

- *The waiting period.* This is the lag time before payments start, usually a minimum of 90 days. (You should have enough savings to cover that gap period.)

- *Term of benefits.* It's most common to purchase coverage to age 65, when Social Security will provide ongoing income. You can save money by purchasing coverage for a shorter period in order to lower the cost, but once disabled, you might need coverage for longer than you ever dreamed.

- *Cost-of-living adjustments.* Many policies allow you to purchase additional benefits without evidence of insurability or guarantee a small annual increase in benefits to keep up with inflation.

Very few insurance companies underwrite disability insurance, compared to the many that provide term and universal life insurance. Those that do are becoming stricter about their definition of disability, frequently restricting claims for mental, nervous, and drug-related disabilities. Among the larger companies in this field are MetLife, Northwestern Mutual, Mutual of Omaha, Boston Mutual, and Principal.

Health Savings Accounts

Health savings accounts (HSAs) are an increasingly popular way to cover your health insurance needs. They are essentially tax-advantaged medical savings accounts that you own. You contribute money (within an annual limit) to an HSA on a pretax basis, much as you would to a traditional individual retirement account. And like an IRA, you can contribute to your HSA account during any calendar year, through April 15 of the following calendar year.

For 2011, you are allowed to contribute $3,050 for a single individual and $6,150 for a family. If an individual account holder or the owner of a family HSA is age 55 or older, an additional "catch-up" contribution of $1,000 is also allowed.

The HSA works in conjunction with a *high-deductible insurance policy* that will provide 100 percent coverage above that deductible level to cover major expenses. The idea is that you will either pay the uncovered expenses out of your own pocket, or using the money you've deposited (and perhaps your employer has matched) in your health savings account.

The money you *don't spend* in your HSA each year can keep growing tax-deferred and be saved up to pay for future uncovered medical expenses. Basically, since you're spending your own money for items that fall within the deductible amount—or using your HSA—you have an incentive to keep costs down and to stay healthy. These plans are particularly useful for younger workers, who otherwise would pay high premiums for health insurance they are less likely to use.

The government sets the minimum deductible for your high-deductible health insurance plan. For 2011, the minimum is $1,200 for self-only coverage and $2,400 for family coverage. The 2011 maximum out-of-pocket limit (the amount you would have to pay) for your high-deductible insurance is $5,950 for an individual or $11,900 for family coverage.

The health savings account combined with a high-deductible insurance plan creates incentives for wise spending and good health. But here's a special note: These high-deductible, lower-cost insurance plans—some with deductibles starting at $1,000 and ranging much higher—are also a way middle-income families can avoid going broke on unexpected major medical expenses. Even if you can't afford the deposit to the HSA, or traditional health insurance with low deductibles, you might get 100 percent *catastrophic coverage* with one of these high-deductible plans. It's worth a look.

To find these high-deductible insurance plans, and plan sponsors for the tax-deductible health savings accounts, go to **www.eHealth Insurance.com**. This website is also an excellent place to search for individual and family health insurance policies if you do not have coverage from your employer.

GETTING STARTED

If you're overwhelmed by the need to consider all these products, there is one combination product that might fill your needs. It's offered by Allstate, and it's called "Good for Life"—a combination of life insurance, critical illness insurance, and severe accident benefits. This "starter" policy offers life insurance benefits of $50,000, $75,000, or $100,000.

Along with the life insurance, it promises a $10,000 immediate payout if you have a severe accident or are diagnosed with a critical illness. And if you have a terminal illness, you can access up to 75 percent of your death benefit if you have less than 12 months to live. You can spend the money any way you want. This policy even allows you to skip up to six payments if your financial circumstances change.

It's a policy designed for younger people, so when you reach age 65 the policy terminates, and you will get a paid-up life policy with $15,000 in benefits—*plus* a return of half of all the premiums you paid along the way.

Read the actual policy terms and conditions for specific details and prices, and to make sure this is an appropriate product for you. You can purchase these elements separately at a more advantageous cost—but will you do it? If not, this is the place to start your basic insurance coverage.

TERRY'S TO-DO LIST

1. Figure out how much life insurance money, if any, you need to really provide for your family or loved ones.

2. Check the prices for level-term insurance to meet basic insurance needs.

3. Consider permanent (whole or universal) life for longer-term insurance needs.

4. Buy policies only from top-rated companies. It's worth paying a bit more in premiums. Check insurance company ratings at WeissRatings.com (for a small charge) or at Insure.com.

5. Take a close look at existing policies. Ask for an in-force ledger to determine current values. If considering a change, contact EvaluateLifeInsurance.org for a policy comparison.

6. Check ownership of policies, and consider creating an irrevocable life insurance trust to purchase new policies and keep ownership outside of your estate.

7. Consider opening a health savings account combined with an affordable high-deductible health insurance policy.

8. Review the need for critical illness insurance and/or disability insurance.

CHAPTER 9

THE SAVAGE TRUTH ON PROTECTING YOUR ASSETS

Your Home, Your Auto, Your Wealth

You've worked so hard to build up financial assets—whether your home, your car, your furniture and other possessions, or even the money you hope to use for retirement. Doesn't it make sense to protect those assets from disaster, especially when insurance is available at a reasonable and competitive price?

But thinking about insurance requires thinking about loss—something we'd all prefer to avoid. The most basic Savage Truth when it comes to insurance is that *not* having insurance is like tempting fate. You can come up with a million excuses, starting with not having enough time, not having enough money, and not understanding the policies. But in the end, if you stare at the ruined pieces of your hard work after a loss, you'll wonder why on earth you didn't read this chapter and take action.

THE SAVAGE TRUTH ON HOMEOWNERS INSURANCE

As a result of the housing and mortgage crisis of recent years, we've all come to have a new appreciation of the meaning of "home, sweet home." If you're fortunate enough to have your home intact, it's time to reconsider how much homeowners insurance is enough and what coverage you need.

A basic consultation with your insurance agent will give you a checklist of the specific coverage and amounts you need. But here's a look at some of the issues you hope you'll never face. My greatest wish for you is that the premiums you pay for homeowners insurance are all "wasted"—that you never need to call upon your insurance because of a fire, a flood, or theft, or because your neighbor injures herself on your property. In that sense, your premiums are never wasted because they pay for your peace of mind.

For most people, the family home is the largest and most important investment you will ever make. And unlike investments in the stock market, you can protect yourself completely against the risk of loss. From that perspective, why would you consider not having complete coverage?

Here are the key ingredients you must consider.

Understand Your Policy Coverage and Limits

Reading through an insurance policy has about as much appeal as going to the dentist. You know it's important, but you don't want to devote a lot of time to the project. A homeowners policy is filled with the word *peril.* A list of those perils (potential losses) sounds like the biblical plagues: fire, lightning, windstorm, smoke, hail, explosion, and riots or civil disorders. There's also coverage for damage caused by vehicles or aircraft (those events make news headlines), and for vandalism or glass breakage. And what about damage caused by a water heater exploding, or frozen pipes, or electrical surges that impact appliances?

That's just damage to the structure. What about your personal property? And what *isn't* covered in the standard policy—floods, earthquakes, wars, and perhaps sewer backups? That's why you need a competent agent to make sure you are appropriately covered.

HOW MUCH?

You'll want to cover the structure of your home for its current market value. (The insurance company won't allow you to cover it for much more, and they will know comparable values for homes in your area.) But don't be surprised if your coverage is less than what you perceive to be the total value of your home, since the land underneath your home is not likely to be destroyed in any covered event. (Earthquake coverage is purchased separately.)

If you have a mortgage on your property, the lender will require you to list the mortgage company as an "additional insured," and to insure at least 80 percent of the value of your home, or 100 percent of the amount of your mortgage. If you insure for less than 80 percent of the value, many companies will place a limit on what they'll pay out, or prorate the coverage based on the percentage by which you are underinsured.

The personal property in your home, including furnishings, clothing, and books and records, will be included as an additional amount—typically a percentage of the total coverage for the structure. See the following if you have valuable items that should be covered separately.

REPLACEMENT COST VERSUS ACTUAL CASH VALUE

This is a critical element of your property insurance. If there's a fire in your living room and you need to replace your couch and other furniture, you want to be sure you have replacement cost coverage. That is, you don't want to receive a check only for the actual cash value of your 10-year-old furniture. It is worth paying more to make sure you have enough coverage to refurnish at today's prices.

If you're smart, every few years you'll make a video or digital photo record of your home interior, pointing out furnishings, carpeting, wall coverings or other decorative items that are unusual and would be expensive to replace. Give a copy or disc of this digital record to your insurance agent for her files. If needed, this could save time and annoyance in getting your home rebuilt.

SEPARATELY SCHEDULED ITEMS

Some items, such as jewelry, artwork, silverware, antiques, coin collections, or furs, would not be covered adequately under the personal property section of your policy, which might allow only $2,500 for "all jewelry." To make sure you have replacement coverage for these items, you will need to *schedule* them and pay an extra premium based on their value. For that purpose, you will need an independent appraisal of their current value. Make sure your agent keeps records of those appraisals so they are not destroyed in a disaster.

DEDUCTIBLE

The *deductible* is the amount you must pay, before the insurance coverage starts. Deductibles can range from as little as $100 to $2,500 or more. Ask for price quotations for a $500 deductible and compare to a much higher level. Raising the deductible can save a substantial amount on annual premiums, but this is wise only if you have the cash and are willing to cover lesser charges, such as the theft of an item from your car, which is normally covered by homeowners insurance.

LIABILITY INSURANCE

If a member of your household is accused of accidentally causing injury or damages to another person or property, this section of the policy pays for a legal defense, and will cover a settlement or judgment up to the limits of your policy. Ask about those legal limits; you might want to pay additional premium to increase them.

GUEST MEDICAL INSURANCE

Your houseguest slips and falls in your shower or on your front sidewalk. Those injuries may be covered by their own insurance, or they may sue you to cover expenses of hospitalization or x-rays or loss of time at work. The guest medical section of your homeowners insurance policy means you will not be digging into your pocket to pay these expenses.

WHAT'S *NOT* COVERED?

Flood and earthquake insurance are purchased separately from your standard homeowners policy. And it's important to know exactly what this means. If groundwater or a sewer backs up into your basement, destroying carpeting and appliances, this damage is not likely to be covered by your standard homeowners policy, but it would be covered if you purchase additional, optional coverage for that possibility. Water backup is only covered by flood insurance, which must be purchased from the National Flood Insurance program (NFIP), if it arises out of general flooding conditions in the area. Rates for flood insurance are set based on the federal flood hazard map, which you can find at **www.FloodSmart.gov**.

Earthquake coverage is expensive and difficult to get these days. If you live in an area prone to earthquakes, then you may find it prohibitively expensive and with a very high deductible.

Ask your agent about how outbuildings such as garages or sheds are covered under your policy. Similarly, you may find that landscaping is not covered. So if wind damages your tree, you'll have to pay for removal. But if the tree hits your roof, or your neighbor's roof, your policy will pay for the damages, and may pay for removal, as well.

ADDITIONAL LIVING EXPENSES

This section of your policy will reimburse you for living expenses if your home is uninhabitable after a fire or other disaster. Make sure you check for this coverage.

Beyond the Basics

The more things you have, the more insurance you need. It's a simple formula. But it's not always a direct ratio. The Savage Truth is *if you have wealth, you become a target for legal actions.* But if you have very little in the way of possessions, a small loss becomes even more devastating. So here are some policy ideas you should consider beyond your standard auto and homeowners coverage.

UMBRELLA LIABILITY

If you fear that the limits of your homeowners liability coverage are not large enough, you can purchase additional liability in the form of an *umbrella* policy, typically for an additional million dollars or more. It must be coordinated with the coverage of your underlying homeowners or auto policy. Ask about the liability limits of your policy per incident, and how this coverage is determined. This coverage is usually relatively inexpensive.

RENTERS INSURANCE

If you live in a rental unit, your landlord probably has insurance to replace the walls and permanent fixtures in your unit. But you are responsible for replacing all your personal property, including clothing, electronics, furniture, and decorations—anything that you own. A fire or smoke damage could destroy you financially if you do not purchase renters insurance. And renters policies also include liability insurance, guest medical protection, and reimbursed living expenses.

CONDO INSURANCE

Your insurance agent should check the condominium association policy to make sure your condo insurance coordinates with the building's coverage. Typically, you are responsible for the interior of your unit, including wall and floor coverings, and decoration beyond the initial surfaces of the building. That could add up to a huge bill if there were a fire in an adjoining unit.

A condo policy also offers liability, guest medical, and reimbursed living expenses. Do not count on the building's insurance or that of a neighbor to make you whole, even if a disaster is their fault. You need your own insurance policy.

SAVING MONEY

There are ways to save money on your insurance needs. One of the easiest is to combine all your insurance needs with one company, including auto, homeowners, and umbrella. That should earn you a discount.

You should ask if there are discounts for fire and burglary alarms, for smoke detectors, or for other safety measures around your home. And seniors may also qualify for insurance discounts.

Insurance is a competitive market today, so you want to shop around for the best price. But in case you actually need to *use* your coverage, you'll want to be dealing with a reliable, well-established company and with an agent you know personally.

THE SAVAGE TRUTH ON AUTO INSURANCE

Every state in the United States has a law against driving without automobile insurance, including a minimum amount of liability insurance. But almost everyone has heard of people being involved in accidents with uninsured drivers. That's why it's especially important that you have full auto insurance coverage.

Even though uninsured drivers are penalized in every state with fines, loss of driver's license, and even jail time, you may find that it is your insurance you must reply upon if there is an accident. If you drive without insurance and are at fault in an accident, you could lose everything you have. That's the Savage Truth. And it should be an incentive to find at least minimal coverage.

That said, coverage requirements vary state by state. Auto insurance policies are very competitive, and price is not the only issue. While the easiest thing to compare about auto insurance is prices—readily available on the Internet through many websites—the premiums are only one part of your policy decision.

If you're concerned enough to read this chapter, you want not only the best coverage for the price, but also an insurance company that will handle the consequences of an accident promptly and efficiently. That's really the extra that you expect your premium dollars to buy, beyond the protection of the insurance policy.

Here are the basics you need to understand.

No-Fault Insurance?

The coverage you need depends on your state of residence. About a dozen states have "no-fault" insurance, where there is no legal recourse to the other driver's insurance to sue for pain and suffering. Your own policy picks up all medical costs regardless of who caused the accident. This portion of your policy is called *PIP* (Personal Injury Protection). As for repairs to your physical damage to your car, you look first to your own collision coverage.

Most states follow the standard *tort* system of law, where the courts may determine who is at fault and whose insurance picks up the tab. You want an insurance company that will pay you promptly and repair your car, using its legal talent to recoup those costs from the other driver's insurance.

Coverage

Bodily Injury Coverage: This feature provides protection if the driver, policyholder, or family member causes bodily harm to someone else. You may find your policy has two limits, such as $100,000 per person, up to $300,000 per accident. (You'll find it written this way: $100,000/$300,000.) If you feel you could potentially be a tempting target for a lawsuit, you'll want to purchase higher limits or an umbrella policy.

Property Damage Liability: This feature covers damages to others' property if you, or someone you allow to drive your car, is in an accident. Make sure you have adequate coverage under this provision in case you hit an expensive car!

Collision Coverage: This is the portion that covers repair to your car (minus the deductible) regardless of who was at fault in the accident. (If you were not at fault, the insurance company will try to collect this amount from the other driver's insurance company.)

Personal Injury Protection or Medical Payments Coverage: This covers medical costs if either the passengers or driver of the policyholder's vehicle are injured, and may also cover lost wages, cost of replacing services, and funeral costs.

Uninsured/Underinsured Motorist: If the other driver does not have insurance, or enough insurance, this portion of your policy will pay the costs, and should also pay if you are hit as a pedestrian. In effect, you're paying the other driver's premium!

Comprehensive Insurance: By this point, you probably think you already have "comprehensive" coverage. But this portion of the policy pays for damage as a result of theft, falling trees, vandalism, or fire and flood. It may also pay for a rental car if yours is stolen.

Rental Car Insurance: This is a good time to ask your agent if your policy also covers collision damages and loss of use (to the car rental agency) if you are in an accident in a rented car. If you have this complete coverage (or if you have it through the credit card you use to rent a car), then you could save a significant amount when you rent a car.

Pricing and Money-Saving Tips

The cost of your auto insurance is based on your driving record, your location, and the kind of car you drive (something to think about before you buy), and can even be based on your credit score. It can also be impacted by a number of other factors that are within your control if you plan appropriately.

You can save money on your insurance premiums by raising the deductible (the amount you are willing to pay). You probably won't make small claims, anyway, out of fear that your claims history will result in higher premiums the following year. So if you are willing to pay the first $250, or $500, or even $1,000 out of pocket, you can save a lot of money on your premiums.

Ask your agent for discounts for safe driving records, for longevity with the same company, for low mileage, or good credit. All can cut your premiums. Bundle your auto insurance with your homeowners insurance to get discounts on both. And you can save a few dollars by paying your premiums either annually, or semiannually, instead of monthly. But don't skimp on basic coverage such as medical payments coverage or bodily injury liability. That may turn out to be penny-wise and pound-foolish.

It's a sad but true fact that if you have an accident claim your premium is likely to rise the next time your policy is renewed. That could be the case even if you were not determined to be at fault in the accident. Many people decide not to report small claims, either because they are under the deductible amount or because they fear rising premiums in the future.

Here's a note of warning: If you decide not to tell your insurer about a minor accident, it may cause problems later. If you get sued by the other driver, your auto policy provider might not cover you because of the time lapse. And if you have not reported the accident to the police, it will be harder to substantiate your claim of not being at fault if the other driver decides to sue.

Double-Check Your Coverage

You've heard all the advertisements about auto insurance features, but don't take your coverage for granted. Does the insurer promise—in print—to "forgive" the first accident? If your car is "totaled" within the first few months, will the insurer give you a brand-new one? Can you get cash to replace a car, or will the insurer demand it provide a replacement? If your laptop is stolen out of your car, is it covered by your auto insurance, or more likely by your homeowners or renters policy?

These are all questions to ask your agent before you jump online to purchase a standard policy. Your experience might not be "standard," and you don't want to find out about missing links when it's too late.

THE SAVAGE TRUTH ON ASSET PROTECTION

Although you can buy insurance to protect your assets from loss as a result of all sorts of perils, there are other losses you should keep in mind when thinking about asset protection. For most people, it will never be necessary to contemplate the loss that could come as a result of lawsuits or bankruptcy. But each state has its own laws about asset protection; if you might be exposed, then you should consult a lawyer about how to handle this eventuality.

Some exposures can be limited merely by the way you hold title to the asset. For instance, owning an asset as *tenants in the entirety* affords more protection than *tenants with the right of survivorship.*

In some states employer retirement plans such as a 401(k) or 403(b) are afforded more protection than an individual retirement account (IRA). That's something to consider before rolling out of your employer's plan.

In case of divorce, some states limit access to retirement plan assets, while others accept qualified domestic relations orders (QDRO), dividing those assets. And in community-property states, each spouse may have an interest in a total property division, including accumulated retirement benefits. The judge may reserve jurisdiction to award each spouse a proportionate share when benefits are eventually paid.

There is no protection for assets given away in contemplation of bankruptcy. If the asset was given away within one year (longer in some states) and if there was not appropriate compensation, or the transfer was made to hinder creditors, the bankruptcy discharge may be denied. However, filing for bankruptcy may protect assets by delaying foreclosure.

As you'll see in Chapter 14, it is becoming more difficult to protect assets from Medicaid, though for years families have given away assets so impoverished seniors could get nursing home care provided by the state. Now *lookback* periods have lengthened, and you don't want to be in a state-funded nursing home, anyway.

There's an amazing array of trusts that have been designed to protect assets, both onshore and off, from creditors and lawsuits. And there's an equally astounding number of scams that prey upon fearful doctors and other professionals.

In all these instances, it's important to get competent legal help— and a second, independent opinion. Even the largest Swiss banks have recently given up lists of Americans participating in tax-avoidance deals that were structured by well-known accounting firms. Your best asset protection is likely to be traditional forms of insurance and a good lawyer—and an honest lifestyle.

GETTING STARTED

How do you get started on purchasing homeowners or auto insurance? The Internet makes insurance comparisons easy. You can get instant quotes at **www.Insurance.com**. But you may want to contact an agent to see if combining homeowners and auto will save you money. Your first step is to fill out this checklist so you can compare coverage. Then make that phone call or go online and start shopping.

INSURANCE NEEDS CHECKLIST

Homeowners Coverage:

❏ Estimated Replacement Value of Home or Condo:
$ _____

❏ Estimated Replacement Value of Contents:
$ _____

❏ List of Items to Be Covered Separately (e.g., Jewelry, Silver, Art) _____

Auto Insurance Coverage:

❏ Liability Limits _____
❏ Collision Coverage _____
❏ Personal Injury _____
❏ Uninsured Motorist _____
❏ Comprehensive _____
❏ Rental Car Coverage _____

Use this checklist to compare. It does you no good to save money on insurance if you don't get complete coverage.

CHAPTER

10

THE SAVAGE TRUTH ON PAYING FOR COLLEGE

Make This Investment Carefully

Going to college has always been part of the American Dream. For a nation of immigrants, a college education meant that children would always do better than their parents. After World War II, a college education became part of the GI Bill that rewarded veterans for service to their country. During the 1970s, the huge baby boom generation impacted college campuses, causing tuition prices to rise even faster than consumer price inflation. Except for federal student aid programs, college might have been priced out of reach.

Then because of all the financial aid (credit) that became easily available, tuition prices started rising at twice the rate of the consumer price index. Caught up in the belief that a good education at a top school would pay for itself over a lifetime career, students and their families increased their borrowing, much as they did on home equity when credit was easy. As a result, student loans have become another recipe for financial disaster.

By 2009, according to the Project on Student Debt, graduating college seniors carried an average of $24,000 in student debt— a 25 percent increase over the debt held by graduates just four years before. And, as the recession progressed, they had an average unemployment rate higher than 9 percent. Clearly, the traditional dream of repaying minimal student loans quickly with a high-paying job has collided with a new reality.

It's an issue I started writing about several years ago, with a column asking whether college is "worth it." Perhaps the most accurate response to that question is that college will certainly be worth the time and money—if you choose wisely not only the school you attend, but the way you pay for that education.

A real education will always be well-rewarded in our Information Age. The wage differences between educated and lesser-educated Americans will grow even wider, as the world is willing to pay for knowledge and creativity. So, yes, your education will repay you many times over, but only if you graduate into opportunity that is not overwhelmed with the demands of debt repayment.

This chapter is designed for you if you're a parent or student facing the college challenge, or a graduate trying to deal with repaying student loans.

A COLLEGE EDUCATION IS STILL WORTH IT

First, let's take a more precise look at the question of whether a college education is worth the money it costs. Again, that all depends on what you pay, how you finance it, and what time period you're looking at. In 2000, the U.S. Government Census Bureau said that a bachelor's degree from college could add more than $1 million over a lifetime of earnings, compared to the income of a high school graduate.

But over the past decade those estimates have dropped sharply. Many current studies say that the lifetime earnings differential is more like $300,000, and less if interest paid on student loans over a long number of years is subtracted. Yet advanced degrees, such as law, engineering, or an MBA *do* significantly increase lifetime earnings.

The declining real worth of a basic college education is bad news for America, because it is important to have a well-educated workforce in this century. And only in years ahead will we see the cost to society if a college education prices itself out of the market for today's high schoolers.

An entire college generation and their parents have been snookered by easy credit and empty dreams. They've taken on huge and unprecedented amounts of debt, which is difficult to repay and cannot be defaulted, no matter what the hardship. College more than pays for itself over the long run, it can be argued. But how do you account for the number of taxi drivers with MBAs or the 25 percent of retail sales clerks with a four-year college degree? And what about the nearly one-third of undergrads who drop out without reaching a degree, yet still must repay their student loans?

So, is college worth it? I'll still give an unequivocal *yes* in answer to that question. But a degree is not the only requirement for success, and college is only a head start to success if you do a good job of managing the process of selection and financing. So the financial "trick" is to figure out how to finance a college education—and how to repay that debt—to produce the best and most productive results from your education dollars.

Think of it this way: You're investing $100,000—or much more—in a college education and giving up four (or more likely five or six) years of earnings in order to get your degree. If you simply invested the cash in a diversified stock portfolio and spent the four years learning about business, you could buy or build your own business and income.

After all, Bill Gates dropped out of Harvard to start his own business, which grew into the multibillion-dollar Microsoft fortune. Larry Ellison, cofounder of Oracle, dropped out of the University of Illinois and still made billions. Quentin Tarantino and David Geffen and countless others in the arts and sports have made lots of money without a college degree. However, relatively few people are going to be sports stars, successful recording artists, or profitable entrepreneurs.

To put the odds of financial success on your side, you'll need a good education. That costs real money. So if you're going to take on all this debt—and spend years in college—you'd better prepare to face the reality of the world when you graduate. That includes considering debt repayment scenarios.

The time for this type of analysis is *before* you choose a college, and while you have time to save, adjust, and analyze the costs and benefits. This is not a topic just for dinner table discussion.

At **www.Finaid.org/calculators**, you'll find a series of online calculators that can give you specifics of costs and the financial aid you can expect. It's a very good place to start your analysis. At the **www.CollegeBoard.com** website, you can click on the "Pay for College" section and then find a calculator that will help you compare the financial aid offers you receive from various schools.

And if you're past that stage and have already taken on a student loan debt burden, read on to the portion of this chapter that deals with paying down and refinancing student loans that you already have on the books.

THE SAVAGE TRUTH ON FINDING MONEY FOR COLLEGE

There are only a few ways to find the money for college. It can come from parental savings or borrowings; it can come from various types of student loans; or it can come as "free money" in the form of scholarships and grants. Plus, of course, some of the costs can be covered by the student's own summer job savings.

Here's the Savage Truth about all those alternatives:

- Parents should limit their debt for a child's education. Don't take out a volatile home equity loan (even if the interest is tax deductible) to put your child through college. And definitely do not take money out of your retirement savings. (Very few college grads will support their parents in their old age, and you don't want to be that burdensome elder.) There are other ways to help, including having your student attend a nearby college and live at home for a couple of years.

- Students need to understand the ultimate burden of loan repayment *before* signing for a loan. In what follows, you'll see websites that help you calculate the total costs over 10 or 20 years of loan repayments—with interest. Being realistic about *total* costs will impact your choice of schools.

- There is some free money, but not as much as you hope. Yes, scholarships are worth checking out at the websites described later, but they typically make a relatively small contribution to overall college costs.

I make these points first not to burst your bubble, but as a reality check. Your high school guidance counselor can be more specific about the financial aid that may be available to your family. But always keep in mind that while the borrowing number may sound huge, the repayment amount will be far greater when you add in the costs of interest.

Several decades ago, the choice of college was based on prestige, getting into the "best" school. Families sacrificed to get their children into top schools and to pay for that degree. Now, it's time for a readjustment. The first step in the process should be finding an *affordable* school. That might involve choosing a local community college for the first two years and having the student live at home. Then she can transfer to a university to get that important degree.

Or, as described later, a more prestigious and expensive school might actually be more affordable because of the financial aid package it is willing to offer. Your decision must be made based on real numbers, not hopes or dreams. So don't avoid applying to prestige schools, even if costs are much higher. They're looking to diversify the student body and so might provide financial aid that makes them more affordable than even your in-state tuition at a nearby college.

Federal Financial Aid

The first place to start the search for college money is at the high school guidance office. It's a process that should start in the child's sophomore year of high school, so the family will understand the requirements for financial aid and take appropriate steps to qualify for the most aid possible. There are also many websites, the best of which are listed later in this chapter. It is never too early to start understanding how the college financial aid system works.

The entire process for parceling out financial aid was revised in the summer of 2010, requiring all new federal education loans to be made through the Federal Direct Loan Program. The loans are distributed through the college's financial aid office with funds provided by the U.S. Department of Education. This includes the Federal Parent PLUS loans in addition to student loans.

Whereas students with loans taken out before July 1, 2010, may have a variety of repayment plans to various lenders, all *new* federal student loans are being made directly from the government, and through the schools. The original Federal Family Education Loans (FFEL) made previously through financial institutions will carry the same terms of repayment, but borrowers who had those loans must complete new Direct Loan applications for future disbursements.

FEDERAL DIRECT LOANS

The Federal Direct Loan Program offers the following types of loans. To get the current interest rate on these loans, check online at **www.ed.gov/directloan/student**.

- *Subsidized Stafford Loan:* For students with demonstrated financial need, as determined by federal regulations. No interest is charged while a student is in school at least half-time, during the grace period, and during deferment periods. The maximum that can be borrowed on a subsidized loan is $3,500 for a first-year student, rising to $4,500 in the second year, and $5,500 for third- and fourth-year students.

■ *Unsubsidized:* Not based on financial need; interest is charged during all periods, even during the time a student is in school and during grace and deferment periods. Maximum borrowing limits are different for dependent and independent students. For example, third- and fourth-year dependent undergrads can borrow up to $7,500 in unsubsidized loans, while independent students can borrow up to $12,500 in those years.

■ *PLUS:* Unsubsidized loans for the *parents* of dependent students and for graduate/professional students. Interest is charged during all periods. With a Direct PLUS Loan, a graduate/professional student or the parent of a dependent student can borrow up to the cost of the student's attendance minus other financial aid the student receives.

PELL GRANTS

Pell grants are need-based grants from the federal government that go mostly to students with family incomes below $50,000. They are available to both full-time and part-time students. For the 2010–2011 award year, the maximum Pell Grant award rises to $5,550. Application is made through the same process as the Federal Direct Loan Program.

PRIVATE LOANS

While the federal loan programs described earlier typically provide the largest portion of most financial aid packages, each college or university will make up its own offer of financial aid. They will combine a variety of the loans described earlier, along with work-study programs and some outright grants that do not have to be repaid, including athletic scholarships.

When the school does not grant enough need-based financial aid, the student and family may have to borrow additional money beyond the amounts they have saved. Parents can use home equity loans, which are dangerous because of interest rate volatility. Or they can cosign for private student loans. That is also a dangerous step, because student loans are not discharged in bankruptcy.

With the 2010 revision of the student loan program, many financial institutions lost out on a profitable business of granting loans that were in effect guaranteed by the federal government. Now, private lenders are still offering college loans to parents or students, but these loans generally have higher initial interest rates that are also variable and pegged to some type of index such as the prime rate. If interest rates rise, these loans could become very expensive to repay. Private loans are also much more difficult to consolidate and offer very little in the way of refinancing if rates drop. They should be considered only as a last resort. Interest rates and fees on private student loans are based on your credit score and typically require a cosigner with a score over 650.

Private lenders such as Sallie Mae or other financial institutions can charge whatever rates and terms they choose to be competitive. But they are no longer offering loans that have any federal guarantee, so these private or "alternative" loans are likely to carry higher rates or variable rates to protect the lenders.

FAFSA: Demonstrating Need

The entire financial aid discussion starts with *FAFSA* (the Free Application for Federal Student Aid). This is the basis for almost every financial aid decision based on need. The information you file on the FAFSA form is used to determine the *expected family contribution* (EFC), no matter which school you attend. Then each school will create an aid package based on the EFC.

You can learn everything about the application and actually apply securely online at **www.FAFSA.ed.gov**. You'll get a PIN, and you can save the information until the application is completed and as a basis for applying in future years. You should fill out the FAFSA form early in January of the year for which you are applying for aid. Aid is often given out by schools on a first-come basis. You'll need to designate the schools to which you are applying when you file the FAFSA.

The process of filling out this form is more intrusive than even the IRS tax return. It asks not only about income of the parent and student, but also about the totality of their financial assets. Thus, although the FAFSA form is first filled out in the student's senior year of high school (and again in every year for which aid is requested), there are important steps to take in the student's junior year—a year in advance of filling out FAFSA—to potentially make the family eligible for the most financial aid.

For 2011–2012, students have an income protection allowance of $5,250, but any money earned above that will be assessed at fifty cents on the dollar! Money in a child's name (such as a custodial account) weighs 3.5 times more heavily against the family in the aid calculations, so these accounts should be spent on justifiable needs well before the application is filed.

Since the assets counted for FAFSA exclude retirement plans, money invested in a family-owned business, and the cash value of life insurance and/or annuities, but do include cash savings, real estate other than your home, and nonretirement stock investments, there are opportunities to adjust your financial picture. You can find similar legal tips at **www.FAFSAonline.com** or **www.PayLessforCollege.com**.

Finding Financial Aid Information

In addition to visiting the high school guidance office, you can find a wealth of information about the student financial aid process on the Internet. Here are some recommended sites for an overview:

- **www.CollegeBoard.com**. Check here to register for the SAT exams and for information about the application and aid process. There is also a calculator to help you compare aid packages from different schools when you receive them.

- **www.Finaid.org**. This is the best site for information on all types of financial aid. It has the most complete selection of calculators to help you compare total costs of various aid packages.

- **www.ed.gov/directloan**. This is the federal government's website on education, with information about the new Federal Direct Loan Program. Or go directly to www.FAFSA.ed.gov to fill out the Free Application for Federal Student Aid (FAFSA) form online.

- **www.ProjectonStudentDebt.org**. You must check out this website for information on loans and costs and to put your financial situation in perspective.

- www.PayLessforCollege.com. This is Reecy Aresty's website.

Evaluating Aid Packages: Asking for More

Students eagerly await the notification that they have been admitted to the school of their choice. Each school will then send information about the amount of aid that will be offered and in which form (subsidized or unsubsidized federal direct loans, work-study programs, grants or scholarships). For most families, the decision relies on which school is ultimately most affordable.

For example, a prestigious and very expensive school might offer a larger aid package—less money for the family to come up with. At first, that might be a compelling reason to attend. But if most of that aid comes in the form of loans that must be repaid with interest, then the calculation shifts to total costs. A local college or university might offer less financial aid, requiring more immediate expenditures, but be a better value in the long run because the student graduates with a lower debt burden. The only way to really compare is to use an online calculator that will show you the *eventual total cost*, including interest that must be repaid. You'll find these at almost every website, including **www.ed.gov**.

One more word of advice from Reecy Aresty of www.PayLess forCollege.com: You don't have to settle for the amount of financial aid in the initial offer from the school. But you do have to have the tools to plead your case gracefully, asking for more money. His website and books are full of tips that could add thousands of dollars to your aid package. You'll also find advice in the latest edition of his book: *How to Pay for College without Going Broke*. And, he's offered a free analysis of your college financial aid package, if you mention this book. Contact him at Reecy@paylessforcollege.com.

Search for Free Money

Let's deal with the truth about private scholarships right up front so you don't wind up paying for free information. Also, remember that any private scholarship award goes directly to the college and may reduce the school's aid offer, dollar-for-dollar! It's natural to start by searching for free money in the form of merit scholarships and grants. But you don't have to pay fees or attend costly seminars to get access to all the information available on these subjects. Still, every year desperate families fall for sales pitches promising access to financial aid. It's all online—and free.

There are two free websites that allow you to search among thousands of scholarships based on your interests, accomplishments, family history, and dozens of other surprising qualifiers. At either **Fastweb.com** or **Scholarships.com**, you fill out a profile to determine a potential match. The sites are free because they are underwritten by companies that want access to market to high school and college students. The time to start searching is early in the senior year because many scholarship and grant applications have early deadlines.

Here's another tip: When searching for college scholarships, don't forget to start at the parents' place of employment, religious or fraternal organizations, or community groups. Small grants can add up to important contributions to the cost of college.

BEST WAYS TO SAVE FOR COLLEGE

If you have young children, start saving as much as you can right now so your money will have time to grow and work for you. But even if you're starting late, tax credits and state savings plans can help build a college fund for your children. Grandparents can easily contribute to these savings plans. And programs such as **UPromise.com** can leverage your everyday spending to add to college savings.

But here's an important reminder: Avoid saving for college in the child's name! There are two good reasons to avoid using custodial accounts or Uniform Gifts to Minors Act (UGMA) and/or UGTA accounts.

First, when the child reaches the age of majority (which is age 18 in many states) the money belongs to him or her. You may have considered it to be savings for college, but your teen might opt for a new car or a vacation.

The second reason is equally hazardous. Money titled in a child's name, even in a custodial account, weighs much more heavily against the family in the FAFSA financial aid calculations. So if you already have money in this type of account, spend it wisely for the child's benefit (perhaps a new computer) well before you file the financial aid application.

That said, here are a few of the best ways to save and invest for college—and advice on how much you should be saving to make a real dent in future college costs.

The Best Education Deal: Section 529
College Savings Plans

By far, the most efficient and effective way to save for college is through a *529 college savings plan,* named for the IRS Code section that created these programs. Very simply, they are a way to save for college that allows all the gains on money invested to be withdrawn free of taxes to pay for college expenses, including tuition, room and board, books, and fees. The law was written so that each state could set up its own plan, with various financial advisors providing money management for funds invested within the state's plan. Some states even offer a break on state taxes for residents who make contributions to the state plan.

That said, you can invest in *any* state's plan and use the money for *any* college in *any* state. And the money in the plan can be allocated to any family member for college expenses, so if one child doesn't attend college or receives a scholarship, another can use the account.

Most plans allow you to start with a very small amount of money; in some cases as little as $50 will open an account. You can then set up an automatic program to make regular additional contributions directly from your checking or savings account. As well, relatives and friends can add contributions to this college account at any time.

These plans are an excellent estate planning tool for grandparents. Without going to the expense of setting up a separate trust, grand-parents can contribute large sums (up to five years of the annual allowable gift tax exemption at one time). So, if the annual gift tax exclusion is $13,000, then Grandma can give $65,000 to little Susie and Grandpa could give an additional $65,000! And they could do this for each grandchild; it is quite a transfer of wealth and an oppor-tunity for all this money to grow tax-free for education.

Of course, there's always the possibility that the grandparents might need this money in their old age. They can get it back. They simply have to pay taxes on all the gains and a 10 percent penalty to take the money back. (It's good insurance that the grandkids will be appropriately loving!)

Best of all, when grandparents make this gift to a 529 plan, the asset is not included in the FAFSA disclosure of the parents. A 529 account owned by a parent for a dependent student is reported on the federal financial aid application (FAFSA) as a parental asset. Parental assets are assessed at a maximum 5.64 percent rate in deter-mining the student's expected family contribution (EFC).

And no matter who owns the plan, the distributions are also treated favorably in the college financial aid formula. A tax-free distribution from a 529 plan to pay this year's college expenses will not be part of the *base-year income* that reduces next year's financial aid eligibility.

Most states give you a choice of investments within the plan, but these are not trading accounts. Changes are restricted to once a year. Or the plan will offer age-based options with the manager typically moving the assets to more conservative choices as the child gets closer to college age.

To find out more about the 529 Plan offered by your state, go to **www.SavingforCollege.com**, where you can find plan details, and compare ratings, which are based on performance and management fees and costs. Or you can go directly to a low-cost provider such as Vanguard or Fidelity to sign up for one of the plans they manage. Remember, you can invest in any state's plan and use the money for any college in any state for any relative.

One other note: Most states have two variations of their 529 plan—one sold directly through the state's plan website and the other sold through financial advisors. The latter plans may have higher internal costs or initial fees to compensate the advisor for time spent explaining the investment. Ask about the differences or read about them at www.SavingforCollege.com.

The 529 college savings plans are the easiest and best way to save for college, whether you're starting with a small amount of money or a large contribution. One drawback: If a 529 plan is owned by a parent (instead of a grandparent), it is a parental asset.

STATE PREPAID TUITION PROGRAMS

Prepaid tuition plans are actually another form of 529 college savings plan. Offered by many states, they are another interesting way to save for college. Basically, you are paying for college tomorrow at today's prices. Since tuition has historically risen at a faster pace than consumer prices, these plans have become very attractive.

Prepaid tuition plans do not carry the risk of the 529 investment plans described earlier. But they do have some limitations. First, the money must be used for a public or private college in the state where you invest. Some states will allow a refund of what you paid in, but without interest, if your child does not use the plan, or a transfer to pay tuition at another school. But there is no guarantee that the guaranteed one-semester purchase at your state school will be enough to pay tuition at an out-of-state college.

Second, these programs are underwritten by the state, and you are dependent on the state to pay off. In these days of troubled state finances, it is possible that the state might renege on part or all of its promise, or that the schools in your state might not be the best choice for your child because of funding cutbacks.

The cost of these plans depends on your child's age when you purchase these tuition credits. Many states add on additional fees, called *tuition differential* fees, to hedge their bets, so the cost of these plans might not be such a bargain. Do the math by comparing the "cost per credit hour" for your purchase against today's actual cost. Or go to www.SavingforCollege.com to check out their analysis and rating of your state's plan. Morningstar also rates, compares, and recommends state 529 college savings plans.

COLLEGE SAVINGS BANK 529 CDS

The College Savings Bank (**www.CollegeSavingsBank.com**) is a federally insured financial institution offering variable-rate certificates of deposit called CollegeSure CDs. These are FDIC-insured bank certificates of deposit, with the variable rate indexed to college costs and designed to meet the future cost of college. (For example, on July 31, 2010, the college inflation rate measured by the College Board was 4.15 percent.) These certificates of deposit are offered in 1- to 22-year maturities, and can be purchased with as little as $100 per month in direct deposit from your checking account. These CDs can be purchased inside a 529 plan offered at the bank website, so they offer the same tax-free growth for education opportunities as your state's plan.

The College Savings Bank also offers a CD that is indexed to return a portion of the gains on the S&P 500 stock index, with no downside risk. On the upside, you may reap between 85 and 100 percent of the index's gain (not including dividends, which are a critical part of total return). If the market falls, you get your money back, but no interest for the period.

Each of these CDs can also be purchased inside an IRA or a Coverdell Education Savings Account (ESA). Signing up is easy at www.CollegeSavingsBank.com.

Coverdell ESA

Coverdell ESAs are another way to save for educational expenses; however, they are limited in the amount you can contribute ($2,000 in 2011) and must be used by the time the beneficiary reaches age 30. These plans at one time were used to save for private school tuition or other expenses in grade and high schools, but since January 2011, the money in Coverdell ESAs can be used only for college tuition. There is also an income limit for eligibility to contribute. Recent changes have made the Coverdell ESA very unattractive compared to state 529 plans.

Series EE U.S. Savings Bonds for College

Although I no longer recommend Series EE savings bonds as an investment (see Chapter 4) because of the change to fixed rates, they do offer an interesting feature for college savings. Many parents purchased EE bonds for just this purpose and should be aware that they do still carry a special benefit. For middle-income families (under $70,100 AGI for singles, under $105,100 for married couples in 2010), savings bonds *owned by the parents* and cashed in the same year the money is used for college tuition and fees (but not room and board) are completely free from federal taxes.

This benefit is not great enough for me to recommend current purchase of EE bonds, with their low fixed rates. However, if you are a parent holding bonds purchased since 1989 when this provision was enacted, you might want to take advantage of the tax break if you qualify. For more information, including current income level restrictions, go to **www.TreasuryDirect.gov**.

Tuition Tax Deductions

The cost of paying for college can be reduced through careful use of some tax deductions. The IRS allows a deduction for tuition expenses as well as a credit for post-high-school education-related expenses. Expenses must be decreased for any scholarships or grants received, as they reduce the amount of money you actually spent. You can claim the deduction and/or credit for yourself, your spouse, or your dependents.

The Lifetime Learning Credit and the ability to deduct tuition, along with the temporary American Opportunity Credit (which replaced the Hope Credit in 2009), each have complicated income limits and phaseouts. I suggest searching the Internet for the numbers that apply in any year and to make sure these programs are still in existence.

REPAYING STUDENT LOANS

Now comes the tough part—repaying those student loans. Once you graduate, you have six months to start repaying most student loans, although Perkins loans have a nine-month grace period. But within weeks of graduation, student borrowers receive an information packet asking them to choose repayment terms and establish a monthly payment program for each student loan.

PLUS loans made to parents and graduate students may actually require repayment to start immediately upon disbursement of the final loan amount. But there is a complicated set of PLUS loan repayment rules depending on the date when the loan was disbursed and whether the student is still in school.

Here is the bottom line: As graduation approaches, it's important for students and their parents to contact their lender about making payments. You will have some choices. The most tempting is to stretch out payments over as long as 25 years. That results in a lower monthly payment, but a much higher interest burden over the long run.

REPAYMENT OPTIONS

Making smart choices could shave many years and many dollars of interest off the repayment program. The first step is to get organized and be able to track your loans.

If you have loans from multiple lenders, or can't remember which lenders have which loans, go to the National Student Loan Data System at **www.nslds.ed.gov**. You can log in and see the loan amounts, lender(s), and repayment status for all of your federal loans. If some of your loans aren't listed, they're probably private (non-federal) loans. Your school would have a record of those, or you should have a copy of your original loan papers.

If you have federal student loans taken out before 2010 under the FFEL program (where private lenders disbursed the loans), you may get a break on interest rates if you agree to automatic monthly deductions and if you have an unbroken record of on-time payments for at least five years.

If you have government loans, there are two basic repayment plans: the standard 10-year plan, and a stretch plan that allows you to stretch out payments for as long as 25 years. If you take this route, there are two payment options. You can choose a fixed payment every month, or graduated payments that start low and increase every two years.

The government also created an *income-based repayment (IBR) plan*, starting in 2009, which is available for federal student loans. Your monthly payment is capped, and recalculated each year based on your income (plus a spouse's income if married) and the size of your family. To learn more go to **www.IBRinfo.gov**.

Most borrowers will have a monthly payment under income-based repayment that is less than 10 percent of gross income, assuming single borrowers with less than $50,000 in income and married borrowers with two children who have less than $100,000 in income. If you have made payments under this IBR plan for 25 years and have not fully repaid your loan, the balance will be canceled.

There is also a new Public Service Loan Forgiveness Program that will forgive the balance of federal student loans after 10 years of public service. And there are other income-sensitive repayment options offered under the Department of Education. In fact, you almost need a graduate degree to understand and compare all the alternatives! For more information on these programs, as well as current interest rates and calculators, go to studentaid.ed.gov or **www.Finaid.org**.

Deferment, Forbearance, Default

Especially in these difficult economic times, it might be tough to pay your student loans. Unlike most types of debt, student loan debt cannot be erased through the bankruptcy process. Even if you don't pay for years, the debt will stay on the government's books. You might even find money taken out of your Social Security benefits years down the road.

If financial circumstances make it difficult or impossible to pay your loan, you must contact your loan servicer immediately. If you have federal student loans, you might be able to change your repayment plan to lower your monthly obligation. That's less likely if you have private student loans. You might also qualify for a deferment, forbearance, or other form of payment relief. But you must be proactive and deal with the problem before you are charged late fees or fall into default.

The most likely result is that you will be granted a *deferment* for a defined period of time. A deferment is a temporary suspension of loan payments for specific situations such as reenrollment in school, unemployment, or economic hardship. You don't have to pay interest on the loan during deferment if you have a subsidized Direct or FFEL Stafford Loan or a Federal Perkins Loan. If you have an unsubsidized Direct or FFEL Stafford Loan, you're responsible for the interest during deferment. If you don't pay the interest as it accumulates, it will be added to the loan balance.

You have to apply for a deferment to your loan servicer, and you must continue to make payments until you've been notified your deferment has been granted. Otherwise, you could become delinquent or go into default. If you're in active military service, you can also seek a deferment of payments on your student loan.

Forbearance is another way to deal with student loans, and it works much like a deferment. Forbearance is a temporary postponement or reduction of payments that you can receive if you're not eligible for a deferment. Unlike deferment, whether your loans are subsidized or unsubsidized, interest will accrue, increasing the outstanding balance of your loan. Forbearance can be granted in intervals of up to 12 months at a time for up to three years. You have to apply to your loan servicer for forbearance and you must continue to make payments until you've been notified your forbearance has been granted.

If you *default* on your student loans—fail to make payments as scheduled—there can be serious consequences. The college, or the financial institution that made or owns your loan, or your loan guarantor, and/or the federal government all can take action to recover the money you owe. If you default, the lender will notify the credit bureaus, impacting your credit score and making it difficult for you to buy a home or a car. Your wages could be garnished, forcing a deduction from your paycheck to repay the loan. Federal and state tax refunds may be withheld to satisfy your outstanding loan. And the process adds late fees and collection costs to the balance of your loan.

As noted earlier, most student loan debt cannot be discharged through bankruptcy, even if it is a private loan. The best you can do if you fall into a hardship category is to deal with the issue head on, consulting the lender or servicer and making arrangements to pay what you can, when you can.

Some Student Loan Interest Is Deductible

Depending on your income level, you may be able to deduct up to $2,500 in interest you pay on your student loan each year. The deduction for student loan interest is found in the "Adjustments to Income" section of Form 1040 or 1040A. That means you can take the deduction even if you don't itemize, or in addition to other itemized deductions.

Your lender will send you Form 1098-E, showing the amount of interest you paid for the year. You can deduct student loan interest on loans issued for yourself, your spouse (if you file jointly), or your dependents. But you must fall within certain income limits (changed annually) to claim the deduction.

If your income is under $55,000 for singles or $115,000 for married filing jointly, you can take the full $2,500 deduction. Above those levels the deductibility of student loan interest phases out. Check on the income limits every year. Also, starting with the year

2013, the deduction is scheduled to revert to an older law in which student loan interest will be deductible only for the first 60 months of repayment. Obviously, that could be changed by the political process, which is why it's important to check for tax law changes every year.

Consolidating Student Loans Can Ease the Burden

Consider consolidating your loans if your monthly payments are too large or if you have many loans and the multiple payments have become a hassle. By law, you cannot be charged fees for consolidating your student loans, and the interest rate is capped.

You can consolidate your federal student loans through the Direct Loan Program, and there is a calculator at **www.LoanConsolidation .ed.gov** that can help you figure out what your interest rate would be. Some older loans may have lower rates than the consolidated rate, which is a weighted average of all your loan rates.

If you have private loans, you'll find it difficult to consolidate these days. Be sure to read the fine print on any contract, including the potential for rate increases. Never consolidate federal loans into a private student loan, or you'll lose all the federal repayment options and benefits such as unemployment deferments and loan forgiveness programs.

If you still have unconsolidated Stafford loans issued before July 1, 2006, you can consolidate them at very low rates now. Check into the current rate, based on Treasury bills, which changes every July 1 but is announced well in advance.

Time Is Money

You signed on to your student loans because you believed your education would have continuing value and increase your earning power over your lifetime. And despite recessions and job challenges, you will have a better future with an education. Still, the sooner you can pay off your student loans the better. As rates dropped, many student loans that once looked attractive failed to adjust interest rates downward. As a result, your student loans may become relatively expensive and not look like such a bargain.

None of the repayment plans prohibits additional payments. So if you do have a job and get a bonus or a raise, consider adding to your payments to pay down the loan faster and with less interest expense.

In the end, college will be worth it only if you make good use of your time *and* the money you borrow.

GETTING STARTED

FOR PARENTS OF YOUNG CHILDREN:

Go to www.SavingforCollege.com and check out your state's 529 college savings plan. Then open an account even with a small amount of money and ask relatives and grandparents to add to it.

FOR PARENTS OF HIGH SCHOOLERS:

Go to www.FAFSA.ed.gov to learn about federal financial aid and start the online application process. Do this before the student's senior year so you can rearrange your finances to qualify for the most aid possible.

FOR RECENT GRADS:

Go to the National Student Loan Data System at **www.nslds .ed.gov** to find the loan amounts, lender(s), and repayment status for all of your federal loans. Then get started on a repayment plan within six months of graduation.

TERRY'S TO-DO LIST

1. Don't be intimidated by the high cost of college.

2. Start saving as early as possible, using 529 college savings plans.

3. Avoid putting money in custodial accounts if you're going to apply for financial aid.

4. Study the aid process early so you can adjust family income to qualify for the most aid.

5. Check Scholarships.com or Fastweb.com for "free money," but start in your junior year or sooner.

6. Use student loans knowledgeably and repay them on schedule.

CHAPTER

11

THE SAVAGE TRUTH ON WOMEN AND MONEY

We Live Longer, We Need More

I t's a statistical fact: Not only do women live longer, on average, but we need more money to provide for ourselves in those later years. Although I've updated statistics in this chapter, these basic Truths have only become more apparent since the first edition of this book.

For many years, I resisted the idea that women have special financial planning needs. Yet, the numbers force us all to recognize that women have not made significant gains in financial security over the past few decades. Women are still paid less for comparable work, and many still work in jobs that are inherently lower paid.

Even worse, we have failed to save and invest for the future. A 2010 report by the Society of Actuaries says four out of ten women over age 65 living alone depend on Social Security for virtually all of their income. That portends a dismal future, since many of those women will live well into their nineties. This is the most critical financial difference for women and a basic Savage Truth: *Women live longer.*

Younger women are not getting the message. Studies of assets in 401(k) plans show that younger women have actually grown more conservative in their investments or cut their savings rate in the wake of market volatility. Instead they should be saving *more* to offset their expected longer lifetime.

Here are the simple facts every woman must face:

- Odds are you will live longer than men who are your age now.
- Odds are you'll wind up alone.
- Odds are you'll need more retirement assets than a man.
- Sure thing: You can deal with that financial reality if you start saving and investing *now*.

The most basic Savage Truth applies here: *Time is money*. And time leverages money, so that if you start to set money aside productively, it will do most of the work for you.

Age is just a number, as my mother always said. But financial reality involves a realistic look at the numbers now, and sensible projections about the future. In this chapter, you'll find advice and resources, no matter what your age.

If you're lucky or smart enough to read and heed this advice in your twenties or thirties, then the automatic saving and investment programs described in Chapter 12 will get you going. Your *individual retirement account* (which can be opened for as little as $50, and $50 per month at T. Rowe Price) or your *401(k)* plan at work will provide the basis for your retirement planning. All you have to do is make the commitment to stick with the plan and keep increasing your contributions as you earn more.

The moment of truth is upon baby boomer women, now approaching the age at which they would like to retire. They look at older women, their role models, and what they see is poverty. At the very least, we owe it to younger women to encourage them not to fall into this trap. We need to confront our situation at every age, and be willing to speak openly about the challenges. But first we need to share the reality.

There Are No Special Truths on Money for Women—Only Special Situations

When you deposit money in the bank or open an investment account, the money doesn't know you're a woman. The same rules of investing apply, regardless of gender or age. But there are some different realities for women, which need to be taken into account. They should not make us more fearful, but serve to encourage us to make smart decisions along the way.

- Women who reached age 65 in 2008 are expected to live, on average, an additional 20 years compared with 17.7 years for men.

- One-third of women who reach age 65 can expect to reach age 90, and at age 85 there are twice as many women as men still alive.

- Women still earn, on average, only 77¢ for every dollar that men earn, resulting in lower Social Security and pension benefits.

- Social Security reported that in 2008, the average annual Social Security income received by women 65 years and older was $11,377, compared to $14,822 for men.

- The latest analysis shows that 46 percent of all elderly unmarried females receiving Social Security benefits relied on Social Security for 90 percent or more of their income.

- The poverty rate for women 65 and older in 2009 was 10.7 percent—nearly double the poverty rate for men 65 and older (6.6 percent).

- Half of women over 65 are divorced or widowed.

- Women make up three-fourths of the elderly poor.

- 80 percent of women living in poverty were not poor before their husbands died, according to a General Accounting Office report.

- And here's a classic: On average, a woman's standard of living drops 45 percent in the year following a divorce while a man's *rises* 15 percent!

Survey after survey reveals that what women fear most is poverty. And with good reason: The "bag lady" syndrome haunts our consciousness. Yet, in spite of that fear—or perhaps because of it—too many women are paralyzed into inaction or pushed into the wrong actions. Risk avoidance becomes a prescription for poverty. Yet the opposite extreme of turning money over blindly to an "expert" is also a recipe for financial disaster.

There is some reason for optimism. Today, female wage earners hold 53 percent of all professional positions and own nearly eight million businesses, doing more than $1.2 trillion in sales. Despite the impact of the recession, more women are in a position to make informed financial decisions about their purchases and investments. And the investment community, led by women who have reached positions of power and authority, is focusing more of its resources on educating and advising women on financial decisions.

So what are the Savage Truths women need to know about investing, retirement planning, divorce, widowhood, and other money topics? You'll find them not only in this chapter, but throughout this book.

A decade of economic boom, then recessionary bust, has driven home the need to be self-reliant and empowered. The words *financial literacy* have entered our vocabulary, yet the soaring bankruptcy statistics show women outpacing men when it comes to filing for bankruptcy.

We can no longer blame a discriminatory education system for our financial situation. In the end, the wealth we create, or the poverty we endure, does not discriminate by gender. It's time to own *all* the facts so we can make smarter decisions.

THE SAVAGE TRUTH ON WOMEN AND MONEY AND PLANNING FOR THE FUTURE

It's Easy for Women to Be Overwhelmed by Money Decisions, but Men Are, Too

Money is both an abstract concept (power) and a very real resource (cash or credit). The actual process of dealing with money decisions is simply a matter of learning the facts and the rules and then improvising based on common sense. Women are especially good at this type of logical thinking that combines study, observation, and improvisation.

That's how we learn to cook—by reading a recipe book or following a family example. That's the way we learn to raise children—again, by reading books, talking to friends in a similar situation, and improvising a bit based on our instincts. It's the way women have become the leading wave of entrepreneurs—perceiving a need and creating businesses to fill that need, often without any formal business training. That's even the way successful career women have managed their climb up the corporate ladder without a rule book or role models: They observe what works for men and then modify the formula to suit their own needs.

There isn't one woman who hasn't burned the roast, spoiled the child, or made an embarrassing mistake on the job. But that has never stopped us from learning a lesson and then forging ahead to do better. Only when the subject is money do many women become too intimidated either to take the first steps to financial independence or to carry on after making an inevitable mistake. Perhaps that's because power is such an integral part of money management.

Some women who are successful in other aspects of their life confess they are tied in knots when it comes to making money decisions.

Many rely completely on someone else's advice. Women who usually recognize that asking questions is the only way to get answers become silent and nod assent when investment advice is offered. It's not that men aren't as dumbfounded; they are, but they've been trained not to show it. In an attempt to demonstrate bravado, most men drive on through the process, unwilling to stop for directions. When they make mistakes, they turn the corner and try another avenue.

Once you recognize that money mistakes have no gender, it becomes easier to trust those natural instincts to ask questions and use your own logic in assessing choices. Still, you need to follow some rules and recipes—and that's what you'll find here.

It's Easy If You Know It!

If you're just starting to deal with financial issues, you must recognize that money is an overwhelming topic only if you stand at a distance and contemplate the task of learning everything about it. But the truth is, you don't have to know *everything*—just the facts that apply to the current situation. Once you narrow down your search for information, the topic becomes much more manageable. Suggesting that the mother of a newborn first child start studying the "terrible twos" or the issues of teenage driving would be intimidating; she needs to contemplate the problems at hand, such as getting the baby to sleep through the night.

Taking any subject step by step makes the learning process much easier. Once accomplished, you can look back and realize that it was far easier than you anticipated—and you somehow made your way through the hazards. It's that way with money, too. It's easy if you know it!

Money Is a Singular Subject

We start out single, and since women outlive men by nearly seven years on average, it's likely that we'll end up single. More and more women are happily choosing to spend large segments, or entire lifetimes, as singles. Even women who assumed they'd be part of a couple find themselves living alone. The Savage Truth is that even when married, we're often single-minded!

Whether you're on your own, married, living as a part of an unmarried couple, or heading a single-parent family, it's important to be on top of your personal financial situation. Being single makes some financial details even more urgent. When it comes to record keeping, for example, singles have to be organized and well planned. Who else will sort out your affairs if you can't do it yourself?

So, whether the goal is the purchase of a home, a secure retirement lifestyle, or the ability to travel, it is every woman's individual responsibility to plan and invest for the future. And all of the regular financial advice in this book applies equally.

A single woman needs not only a will or living trust (see Chapter 15), but a trusted friend or relative who is willing to accept responsibility for everything from health-care decisions to care of a pet in case of emergency. Estate planning and taxation issues take on new importance for a single person who cannot pass an unlimited amount of assets to a spouse.

Life insurance needs may differ for singles. If there are no dependents, there may be little need for life insurance, except to cover funeral costs. However, singles living together might want to purchase life insurance to cover the cost of maintaining a shared mortgage that is dependent on two incomes. And single parents definitely need to examine the life insurance needs of raising dependent children in the absence of a supporting parent.

Being single has financial advantages and disadvantages. Singles may find it less expensive to get health insurance, but may need to pay for disability or critical illness insurance (see Chapter 8) so they can be cared for in case they are alone and cannot work. Single parents may receive child support to assist in covering costs, but they may spend more money on child care and have less to invest in a retirement account.

Whether single or married, having control over your finances, setting personal financial goals, and creating financial independence gives you the power to enjoy life in a way that's impossible when you're in an emotional meltdown about your money.

Marrying for Money Is a 24-Hour Job

(*Update:* We've come so far in the past decade, that the concept of "marrying for money" seems almost quaint, or at the very least as likely to apply to men as to women. But in case the myth lingers on that marriage is an easy way to get rich, I decided to leave this section intact. Perhaps I should also include a warning or two about the dangers of men looking for a free ride from all of you successful women!)

Although today's intelligent woman is past the fairytale stage of believing that Prince Charming will rescue her from financial worries, there must be some genetic imprint on many women about the saving grace of a rich husband. I highly recommend *Prince Charming Isn't Coming* (Penguin, 2007), a book by Barbara Stanny, the daughter of the founder of H&R Block tax preparation service. Stanny shows how even a wealthy young woman could fall victim to this myth and turn her finances over to a charming but ne'er-do-well husband. Her story of regaining control after losing much of her fortune is both educational and inspiring.

Another helpful book, *Marriage Shock: The Transformation of Women into Wives,* by Dalma Heyn (Delta, 1998), postulates that since the Middle Ages women have been transformed from the equal work-mate and helpmate into the dependent, self-sacrificing, nurturing "ideal wife." Heyn says that culturally imprinted icon confronts even the most independent career women when they marry. One way it manifests itself is in acceptance of male dominance in financial decisions.

There is certainly a middle ground between the extremes of financial submissiveness and financial stubbornness. That mutual respect is best developed between two people who are willing to contribute and converse about financial issues. The Savage Truth that "money is power" is often played out in marriage as money becomes a basis for control. Once ceded, control takes with it self-esteem. There is no price great enough to pay for loss of self-esteem. Far more difficult than climbing out of debt is the struggle back to self-respect.

THE SAVAGE TRUTH ON MARRIAGE AND MONEY, DOLLARS AND DIVORCE

Savers and Spenders Attract Each Other

Half of all marriages end in divorce, and in many cases money is the source of friction. I've often said that there are only two types of money personalities: the savers and the spenders. For better or worse, they tend to marry each other, and that inherent difference is the source of many problems.

That's why it's important to talk about money *before* marriage. Only in recent years have couples come to marriage with their own financial assets and prospects. Financial parity requires a different set of rules than those of a few generations ago. At the start of the twentieth century, women still didn't have the right to vote. Young women came into marriage with a dowry—possessions the girl's parents would hand over to their prospective son-in-law. Women had few property rights and a cultural expectation that they would not "trouble their pretty little heads" with such mundane concerns. Yes, we've come a long way in just one century.

We've Come a Long Way

Today, women have their own jobs, checking accounts, investments, and retirement plans before marriage. Although women still take time out of their careers to raise children and care for parents, younger women have a new respect for the importance of a paycheck in preserving their financial independence now and in the future. That is not to say that a young woman might not choose to work flexible hours, telecommute, or start a home-based business to balance her lifestyle. But women now understand the importance of a paycheck to provide a base for retirement investing.

This duality of income and mutual acknowledgment of careers requires some careful discussion about prospective money management and organization. These discussions are better undertaken when each party is on solid—and separate—ground.

Money Melts in Marriage

If you decide in advance how your financial issues will be determined, there is less opportunity for disagreement. Once you are married, your finances may be commingled by law. Keep in mind that in most states, a couple who purchase a home together will automatically create a joint credit report, since both incomes contribute to the mortgage payments. In community property states (Arizona, California, Idaho, Louisiana, Nevada, New Mexico, Texas, Washington, and Wisconsin), both spouses are viewed as equal owners of all marital property; similarly, they are viewed as equally liable for purchases made on credit.

When it comes to federal income taxes, if you file a joint tax return, each spouse who signs the return is responsible for the total tax liability and any challenges or penalties from the IRS—now and in the future, even though you may divorce. (It is possible, but difficult, to claim status as an "innocent spouse" if the IRS challenges a joint return that you signed.)

When it comes to estate planning, in most states it is impossible to disinherit a spouse unless there is a valid prenuptial agreement on this point. A spouse has pension rights, unless they are specifically waived in writing, and these benefits can be the subject of litigation in divorce when they are considered marital property. Even a divorced spouse has certain Social Security rights to an ex-spouse's benefits.

"I Do": Money Vows Matter

When women understand the basic legal facts about marital finances, it becomes clear that money vows are better discussed *before* marriage. Consider these questions, which apply to all marital unions:

- Will you keep your finances completely separate and contribute only a specific amount to a joint checking account to pay for mutual household expenses?

- If you establish a joint household account, will you contribute an equal amount, or an amount proportionate to each person's earnings?

- Will you keep your retirement accounts separate at work but commingle a mutual savings or investment account for things like a home or a child's college education?

- Will you maintain separate accounts for assets acquired before marriage? (*Hint:* If you never change title to an account acquired before marriage and do not add to it during marriage, it's less likely to be considered a marital asset.)

- Will you share your investment strategies so that your future investment plans are well balanced?

- How would these agreements change if you had children, or a parental health crisis, and one of you had to take a temporary but unpaid leave of absence from work?

- In the case of a second (or third) marriage, are you in agreement about how previous child support and spousal maintenance payments will be made? Are you willing to create an estate plan that provides for children of a previous marriage?

It's impossible to plan for all financial contingencies, but a discussion of these issues is sure to reveal potential financial conflicts. Take these disagreements seriously and attempt to resolve them now, because they won't go away after marriage. The decisions you make may even become the basis for a prenuptial agreement about material division of property.

Prenuptial Agreements Are Marriage Insurance

Many would argue that a prenuptial agreement takes all the romance out of a relationship and makes divorce inevitable. However, experience shows that so many of the financial penalties of divorce come because of the desire to inflict financial punishment that matches the emotional distress of the parties. An agreement in principle, arrived at in advance, can save a fortune in fees paid to divorce attorneys.

Even a couple who live together and purchase property together, but do not plan to marry, might benefit from a legal agreement covering financial issues in case of a future separation. Remember, this is all about thinking logically during a moment of positive emotion while you are committing to a relationship. It is far better to think ahead than to look back and regret.

A caution regarding prenuptial agreements: Each party must be represented separately by a competent attorney and each party must reveal his or her complete financial picture so there can be no later charges of concealment.

A prenuptial agreement does not have to specify dollars or specific property to be divided. It can set the terms under which the couple's assets will be divided and the financial terms under which the parties agree to live during the marriage. A prenuptial agreement is not a power play for one of the parties at the expense of the other. A properly negotiated prenuptial agreement should be in the best interests of *both* parties. No matter what your circumstances, it is neither unromantic nor unfeminine to insist upon having one.

Divorce Discussions Require Financial as Well as Legal Advice

A woman needs more than a divorce attorney to guide her through one of the most emotional times of her life. She needs her own independent financial planner to advise her of the future consequences of the agreements made today. Unfortunately, too many women rely on divorce attorneys who may be motivated by the immediate financial concerns of women rather than their future security. Consider the following issues:

On an emotional basis, many women would trade an equal cash value share in a spouse's retirement plan for full ownership of the family home, especially if young children are still living there. That may be the worst trade ever, even though the dollar amounts are equal today. The home will require upkeep and repairs as well as potentially higher property taxes. Future growth in value of the home may be limited, based on inflation. However, the retirement account has tax-deferred investment growth potential. Giving up its cash value today could mean sacrificing a much larger amount of future security.

Tax advice can also help a woman make smart decisions about the value of an immediate cash settlement versus ongoing maintenance payments. A division of property may not have tax implications, whereas alimony or maintenance may be subject to income taxes. Similarly, if the value of the marital estate is tied up in company stock that is not public, financial experts may place differing values on the shares being offered. If there is not a public market for the stock, it may be valued at a discount because it will be difficult to sell. However, a future public stock offering could create quite a premium value for those same shares.

Lawyers may insist on life insurance to guard the value of future payments for child support or college education. But the smart woman will insist that *she* own the policy and make the premium payments so that her ex-spouse cannot drop the policy or change beneficiaries. The amount of her settlement should include the cost of annual insurance premium payments.

It's important to get all the legal work done at the time of the divorce, when legal bills may be divided equally. If the court agrees that either spouse has the right to a portion of a spouse's existing retirement account, a specific and separate order should be entered in judgment. That order is called a *qualified domestic relations order* (QDRO—*quadro*) in most states. It should be given immediately to the spouse's pension trustee, who will then carve out a specified amount in a separate account for the spouse. Make sure that any QDRO you receive is enforceable upon your spouse's pension plan, or else demand other assets to make up for the future value of the pension benefits.

Once you're finally divorced, you'll have a new set of financial responsibilities. The income you receive may require you to make quarterly estimated income tax payments. Your financial planner will work with your own accountant or tax advisor to make sure the taxes are paid on time and that your investments or work generate enough cash to cover the payments.

THE SAVAGE TRUTH ON WOMEN AND MONEY AND GROWING OLDER

Men Retire into Leisure; Women Retire into Work

While the financial advice in this book applies equally to men and women, there are some special financial issues and pitfalls for women as they age. The fastest growing categories of poverty in America are children under the age of five and elderly women. (See Figure 11.1.) They share one common trait: They are the most dependent in our society.

Certainly, there's a danger in generalities. The image of the wealthy widow plays large in fiction, and sometimes in fact. But today's older women, whether widowed, divorced, or never married, are less likely

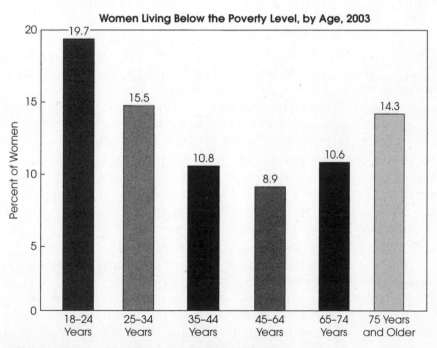

Figure 11.1 Poverty Rate among Older Women
Source: U.S. Census Bureau, Current Population Survey.

to have financial independence. During their strongest potential earning years, they were more likely to take time out from the workplace to rear children, care for elderly parents, or contribute their services in low-paying or volunteer community service. The value of their work was not recognized, financially or legally.

Today, the retirement laws are more favorable to women. Even nonworking spouses can contribute to an IRA account, something not allowed when the law first passed. Traditional pension plans have been abandoned in favor of 401(k) plans that allow for immediate vesting of contributions and the rollover of those contributions to a continually growing, tax-deferred IRA when leaving a job. (See Chapter 12.) But women must still recognize the importance of substituting current consumption for future wealth by making regular contributions to *their own* retirement plans and by taking appropriate investment risks.

Widowhood Often Means Poverty

Far too many of today's elderly widows live in poverty because they either did not work or did not participate in the financial planning process. Widows need to understand their rights to Social Security benefits and pension plans under their husband's accounts. Currently, there are about five million widows and widowers receiving monthly Social Security benefits based on their deceased spouse's earnings record—making a big difference in their lives.

Check in at **SocialSecurity.gov** for a complete explanation of benefits for widows and widowers. For example, if you will be entitled to Social Security benefits based on your own work record, you'll want to compare those figures with what you would receive as a widow. In most cases, a widow who remarries after age 60 can continue receiving her widow's benefit from Social Security (or benefits at age 50 if he or she is disabled). A young widow can take a reduced widow's benefit until she reaches retirement age and then claim full retirement benefits based on her own work record.

And divorced ex-spouses have rights to their former spouse's Social Security benefits, if they were married for at least 10 years, even if the ex-spouse is deceased. Thus, more than one woman could be collecting benefits on the same man's work record, and the amount each can receive will not be impacted by the benefits paid to the other.

Similarly, you may have choices about payment options from a deceased spouse's retirement plan. If your husband had not already retired, some plans let you decide whether to delay payments, take a lump sum, or take an annuity (regular monthly payments). Most corporate 401(k) plans proved for a rollover into your own name if your spouse had not already started receiving monthly benefits.

If there is a choice to be made, your tax advisor can help you take the best course. If your spouse was already receiving benefits, you may find your monthly income reduced by as much as half. When a husband is retiring, a woman should *never* sign away her rights to a future payment after his death in favor of a higher current payment. Remember, the odds are you'll outlive your husband and will need a continued monthly income.

The most difficult time to learn the basics of money is under the stress of bereavement. A husband who keeps his wife in the dark about estate planning, life insurance, and retirement plan benefits is leaving a legacy of grief—and the very real possibility that assets that took so long to accumulate will be dissipated out of ignorance.

Savage Truth: *A wife who does not demand to be included in family finances and estate planning buys short-term peace at the expense of potentially longer-term poverty.*

When in Doubt, *Don't!*

Women should find trusted financial advice starting at an early age. The biggest mistake women make is turning their finances over completely to someone else under the mistaken impression that action must be taken immediately. Although you shouldn't postpone important financial decisions—whether they relate to investments, insurance, or estate planning—there's never a reason to rush into a commitment. Always take the time to get a second opinion or to think over the consequences of your actions. That holds true for advice given by family members, lawyers, financial experts, or friends.

THE SAVAGE TRUTH ON WOMEN AND THE ESTATE PLANS DESIGNED TO CONTROL THEM

Many Estate Plans Use Marital Trusts to Control the Widow

When it comes time for estate planning, it's easy to be overwhelmed by technical jargon. Some of the best techniques for saving on inheritance taxes and distributing wealth involve the creation of trusts. Estate laws require some trusts to use an independent trustee to make investment decisions and distributions in order to qualify for an exemption from estate taxes.

All too frequently, even the portion of the estate intended to benefit the spouse directly is left in a *marital trust,* with someone else—an attorney, bank, or relative—appointed as trustee. That arrangement can result in a widow being forced to justify her needs or plead for money to the trustees appointed by her deceased spouse.

From an estate tax point of view, the marital trust contains money or other assets that could just as well be left outright to the widow with no restrictions. That's because one spouse can leave an unlimited amount of assets to a surviving spouse, completely free from estate taxes. But concern over how the grieving widow might spend the inheritance, and what would happen to the assets in case of a bad second marriage, often leads estate planners (and husbands) to put significant restrictions on the marital trust. The time when a woman must raise the issue is when the estate plan is being created.

For the record, not all marital trusts are alike. In order to qualify for the estate tax-free conveyance to the wife, the trust must meet only the following criteria:

- Allow the spouse the right to all of the income of the trust for life.

- Designate the spouse as the only person allowed to receive income or principal from the trust during her lifetime.

- Allow the spouse to direct the trustee to invest all the trust assets into income-producing investments.

This type of trust is called a *qualified terminable interest property* (*QTIP*) *marital trust.* As you can see, a wife may be told that the estate's marital trust is for her benefit, but she may receive limited income during her lifetime. She may also find that she has no control over how the remaining trust assets are distributed after her death. That's the "terminable" part of the title.

This is a technique frequently used in second marriages to make sure that most of the estate's assets ultimately pass to the children from the first marriage. While this is certainly appropriate in some situations, women should always be aware of any restrictions placed on their control over the marital trust.

And, if you are a wealthy woman making an estate plan in contemplation of marriage, it is a technique that you might use to safeguard your own assets. (Read more about estate planning issues in Chapter 15.) As women gain more wealth, these estate planning strategies work both ways!

Participate in Estate Planning

I've spoken with numerous estate planning attorneys who verify that wealthy spouses typically create marital trusts like the one just described. To be fair, a wealthy woman who marries a second time might use this technique equally well to make sure her second husband is provided for during his lifetime while passing on the majority of her estate to her children or other relatives.

If everyone understands the restrictions on how the trust works, there should be no problem. But all too frequently, a naive wife is told that all of these assets are being set aside at death in a trust "just for her." She's never apprised of the trust's restrictions on her ability to withdraw cash, change investment advisors, or direct the assets after her death.

The solution is simple: Participate in the process and ask questions. If you suspect that your rights to an inheritance may be abridged, take a draft copy of the proposed plan to another attorney for review. Conflicted spouses might hire separate attorneys. Creating separate estate plans will not be a problem as long as the attorneys coordinate the provisions—and make sure the estate plan coincides with the requirements of any prenuptial agreement. It's far easier to discuss these issues in the planning stage than it is to contest the provisions of a will or trust.

Marital trusts may serve a legitimate purpose to reduce estate taxes upon death and to protect assets from creditors. But there is no restriction on naming the widow as one of the trustees of the marital trust—with the power to remove or replace the other trustees or the investment advisor. She may also be given the power to distribute the trust assets after her death. To do otherwise demonstrates a lack of trust.

Spouses Can Be Disinherited

Some women take solace in the belief that they are entitled to a share of marital assets upon divorce or death. It's true that it's almost impossible to disinherit a spouse. Almost every state provides that a surviving spouse is entitled to a percentage of the estate. In some states it is one-third of the deceased spouse's estate; in others it is one-half.

All property titled in the name of the deceased spouse, including property transferred out of the spouse's name within one year of death without adequate compensation (i.e., attempts to give money or assets away), is considered a part of the estate. There is a time limit for making a claim on the required spousal share of an estate, so a surviving spouse should immediately consult an attorney if she suspects she's not getting her fair share.

There *are* circumstances under which a surviving spouse could be excluded from the estate. This occurs most frequently when a spouse has signed a prenuptial (or legitimate postnuptial) agreement waiving rights to the other spouse's property on death. Also, if you live in a community property state, assets owned before marriage or inherited and kept separate from the couple's community property do not have to be divided equally upon the death of one spouse. And, in a few cases on record in some states, a spouse has been allowed to transfer property into a separate revocable living trust and disinherit the other spouse.

A Promise Is No Substitute for an Estate Plan

There has been a bitter battle over the estate of novelist Stieg Larsson (*The Girl with the Dragon Tattoo*), who died in 2004. Larsson had spent his entire life with partner Eva Gabrielsson. But since he died without a will, all of his assets, and future royalties from his best-selling books, went to his family, triggering a bitter fight.

The estate of noted newscaster Charles Kuralt made the news because of a relationship he had with a woman who was not his wife. He promised to give her a ranch they shared upon his death, but he never put it in writing. If he had titled the property in joint tenancy with right of survivorship, it would have all passed to her. Since he did not, there were competing claims upon his estate.

These stories become public because the participants were involved with celebrities and there's a lot of money at stake. But the financial distress is equally painful when it occurs outside the media glare. These examples should serve as a reminder: All the promises in the world, even if a couple is living together, are no substitute for a legal document.

GETTING STARTED

"GETTING TO GO" ON AN ESTATE PLAN

One of the most difficult discussions for loving spouses or partners is the importance of creating an estate plan—especially if the idea is generated by a woman. Thinking about making a will may be even more painful if you're on your own. The estate planning details that should be considered are discussed extensively in Chaper 15. But getting started on the process is the most difficult part. And convincing an unwilling partner to participate is often a Herculean task. So, here are two potent incentives:

1. *Invoke superstition!* Simply, remark that not being prepared is to invite disaster. This is a subtle concept that works on the mind of the stubborn and is often convincing!

2. Make an appointment with an estate planning specialist, and if necessary, go alone. To find an attorney in your state and city, go to **www.search-attorneys.com**. Or ask a senior banker or the trust department of your nearby bank for a recommendation. When confronted with a prepared document, even the most reluctant will get involved.

TERRY'S TO-DO LIST

1. Make a commitment to control your money, one step at a time.
2. Think about how your personal fears affect your money decisions.
3. Set up your own retirement plan, even a spousal IRA for nonworking spouses.
4. Make an investment on your own.
5. Review your estate plan—and that of your spouse.
6. Ask one money question every day.
7. For more information and advice go to **www.WiserWomen .org**—the Women's Institute for a Secure Retirement.

CHAPTER

12

THE SAVAGE TRUTH ON INVESTING FOR RETIREMENT

Start Now—It's Never Too Late

No matter what your age, it's your responsibility to think about the future, and the possibility that you will be able to retire to a new lifestyle at some point in the future. We've come far beyond the idea that retirement means years of playing golf or sitting on a beach. As our lifetimes expand, and as the economy changes, we've all come to reevaluate the concept of traditional retirement.

But if you plan wisely, there is no reason to give up the idea of an enjoyable retirement. In fact, with careful planning and some simple self-discipline you can structure a life that will be fulfilling at all stages and never boring.

There are two simple stages to retirement planning: *saving up* and *drawing down*. The trick is to balance your efforts so that you can enjoy life in both stages. Since there are no guarantees in life, it hardly seems reasonable to postpone all the pleasures that you work so hard to enjoy. And it hardly seems wise to enjoy life fully now, without sacrificing a bit for a more secure future.

It's easier to balance those objectives than ever, now that we have the tools of technology to guide us. You have access to sophisticated advice that can help you invest and diversify appropriately within your retirement plan, and programs that can help you create a withdrawal scenario that gives you assurance that your money will last your lifetime.

We'll deal with the issue of scheduling and using your retirement withdrawals in the next chapter, as well as answering your most important question: How much is enough? But first, you have to choose the best ways to save and invest. I never heard anyone complain about having too much money in retirement. So this chapter is devoted to helping you accumulate retirement savings.

GETTING STARTED ON SAVING FOR RETIREMENT

The Savage Truth: *The first step is always the hardest—getting started.*

There is never "extra" money to save for retirement. So don't bother looking for it! Instead, take a look at your paycheck. You'll see a little box marked "FICA." That's Social Security—and it takes a nice hunk out of every paycheck.

Do you know what the initials *FICA* stand for? *FICA* is the acronym for *Federal Insurance Contributions Act.* You're making a *contribution*— but likely not to your own retirement. Instead, the money coming out of your paycheck this week will be on the way to your parents or grandparents on the first day of next month in *their* Social Security checks!

When Social Security first started, there were many more people working than there were retirees. And those retirees didn't live as long as they do today. As a result, Social Security is no longer the well-funded retirement plan for your future. Instead it has become a transfer payment—from those still working to those who have already retired. And in years to come, it will likely be a "means-tested" program—offering benefits only to those truly in need, despite the fact that all workers contributed to the plan.

The point here is not to debate the future of Social Security. Instead it is to give you an incentive to save on your own. You'll notice the word *contribution* in the FICA name. Mostly when that word is used it connotes a voluntary giving. But don't walk into the HR office at work and tell them you "can't afford to contribute to FICA this month." It's not optional!

Instead, you should take note of that money being taken out of your paycheck before you can see it and spend it. Then set up another deduction for your own retirement. If your employer has a

401(k) or *403(b)* or *thrift savings plan*, take advantage of it. Don't tell yourself that you "can't afford it." In reality, you can't afford *not* to set money aside for your own retirement.

If your employer matches all or even part of your contribution, that's free money—a riskless gain. Yet, amazingly, major corporations report that a significant percentage of employees fail to contribute enough to the plan to get the matching dollars. No excuses: Increase your contributions.

The Savage Truth is: *If you don't see it in your paycheck, you won't spend it!*

If your employer doesn't offer a plan that will take automatic deductions from your paycheck, read the next section about setting up an *individual retirement account* (IRA) or a *Roth* IRA. They'll take automatic deductions from your checking account every month before you see the money and spend it!

Time Is on Your Side

Time leverages the power of money through compounding. The earlier you start making regular contributions to a retirement plan, the less you have to contribute along the way to build your assets. Consider the story of Tom and Mary. (By the way, in my stories the woman is always the smart investor!)

Tom and Mary both start work at age 25. They're asked if they want to make pretax contributions to the company's 401(k) plan. Mary decides to contribute $200 a month. She does so for 40 years, until she retires at age 65. Over the years, she contributes a total of $96,000 ($200/month × 40 years). The money grows at an average annual rate of 9 percent, sheltered from taxes inside the plan. At retirement, Mary's account is worth **$850,000**.

Tom, on the other hand, feels he is way too young to start thinking about retirement at age 25. But at age 45, he notices that his hoped-for retirement is now on the horizon and he realizes he needs to catch up. Tom decides to contribute $400 a month (twice what Mary is putting in), which he does for 20 years. When he retires at age 65, he has contributed a total of $96,000 (400/month × 20 years)—the same amount as Mary—and his account also grows at an annual rate of 9 percent inside the plan.

But at retirement, Tom's account is worth only **$257,000**—*far* less than Mary's. The big difference is due to the time the money had to grow within the plan. The fact is that if Mary had stopped contributing when Tom started, she'd still have more than *twice* as much as Tom at retirement.

If Tom really wanted to catch up to Mary by starting his retirement plan at age 45, he would have had to contribute $1,321 per month—in order to have the same total at retirement.

If Tom and Mary happen to be married to each other, Tom's a lucky guy. Here's another thought: Even if you are married, each individual should be setting aside money in his or her separate retirement plan.

The bottom line: The younger you are when you start saving and investing for retirement, the less you have to save along the way. It's a lesson we must pass on to every young worker. But don't be depressed if you've fallen behind. There's another Savage Truth that applies to you: *Better late than never!*

Better Late than Never

Don't be paralyzed by fear of taking the first step. There are several ways to leverage the growth of your retirement dollars even if you're late in getting started. There's an old saying that even a small percentage of *something* is better than 100 percent of *nothing*. If you're a late starter, there are three basic alternatives: save more, take more risk to earn a higher return, or delay taking withdrawals as long as possible.

First, look at the effects of saving more. Consider the earlier example (in Chapter 1) of the person who contributes $38.46 a week for 31 years to amass $364,000 in his or her retirement account. You could start at age 40 and have that much by age 71, when you'd be required to start making withdrawals.

Would you rather have $1 million in your retirement account? Of course you would. So let's do some rounding and figure that you'd have to save about three times that amount, or $120 a week, or about $500 a month, to reach your goal. (That's assuming a long-term average investment return of about 10 percent, the historic average return of the stock market with dividends reinvested.) Ask yourself if it would be worth it to you to earn that much more every month, perhaps in a part-time job, or to spend that much less every month.

In fact, that additional amount could be partly made up by your employer's matching contribution to your retirement plan. That's what you miss when you fail to see the big picture. A match of

50¢ on the dollar is like buying a stock that goes up 50 percent overnight.

Now consider what happens to Tom and Mary if the company retirement plan matches their investment for the typical 50¢ on the dollar. Mary's account would be worth $1,275,000 at age 65, and even late-starter Tom would come out with a much better result. After 20 years of contributing $400 a month with a match of 50¢ on the dollar, his account would be worth $386,000 when he reached age 65.

Certainly, it's better to start early. But even a late-starting program of regular retirement investing, using every opportunity to leverage your investment dollars while taking only acceptable risk, will bring you far closer to a secure future. And if you're still worried about stock market risks, reread Chapter 5, and I'm sure you'll conclude that the greater risk is in *not* investing for the long run.

THE SAVAGE TRUTH ON INVESTING FOR RETIREMENT

Here's a sad Savage Truth that many people learned the hard way over the past decade: *Your investment discipline should match your time horizon.* The years since the market crash in 2000 created a whiplash effect for many people's retirement accounts. Reflecting those powerful emotions—fear and greed—many bought recklessly at the top, or sold emotionally at the bottom. Of course, that only becomes obvious in hindsight.

The lesson to be learned is that retirement savings is a long-term process. If you continue to contribute to your account every month, you'll never pick the top or be fortunate enough to buy at the bottom. But you will accumulate more shares, as explained in Chapter 5, and they will give your account a powerful boost when the market rises, as it eventually will. Even if you're just a few years from retirement, you'll need some form of growth in your investments for the extended period in which you'll live during retirement.

If you have a long-term goal in your retirement savings, you don't want to be making short-term investment decisions. Unfortunately, with today's technology you can check your balances every night. And most retirement plans let you make immediate changes to your portfolio with a click of your mouse. That can lead to big mistakes because of impulsive decision making.

Taxes are another issue to consider when you start your program of retirement savings. Traditional programs such as 401(k) plans and most individual retirement accounts give you an immediate tax deduction for the money you save. And the money you invest grows tax-deferred. That means you'll pay ordinary income taxes when you withdraw the money at retirement.

It was always simply assumed that you'd be in a lower tax bracket at retirement, as you start withdrawing. Now, however, given America's huge debt and the propensity to increase tax rates, that might not be such a wise assumption. So you might want to do both pretax and after-tax savings.

The best way to accumulate after-tax savings is a Roth IRA (described below) in which you pay taxes now (or upon conversion from a traditional IRA), and can withdraw all the money, including the growth, on a tax-free basis. The details will be discussed later, but the concept of tax planning is growing ever more important.

Don't let those considerations deter you from your main objective: setting aside money today and making it grow for your future. The best place to start is your employer-sponsored retirement plan.

401(k)—The Easy Way

Your 401(k) or 403(b) or thrift savings plan is the easiest way to set aside money for retirement. These plans, offered by corporations, nonprofits, and government agencies, have mostly replaced the traditional pension plans, which promise a lifetime monthly check at retirement.

Instead, you've been made responsible for your own retirement lifestyle. It will depend on how much you contribute and how wisely you invest. Surprisingly, for the first two decades of these *defined contribution* plans, employers were mostly prohibited from—or felt they could be liable for—offering investment advice that went beyond simple education. So employees were left on their own to make important decisions.

In recent years, that situation has improved. Most employers now automatically "default" new hires into the company plan. And instead of defaulting them into a conservative money market fund, which won't bring desired growth, employee contributions may be automatically placed into *safe harbor* investments—funds that balance the need for safety and the opportunity to grow your retirement money.

These funds do not guarantee returns, but over the long run they are likely to provide better results.

Still, the choice is yours, and since it's your money, you should understand the alternatives. Here are a few simple ways to make investing in your employer plan easier and more profitable in the long run.

Target-Date Funds

Target-date funds, as explained in Chapter 6, are managed mutual funds that are invested to reflect a growing conservative stance as you approach your hoped-for retirement date. They typically come in a series—about five years apart—allowing you to choose the target-date fund closest to your planned retirement. These are often the *default* option in 401(k) plans for employees who do not choose among the other funds offered.

It's important to understand that target-date funds always maintain a portion of their assets in stocks, even as the target date approaches. This reflects the understanding that you will need some growth of your assets offered by stocks during your years of retirement. Many investors who were close to retirement were shocked by losses in these funds during the market crash in 2008–2009. They knew they didn't have years of continuing contributions to make up for the losses they suffered. Some panicked and sold out right at the bottom. They never had a chance to recoup those losses when the market rebounded.

So if you're using target-date funds in your 401(k) plan, then you might also want to set aside a money market fund component that will cushion both your balances and your emotions if the market declines just before you're ready to retire.

Choosing Among Plan Investments

If you really want to be involved in choosing among your 401(k) plan alternatives, your company is likely to give you plenty of choices.

Typically, a 401(k) plan should allow you to choose an index fund that represents the large-capitalization domestic stocks, such as an S&P 500 stock index fund. There should also be a fund that is growth oriented, one that is balanced between growth and income, and one that concentrates on stocks of smaller companies. Most companies also offer one or more international mutual funds.

A well-run plan also gives employees a chance to invest in bonds, or it may include a guaranteed income contract (GIC) fund that is invested in insurance company promissory notes or bank CDs. Or you could find a stable value fund that is designed for income with little price volatility. There should also be a money market–type choice for those nearing retirement, although many employers worry that their younger employees will invest too conservatively in this type of fund.

Under the ERISA rules, a 401(k) plan must be run profession-ally, with an appropriate choice of low-cost investments. If you don't like the company investment choices, or the costs associated with the plan, get a group of employees together and complain loudly! Management should understand the liabilities for providing a poor range of choices or high-cost alternatives.

Getting 401(k) Investment Advice

You can learn the lessons of 401(k) investing by experience—the hard way. Or there is guidance and advice you can seek for diversifying the investments inside your plan. Most of the major Fortune 100 companies use a computerized modeling service called Financial Engines to offer 401(k) advice or money management services to their employees. This service helps employees appropriately diversify among plan options based on their individual goals and financial situation.

If your company doesn't offer that program, you can get a free one-year trial by going to my website, **www.TerrySavage.com**, and clicking on the box on the home page marked "Financial Engines."

If your company offers the service, they'll automatically insert your existing investments for the computer to model. If you do it on your own, you'll have to fill in the blanks. You can also include your nonretirement savings and investments. It's a personalized service based on your age, goals, and risk tolerance, which will be computed as you fill out an online Q&A form. Financial Engines, created by a Nobel Prize–winning economist, is a lot better than listening to your emotions—or your best friend—for advice on investing within your retirement plan.

Roll Over—Don't Withdraw

What happens if you leave your job or retire? When switching jobs, it's very tempting to simply take a check and use the accumulated money to pay off current bills. Don't yield to that temptation.

If you withdraw money from your 401(k) account before age 59½, you'll pay ordinary income taxes on all your withdrawals, plus an additional 10 percent federal tax penalty. You may also owe state income taxes. (There is an exception to this penalty for people over age 55 who retire.)

When you add it up, half of your early withdrawal could be lost in taxes. It's a huge mistake because you not only pay taxes and the penalty now, but you lose all the future tax-deferred growth on the money you take out.

When you leave your job, some companies will allow you to leave your funds within the company plan, although you may make no more contributions and will receive no more matching dollars. But you may prefer to make your own, different investment choices under your own control. In that case, you should roll over the plan assets directly into a *rollover IRA* at a bank, mutual fund, or brokerage firm, or into your new employer's plan. Doing a rollover gives you the opportunity to choose a new *custodian* that offers a wide variety of low-cost investment options.

The critical point is that you *do not touch the money or cash a check* from your existing plan. Instead, notify your new custodian and they will handle the transfer process to avoid taxes and penalties.

If you're retiring, there are additional reasons to do a rollover to an IRA. First, the investment choices in your employer's plan are likely designed for the accumulation period of younger workers, and may not be suitable or broad enough for a retiree. Second, it is easier to name a beneficiary (or joint beneficiaries) for an IRA or to divide your rollover into several IRA accounts with different beneficiaries.

But here's an important word of warning: If your company retirement plan includes highly appreciated company stock, do *not* roll that stock into an IRA. You may be able to take advantage of a special tax provision for net unrealized appreciation (NUA) on this stock, a tax benefit that could turn your stock appreciation into capital gains, instead of the ordinary income tax treatment generally accorded to IRA withdrawals. Consult your tax professional.

Name a Beneficiary

Be sure you *name a beneficiary* for the money that is growing in your retirement plan. And be sure to update that designation as your life situation changes. The money in your retirement plan passes directly to the named beneficiary, outside the court process of probate. As you'll see in Chapter 15, depending on this designation, your beneficiary will have the option to stretch out payments from an inherited retirement plan over his or her lifetime, allowing the money to continue to grow.

Borrowing from Your 401(k) Is Costly

As noted in Chapter 3 on debt, borrowing from your 401(k) plan is allowable, within limits, but more costly than you may realize. Sure, you're borrowing from yourself—and at a cost that may be only one or two percentage points over the prime rate. That's a lot less than you'd pay in credit card interest, but you're also borrowing *opportunity* from yourself. You lose not only the investment earnings for the period you borrowed the money, but also all the future growth on the money you didn't earn while your cash was out of the plan. And you'll be repaying that loan with after-tax dollars. So while that pool of money may be tempting, or your only choice in tough economic times, you need to be aware of the true cost.

There are some other drawbacks to borrowing from your 401(k) plan. Loans must be repaid within five years (unless the money is used to buy a house), and repayments are made from paycheck deductions. If you lose your job, your loan must be repaid within 60 to 90 days in most cases, or else it is considered a withdrawal subject to taxes and penalties. So instead of considering your 401(k) plan a first resort in a cash shortage, it should actually be your last resort for borrowing.

Most employers allow actual withdrawals from a 401(k) plan in cases of real hardship, such as medical expenses or to prevent eviction from your house. Ordinary income taxes and penalties still apply, and these withdrawals mean future growth on this money is lost forever.

The realization of how costly it is to borrow or withdraw from your 401(k) should lead you to another important awareness.

Your 401(k) Can't Be Your *Only* Savings Plan

Having extra cash set aside for a rainy day seems like a waste of money, until you need it. If your only recourse is to borrow from your retirement plan, you'll probably sell out at just the wrong time, especially if your plan assets are invested in stock market funds.

And if you lose your job while a loan is outstanding, it will almost immediately become a taxable withdrawal. Even if you think your job is secure, you need a savings cushion because secure jobs are lost only when economic times are worst. And when economic times are bad, the stock market is likely to be down. You could face the double whammy of being forced to liquidate your retirement plan assets when prices are lowest.

If you're going to mentally segregate your retirement plan assets for retirement, you must have other liquid assets for the emergencies that are bound to come between now and then. Otherwise, you're fooling yourself about your true level of financial security.

This advice about having extra savings was written a decade ago— a Savage Truth that became apparent only in the Great Recession. The advice still stands: You need more liquid savings *outside* your retirement account in order to have confidence (and the financial ability) to stick with your investment plan in tough times.

Repaying Debt versus Contributing to a 401(k)

People have always asked me whether they should repay consumer debt or contribute to a 401(k) plan. I have one standard answer, which is guaranteed to displease: *Do both.* As we've moved through tough economic times, this question takes on more urgency. Many people had no choice but to dip into their retirement plans, merely to survive. But as the economy and jobs return, it's important not only to repay plan loans, but also to continue to save for the future. So my original advice still stands. If you haven't wiped out your debt through bankruptcy, you must not only repay it but restart your retirement savings plan.

In the original edition of *The Savage Truth*, I explained the choice as follows: This is not really an either-or question, but it's often posed that way based on an erroneous assumption that there is only a finite amount of money above and beyond your current consumption needs that can be diverted either to repaying debt or to saving for the future. That's like asking whether you should eat or sleep. If you knew you were required to do both, you would find a way. It's the same story with your financial life. Find the funds, either by cutting back on current expenditures or by earning more money.

Paying interest on consumer debt is the least productive and most burdensome financial situation. But failing to contribute to a

401(k) plan does not solve your cash flow issues today and only compounds your future financial problems. To get ahead, you must solve both problems at the same time. As the economy recovers and jobs return, this advice will be easier to follow!

THE SAVAGE TRUTH ON IRAS

They're called *individual retirement accounts* for a reason. It's up to you—the *individual*—to open the account, keep contributing, make smart investment decisions, and plan for eventual withdrawals. No employer, no spouse, no one but your own conscience will motivate you to contribute. However, you will be the one to benefit from your decisions.

Even if you have a retirement plan at work, and some additional savings outside a retirement plan for emergencies, you might want to stash some extra money away in an IRA. And, even if you don't work outside your home, the government has recognized your right to individual saving, based on your spouse's work record.

Roth versus Traditional

There are two types of individual retirement accounts. A traditional retirement account is typically made using pretax dollars. That is, you can deduct the amount of your contribution on that year's tax return. (The actual contribution may be made up until the date that year's return is due, in April of the following year.)

The money in a traditional IRA grows tax-deferred, but when it is withdrawn all the money is taxable. If you withdraw money before age 59½, there is also a 10 percent federal tax penalty. After that age, you can withdraw any amount at any time, paying ordinary income taxes on the withdrawals. With a traditional IRA, there are rules that require you to start a systematic, lifetime program of withdrawals in the year after you reach age 70½.

A Roth IRA gives you no tax deduction in the year in which the contribution is made. But the contributions and all the investment gains in the account can be withdrawn tax-free in the future. There is no requirement that you withdraw money from a Roth, so it can keep growing tax-free, to be distributed to your heirs upon your death if you do not need the money in retirement.

Your withdrawal from a Roth IRA is considered a *qualified tax-free distribution* if you have had your Roth account for at least five years and you are age 59½. If you do not follow those rules, then the portion of the withdrawal that comes from *investment earnings* may be subject to ordinary income taxes and the 10 percent early withdrawal penalty. (See more on withdrawal rules later in this chapter.)

Whichever type of IRA you select, the most important thing is to get started early.

Contributing to an IRA

You would think the government would encourage the maximum amount of savings, but instead there are limitations on how much you can contribute to your IRA each year, and on the income levels at which an IRA contribution is allowed.

The amount you are allowed to contribute to an IRA has risen over the years, reflecting inflation. For 2011, you can contribute up to $5,000 of earned income to any type of IRA, and if you are age 50 or older at the end of 2011, you can contribute $6,000.

But your income and the availability of workplace retirement plans may also limit the amount of contributions you can make, and impact the tax-deductibility of your contribution. First, as noted, the money you contribute must come from earned income—not from savings or dividend or pension income. Only nonworking spouses, filing a joint return showing earned income, can make IRA contributions without having their own personal income.

Traditional IRA Contribution Limits

If you are covered by a retirement plan at work, and are also contributing to a traditional, tax-deductible IRA, there are income limits beyond which you will not get the full deduction for your contribution. In 2011, singles get a full deduction if their income is $56,000 or less ($90,000 for married filing jointly) and that deduction phases out completely if singles earn more than $66,000 ($110,000 if married, filing jointly). If you're in doubt as to your income eligibility for an IRA contribution, you can wait until you prepare your taxes, since the IRA contribution can be made until the tax deadline (not including extensions).

If you are not covered by a retirement plan at work, there is no earnings limit for a full tax deduction on your traditional IRA contribution. But remember, you can contribute only if you have earned income (except for spouses). Even if you spent all of the income you earned, you could contribute to your IRA out of other savings. Or parents could help children set up an IRA by gifting the amount of the allowable contribution, assuming the child is reporting earned income.

Roth IRA Contribution Limits

The allowable contribution amount is the same each year for Roth IRAs as traditional IRAs ($5,000/$6,000 in 2011). However, there's a completely different set of income limits for Roth (after-tax) IRA contributions. Opening and contributing to a Roth IRA in 2011 is restricted to singles with an adjusted gross income (AGI) under $122,000, and married couples filing jointly with an income under $179,000. Above those levels, your allowed contribution amount is reduced and quickly eliminated.

Contributions to a Roth IRA can be made at any age and no withdrawals are required, unlike traditional IRAs, which do not allow contributions after age 70½ and require withdrawals to start at 70½. Those differences create some interesting financial and estate planning opportunities.

Since the allowable contribution amounts and the income limits may change, you should check at **www.IRS.gov** for updates.

Investing Your IRA

You'll be faced with a wide array of choices for investing your individual retirement account. Mutual fund companies, banks, insurance companies, and other providers all will be competing for your business. In Chapters 5 and 6, you learned about the importance of long-term growth in a retirement account and the products that provide it.

Those products all have different costs and may have restrictions that limit your ability to switch when your investment outlook changes. Those are all questions you should ask *before* you open your IRA. You'll want to know whether there are annual maintenance fees for your IRA. Ask how much is deducted from your account yearly for a management fee, as well as whether up-front commissions or back-end charges will impact the amount of your investment.

If you make a mistake, you're not stuck, unless you've chosen an account with early withdrawal penalties. Simply contact a new custodian and they will handle a rollover. Or you can open a new account for this year's contribution, and also for future contributions. It's a lot easier than you think.

Many of the major mutual fund companies allow you to open an IRA account with less than their regular minimum, typically $1,000. And all will set up a plan to automatically deduct a monthly contribution from your checking or savings account. That solves the problem of "not having enough" money to set aside. It will be taken out of your account before you see it and spend it.

But don't let those big numbers intimidate you. In the "Getting Started" box at the end of this chapter, I introduce you to an IRA you can open for just $50 and a contribution of less than $2 a day!

Conversion to a Roth IRA

If you fear rising tax rates in the future, you might want to convert your traditional IRA or IRA rollover account to a Roth IRA, where the money will then grow tax-free. For many years, there were income restrictions on converting a traditional IRA to a Roth IRA. Those were eliminated in 2010, and now you have a choice of converting your traditional IRA, or rollover IRA, into a Roth, regardless of income level.

There's one big caveat. You must pay the federal and state income taxes at the time of conversion! That means, if you're in the 28 percent tax bracket, and convert a $100,000 traditional IRA to a Roth, you'd owe $28,000 in taxes! (You do have the option to do a partial conversion of your IRA, to make the taxes more affordable.)

There's an even more important consideration. Those taxes should be paid with money held *outside* your traditional IRA. Otherwise, you'll pay taxes (and a 10 percent early withdrawal penalty if under age 59½), on the money you withdraw to pay the conversion tax. After all, the whole idea of a conversion is to keep the maximum amount of money growing tax-free for the longest time.

Money in converted Roth accounts must be held for five years and account holders must be at least 59½ before money can be withdrawn tax-free. Starting with conversions done in 2011, you must pay taxes on the converted amount in your tax return for the year in which you do the conversion, at ordinary income tax rates.

There are opportunities to undo the conversion, or *recharacterize* back to a traditional IRA, if your tax situation or your investment results change. But the recharacterization must be done before

April 15 of the year that tax return is due (or later if you apply for an extension). This is a matter to discuss with your tax professional.

Roth IRA conversions make sense if you have the extra money, and if you find yourself in a low-earnings year. But you need to consider the impact of paying taxes now instead of later. If you either have time to let the money grow tax-deferred to make up for the early tax payment, or don't plan to use the money in your Roth and want to leave it to your heirs, then a conversion may make sense.

Remember, a Roth IRA left to your heir may result in minimum required distributions, but those distributions from the value of your Roth at your date of death will be withdrawn tax-free, providing the account was open for five years. Think carefully about naming a beneficiary for your Roth, because a very young beneficiary can stretch out that tax-free growth over a long lifetime, with minimal withdrawals. Your estate planning attorney or CFP can explain the possibilities and tax benefits.

Don't forget that converting to a Roth IRA will increase your income in the year of the conversion. That could impact other income-sensitive situations, such as eligibility for student financial aid or for other federal benefits. Discuss this with your tax professional.

There's one other consideration before doing a conversion and paying taxes now. Do you believe the government will keep its promise of future tax-free withdrawals from Roth IRAs? Or, like Social Security, will it change this promise (as it did with municipal bond income) and make it dependent on your overall income (or asset) levels? These are all things to think about before doing a Roth conversion.

Roth IRA or 401(k)? Do Both

One of the most attractive features of a Roth IRA is that it allows you to open an account, as long as you qualify based on income, even if you are covered by an employer plan, such as a 401(k) or 403(b) plan. Given a choice, invest in both.

If your employer matches your contribution, you should at least contribute up to that level. There's no sense passing up "free money." Some companies actually offer a Roth 401(k) plan, which works the same as the traditional plan, except that you don't get a tax deduction and the money grows tax-free, as in a Roth IRA.

If you can manage more savings, and don't need the tax deduction, it would be good to grow some of your money on a tax-free basis in a Roth, as well as your employer's tax-deductible plan. I never heard anyone complain about retiring with too much money! And hedging your bets on the taxation of withdrawals is a smart move.

THE SAVAGE TRUTH ON SMALL BUSINESS RETIREMENT PLANS

There are other types of retirement plans available for small business owners to create for themselves and their employees. These plans don't have to be costly or create a mountain of paperwork. But they can provide an incentive for good employees to stick with the company even through periods of pay cuts.

Consult the major mutual fund companies for more information on these plans. They will help you set them up, and they will handle the record keeping, as well as providing investments. Here are some of the basics:

Simple IRA

This plan is designed for small businesses, generally with fewer than 100 employees. The employer does not have to make complicated filings, but does have to contribute to each employee's plan—either a 2 percent of wages contribution for each eligible employee, or a 3 percent matching contribution for each employee who contributes.

It's up to the employee to decide whether to contribute, but for 2011 the employee may not contribute more than $11,500. All of the money, including matching contributions, belongs to the employee. Withdrawals taken before age 59½ incur the standard 10 percent early withdrawal penalty, plus income taxes. But withdrawals made during the first two years face a 25 percent tax penalty.

SEP-IRA

A SEP-IRA is an acronym for *self-employment pension*—a plan available to individuals, or small business owners with fewer than 10 employees. The employer makes the tax-deductible contribution each year, ranging from zero to 25 percent of compensation, but each employee must receive the same percentage contribution. For 2011, the maximum contribution is $49,000.

Contributions are optional each year. All contributions are made by the employer, but each employee maintains his or her own SEP-IRA account and investments.

Keogh Plan

A Keogh plan is a tax-deferred retirement plan for the self-employed. It works much like an IRA, but the contribution limits are higher: $49,000 in 2011. There are two types of Keogh plans: *defined benefit* and *defined contribution*. A SEP-IRA plan is a type of defined-contribution Keogh; other types include profit-sharing Keogh plans.

Each of these plans for self-employed or small business employers has slightly different rules and uses. Consult your tax advisor or the major mutual fund and insurance companies that set up these plans to find the one that is best for your situation. Among the variables you'll want to compare is the amount that must be contributed each year, and whether you have the flexibility to discontinue contributions in tough times and still keep the plan going.

THE SAVAGE TRUTH ON TAKING MONEY OUT

In Chapter 13, we'll talk about planning your retirement withdrawals. There are excellent strategies for calculating how much you can withdraw in order to make your money last your lifetime. But just as the government limits how much you can save on a tax-favored basis for retirement, it also wants to make sure you don't pass it all on to your heirs before they get a crack at collecting taxes.

As explained earlier, there are restrictions on retirement plan withdrawals before you reach age 59½. Otherwise, you'll pay not only ordinary income taxes, but a 10 percent penalty. Companies set their own "borrowing" rules on 401(k) plans, but the government sets the rules about when withdrawals from company plans or IRAs will be subject to penalties.

For instance, you can withdraw up to $10,000 from your IRA, penalty free, for the purchase of your first home. (You still have to pay income taxes on the withdrawal.) Or you can withdraw any amount to pay for higher-education expenses for your immediate family members. Or you can take money out penalty-free to pay medical insurance premiums, if you've been unemployed for longer than 12 weeks. You can even withdraw penalty-free to pay for unreimbursed medical expenses that exceed 7.5 percent of your adjusted gross income. And there is no penalty for withdrawals if you become disabled, or for your estate if you die before age 59½.

If you retire at age 55 or older, you can take penalty-free withdrawals from your workplace retirement plan, although you still pay income taxes. If you retire at a younger age, you can take substantially equal distributions from your workplace retirement plan or IRA over your lifetime without incurring a penalty.

All of these early withdrawals are exceptions to the rule that you want to keep your retirement savings growing as long as possible. While the early-withdrawal penalties stop at age 59½, your retirement plan should keep working. No one says you must, or should, take money out as soon as the penalty period expires. But eventually the government will require you to take money out so it can collect taxes!

MINIMUM REQUIRED DISTRIBUTIONS

Thus was created the concept of the *minimum required distribution* (MRD). Those are the required distributions that you must start taking every year once you reach age 70½. While you can always take *more* out of your retirement account after you reach age 59½ without tax penalty, you are required to take a certain amount of money out each year even if you don't need it. If you fail to take out the MRD on time, the penalty is 50 percent of the amount that should have been withdrawn!

How much must you withdraw? There is a standard calculation, the IRS Uniform Lifetime Table, which is based on your age and the amount of money in total in *all* your retirement accounts (except Roth accounts) at the end of the previous year. (There is a separate calculation for those with a spouse at least 10 years younger, which likely will result in a lower required annual withdrawal.)

Any one of your retirement plan custodians will calculate the required amount for you, but you must give a year-end total of *all* your traditional IRA accounts for the calculation. Additionally, many financial sites have online calculators to help you do the computation yourself. You'll find a link at TerrySavage.com, under "Terry's Favorite Calculators."

You can take the withdrawal from any one of your IRAs—or from several IRA accounts—as long as you meet the required minimum. If you also have a 401(k), you must calculate and withdraw separately from that account. Each will send you a tax form, noting the withdrawal, at the end of the year.

Special note: You must start taking these withdrawals in the year you reach age 70½, or you can delay until April 1 of the year *after* you reach age 70½. But in order to avoid a double withdrawal in one year, which may boost your income and impact other federal benefits and your tax bracket, you might want to take your first distribution in the actual year you reach age 70½.

THE SAVAGE TRUTH ON RETIREMENT PLANS AFTER DEATH

Your retirement plan is part of your estate even though it will pass outside probate directly to your named beneficiary. Because it is part of your estate, it may be subject to huge estate taxes, depending on your planning. (See Chapter 15.) In 2011, you can pass total assets of $5 million to your heirs (or an unlimited amount to your spouse) without being subject to estate taxes. That law is likely to change, so stay in touch with your estate planning attorney. The critical point is that all your assets—including your retirement plans—are included in that calculation.

There is a second tax burden on your retirement plan. Unlike assets held outside a plan, which receive a step-up in value to their worth at the date of death, all your tax-deductible contributions to your retirement plan, plus your investment gains, will be subject to income taxes that your heirs will have to pay as they withdraw from their inherited accounts. That has implications for naming a beneficiary.

At your death, your IRA or other retirement plan will be rolled into an *inherited IRA*. All inherited IRAs are subject to IRS minimum required distribution rules, but generally these are taken over the life expectancy of the beneficiary. The beneficiary could also take an immediate distribution of all the assets, paying ordinary income taxes. But that would negate the benefit of stretching out the payout and allowing the balance to continue to grow tax-deferred. Spouses may have additional rollover benefits that can delay the start of minimum required distributions.

The tax advantages come from choosing a much younger beneficiary, whose small (age-based) required lifetime distributions will leave the account to grow for many years. Beware, however, of leaving an IRA to a minor as a beneficiary, as the court may have jurisdiction over the withdrawals and the investments. You can resolve that by naming a trust for the minor, which involves legal expenses. If you select a younger beneficiary, be sure to leave a letter explaining the benefits of taking only minimum distributions, and allowing the account to continue growing.

If you are the beneficiary of an inherited IRA, you must remember to name a beneficiary for your new account, in case you die and there is still money left in the account. That beneficiary can continue withdrawing on your remaining schedule.

If you have questions about any aspect of an IRA, consult your estate planning attorney. Or there is a terrific resource for all IRA questions. Ed Slott is the acknowledged IRA guru, and you can reach him through his website, **www.IRAHelp.com**, where you can post questions on the discussion forum. Slott has also trained and credentialed "elite IRA advisors." You can search for one near you on his website.

If you take your retirement savings seriously, and start early, this could be a huge pool of money by the time you confront these issues. You'll want to plan ahead carefully for distributions after your death.

Of course, there's the distinct possibility that you'll use it all up in your lifetime for living expenses. In fact, making your retirement assets last as long as you do is the subject of the next chapter.

RETIREMENT PLAN PROTECTION

Just in case, you should be aware of how assets in your retirement plans are protected in the event of bankruptcy or lawsuit. Assets in 401(k) or 403(b) plans fall under the ERISA protections of federal law. That makes them generally immune from attachment by creditors. Just ask O.J. Simpson, who is living off pension distributions from his retirement plan, which was structured just for this purpose.

But individual retirement account assets are protected only by state laws, which may vary and change. That means there is a slightly lower degree of protection for those assets in many states. New Hampshire and New Mexico have no laws protecting IRA assets, while Texas, Arizona, and Washington have strong protection from creditors for IRAs.

It's something to check out before you roll over assets from a company plan to your IRA, if you think you might be exposed to litigation.

GETTING STARTED

THE $50, NO EXCUSES, EASY IRA

T. Rowe Price, one of the leading mutual fund management companies, has an incredible offer for those who want to open an IRA. They will let you start with as little as $50 to open the account, if you agree to an automatic monthly contribution of at least $50. That works out to less than $2 a day.

Of course, you can always add more at any time, or increase the amount of your automatic contribution. But this easy program takes away all your excuses for not getting started. To open an account, go to **www.TRowePrice.com** and click on "Individual," then on "View All Mutual Funds."

Scroll down until you find a list of *retirement funds*, with target dates ranging from 2010 to 2055, in five-year increments. Pick the one closest to the year you hope to retire. Or choose from any of their other diversified funds.

Opening up the account and setting up the regular contribution is easy to do online. Or you can call T. Rowe Price at 800-638-5660, and they'll walk you through the procedure.

TERRY'S TO-DO LIST

1. Sign up for the company retirement savings plan or open an IRA today.

2. Try to contribute at least as much to the company plan as your Social Security (FICA) deduction from your paycheck. At least, contribute up to the maximum the company will match.

3. Choose carefully among the investment options in the company plan. Make sure your retirement plan money is also working in growth investments.

4. Don't borrow from your retirement plan. If you have already borrowed, make repayment a priority.

5. If eligible, open a Roth IRA in addition to the company retirement plan.

6. Make sure you have named a beneficiary for your company retirement plan and IRAs.

7. When changing jobs, seek help in creating an IRA roll-over. Avoid withdrawals that create taxes and penalties.

8. Understand the rules for required distributions from your plans after age 70½.

CHAPTER

13

THE SAVAGE TRUTH ON GETTING TO—AND THROUGH— RETIREMENT

Time Is on Your Side

The time to start thinking about retirement planning is well *before* retirement, when you have time on your side and the flexibility to adjust your investments, your lifestyle, and your expectations to meet the reality of living longer. As the 79 million members of the baby boom generation start turning 65, there will be a new definition of *retirement*—one that is likely to include the need for continuing employment, even on a part-time or entrepreneurial basis.

That makes sense. Today's retirees will live much longer than their parents and grandparents, who could sensibly retire at age 65 and expect to live for only a few years. Now, at least one member of a 65-year-old couple can expect to live for another 23 years, to age 88, according to 2010 Social Security data. And there is a 30 percent chance that one of them will reach at least age 92.

The reality of longer lives has a huge impact on retirement planning. On the plus side, it gives us more years to work and save up for retirement. And with new hips and knees, not to mention other medical advances, many seniors are capable of and challenged by the idea of continuing to work. Thirty years on a golf course or at the beach could get very boring!

On the minus side, that longevity not only stretches out your need for income, but exposes you to the potential ravages of inflation or stock market volatility. If you retired at age 65, and had only a four-year life expectancy (as was the case in the 1950s), then you'd divide your money into four parts, and probably spend a bit more than a quarter of your savings in the first year—just in case! But as life expectancy increases, more uncertainty is created.

So the big questions are: How much money do you need, and how do you manage that money so it lasts your lifetime, with maybe a little left over to give to your heirs? This chapter explains how to find rational answers to those questions.

In my book, *The New Savage Number: How Much Money Do You Really Need to Retire?* (John Wiley & Sons, 2009), I deal with these issues in greater depth. You may think this chapter is designed for "older" people, but this chapter is meant for *you,* even if you're just starting your career and family. After all, what good does it do to start planning when you're on the brink of retirement?

As noted earlier, time is on your side if you start early. Even though you're still raising a family, paying off student loans, or saving for college for your children, it's never too early to consider the issues you will face in retirement. And smart retirement planning doesn't end with the official date of retirement. In fact, that's when you'll face an entirely new set of challenges.

THE SAVAGE TRUTH: HOW MUCH MONEY WILL I NEED?

This is the most important question and the easiest one to answer. It's not a matter of guesswork or hopeful assumptions. Instead, the answer to that question requires a calculation that takes many variables into account. There's actually one website that will calculate the answer to that "how much" question in seconds if you're willing to input some current information and make some assumptions.

Go to **www.ChoosetoSave.org**, the website of the national nonprofit Employee Benefit Research Institute (EBRI). When you get there, click on the green icon that says "Ballpark Estimate." That will take you to their interactive calculator, and all you have to do is fill in the blanks.

Some are easy. You'll be asked to fill in your age, salary, current savings, and planned retirement age. Then, you'll need a little more thinking. They're going to ask how much of your current income you'll need to replace in retirement. You may not need 100 percent of your income, because you won't have commuting expenses, dry cleaning charges, or other workplace needs. However, you *will* likely have higher medical expenses, and you do want money to travel or pursue your hobbies. Start with a replacement figure of at least 80 percent of your current salary.

Then the calculator gets a little tougher, which is why you can try it with several sets of numbers. You'll be asked to make assumptions about your wage growth, about inflation, and about investment returns. But the most important question is a simple one: How long do you expect to live?

I can give you a little help with that estimate. Just go to **www.Livingto100.com**, and take their online quiz. You'll be asked about your parents' and siblings' longevity and about your eating and exercise habits. You'll even be asked if you floss your teeth daily! (It seems gum infections can go to your heart and contribute to your mortality.) When you've filled in the blanks, one click will give you the computer's estimate of your life expectancy.

It will be shocking—either way. (When the computer reported I'd likely live to 104, I decided to go back and be more honest about my exercise and eating habits!) Still, you might be surprised to find that you'll live well into your nineties. And that can have a huge impact on your retirement planning.

The current life expectancy for an American at birth is 77.9 years—58 percent longer than in 1900, when the average life expectancy was 49 years. That's just an average, however, and there is a 30 percent chance of living past 92. Plus, don't we all want to be "above average"?

Is this good news, or bad? And since that data is based on the longevity of boomers' parents, could those numbers be extended in coming years?

So go back to the "Ballpark Estimate" and fill in this number—your life expectancy. Now, after filling in a few more blanks, you're ready to click and calculate. The program will instantly tell you how much more you should be saving to reach your retirement income goals. Or how much your lifestyle will be reduced in retirement if you don't adjust your savings. That's how to find your "number."

This number—the Savage Number—is a wake-up call, no matter what your age. Of course, if you're younger, you have more time to make adjustments. And if you're older, you might postpone full retirement, planning to work part-time or become a consultant, or taking up another income-producing lifestyle based on a hobby or talent.

In fact, a recent report by T. Rowe Price, talks about "practice retirement"—a strategy suggested for people in their sixties who are unwilling to defer the enjoyment of their last, best years just so they can have "enough" money to fully retire. Instead, the study suggests, they should keep working and contribute only enough to their retirement plan to get the employer match.

That should free up some extra money to spend on vacations or lifestyle changes while you are young enough to enjoy the good times. Meanwhile, having some current earnings allows you to delay withdrawals from your retirement plan, so your nest egg can continue to grow tax-deferred. For more details on how to evaluate these trade-offs, check the "Practice Retirement" section at **www.TRowePrice.com**.

Clearly, it's important not to view retirement as a cliff off which you will drop at a certain age. You've climbed the mountain to save for retirement. Now the challenge is to stay near the top of that mountain range for the rest of your life.

Whether you can do that will depend not only on your investments and withdrawal strategy, but on your choice of retirement lifestyle. This chapter is about the tools, techniques, and sophisticated advice that will help you achieve your goals. The first, most important step is to face up to the reality of your current situation. Use the "Getting Started" box at the end of the chapter.

CONSIDER YOUR RETIREMENT LIFESTYLE

Now that you know how much more money you may need to contribute to maintain your desired standard of living in retirement, the second step is to take a closer look at your dreams and hopes for a retirement lifestyle. It's entirely possible that you can afford the retirement you want—but it could take some adjustments. Since time is on your side, you'll have to make those changes as early as possible. But you'll also have to examine your personal balance sheet.

Retirement Planning Rebalances Your Balance Sheet

A personal balance sheet is just an assessment of what you *own* and what you *owe*, as you saw in Chapter 3. As you approach retirement it's time once again to confront your assets and liabilities, perhaps from a slightly different perspective. Although the popular view of retirement is as a time to draw down your assets, you might benefit from simply rearranging your assets. And when listing your material holdings, don't forget to include intangibles such as your knowledge, experience, skills, and good health. They may come in handy if you need to rearrange your financial situation.

Retirement is a time to reassess the usefulness of your assets, and you might find that some assets are a cash drain. This analysis could result in the sale of the family residence, if you can get a reasonable price. The purchase of a smaller residence or condo at a bargain price could free up cash for investment or spending, and eliminate mortgage payments.

A change in location could even affect your cash flow if you move to a state with no state income tax. Check carefully, because some states without income taxes, such as Florida, have a *tangible personal property* tax on assets you own. Also, be aware that some states tax pensions earned within their borders, even if you move out of state. And don't forget that a change in state residency will require a review of your estate plan.

You might be able to turn a liability into an income-producing asset. For example, consider turning your mortgage-free home into your pension through a reverse mortgage. As you'll see later in this chapter, a reverse mortgage gives you a tax-free withdrawal of either a lump sum of cash or a monthly check that will keep coming as long as you live there. That can turn your home from a cash drain into a source of cash flow.

Study the liability side of your balance sheet carefully. Credit card debt is particularly burdensome when you're paying double-digit finance charges and earning far less on your savings. Seniors have been among the fastest growing group filing for bankruptcy, since it is tougher as a senior to increase your income to make a dent in the interest expense that keeps piling up. The goal is to enter your retirement years free from as much debt as possible. For retirement planning, you want a lopsided balance sheet—all assets and very little debt.

Cash Flows Differently in Retirement

Next, you and your planner will need a realistic look at your projected retirement cash flow. Start with your expected monthly spending needs in your hoped-for retirement scenario. While some expenses will drop in retirement, others will consume a bigger part of your budget. As noted earlier, you may no longer pay the expenses of commuting to work, dry cleaning, and a business wardrobe suitable for the office.

However, you probably want to spend more money traveling or dining out. And you're certain to have higher medical expenses and copayments than you did when health insurance was provided by your employer. Medicare premiums keep rising, and are even more expensive if you have additional income. You'll need a Medicare supplement and Part D prescription drug insurance unless you have retiree health coverage to take care of those costs.

So even if you think you'll be ready to "cut back" in retirement, don't forget about the new costs that will arise around health care. And remember the lessons of the Rule of 72: Even at a low 3 percent annual inflation rate, your buying power will be cut in half in less than 25 years.

Don't Count on Social Security

Don't expect Social Security to cover very much more than the costs of your Medicare premiums, supplement premiums, and drug plan insurance. Social Security is likely to be reformed in a way that could impact your benefits. The retirement age will likely be adjusted, and the companion Medicare health benefit premiums will increase, depending on your total income. They were already adjusted upward for higher-income retirees as part of the 2003 Medicare Modernization Act.

The government acknowledges the significant reliance of today's elderly population on Social Security benefits. In fact, that's why it has been so politically difficult to make adjustments. For more than half (55 percent) of elderly beneficiaries, Social Security provides the majority of their cash income. For one-quarter (26 percent), it provides nearly all (more than 90 percent) of their income. For 15 percent of elderly beneficiaries, Social Security is the sole source of retirement income.

As of June 2010, there were 53.4 million people, or about one in every six U.S. residents, collecting Social Security benefits. (About a quarter of them were not retirees, but were collecting disability insurance or benefits as young survivors of deceased workers.) The numbers will swell as Boomers retire.

See Figure 13.1 for some perspective on how the "pyramid" that existed when Social Security was first created is rapidly becoming a "square"—with fewer younger workers paying into the system and more older people collecting benefits. Notice, too, that since women live longer there will be a lot of "little old ladies"!

Aging Demographic

Population by Age and Sex: 2010 and 2035

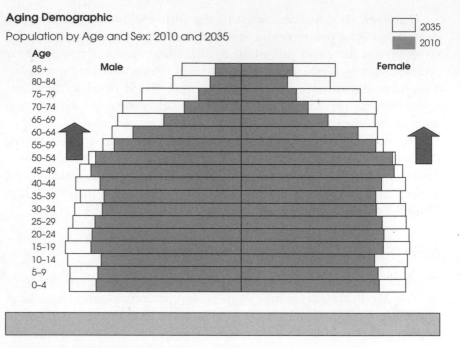

Figure 13.1 "Who Will Pay for *Us*?"
Source: Genworth Financial.

There is simply no way that today's young workers will receive the benefits that their parents and grandparents have taken for granted. So, as mentioned previously in this book, be sure to contribute as much to your own retirement plan as is being taken out of your paycheck for FICA.

Reforming Social Security and gaining control over Medicare expenses will be hotly debated issues in coming years. You're entitled to your own opinion. But a reality check says that in the future you will receive less in benefits—and the benefits you do receive will cost you more. Plan on it.

If you'd like to know what your current projected Social Security benefits will be, go to **www.SocialSecurity.gov** and use the secure online "Retirement Benefits Estimator" tool. Or call them at 800-772-1213.

TAKE YOUR MONEY TO MONTE CARLO!

No, I haven't suddenly lost my mind, but I did want to catch your attention. And I'll explain about Monte Carlo in just a moment.

First, though, you need to get your mind around the concept that if you're going to make your money last your lifetime, you will probably have to dig into your principal at some point in your retirement, unless you have a large enough fortune that you can live off the income. That doesn't apply to most people reading this book!

But if you have saved and invested enough to hope that your money will last as long as your life—with perhaps a bit left over for your heirs—then it's important to come up with a plan for withdrawals of both principal and income.

When planning for your retirement withdrawals, here's an important Savage Truth: *Beware of averages!*

Although we often talk of investment returns in terms of average returns, in the case of retirement withdrawal, averages can be dangerous, as you can see from Figure 13.2, which shows a man who drowned crossing a river with an "average depth" of three feet.

It's dangerous to use historic averages in your retirement withdrawal scenario, because averages mask a wide array of extremes. You don't want to be withdrawing too much when the market is down, or you won't have enough assets left to recover your balance when the market rebounds.

There's a much better way to calculate the probabilities that an investment and withdrawal strategy will be successful. It's called

Figure 13.2 Man Drowning Crossing River
Source: © Jeff Danziger (**www.danzigercartoons.com**).

Monte Carlo modeling—and it has nothing whatever to do with gambling. In fact, the term refers to the science of *probabilities* and was a code name developed at the time the first nuclear bomb was created. Monte Carlo lives on in the modern world as the technique for modeling probabilities when a variety of factors interact.

In the case of retirement planning, a sophisticated computer can quickly do the Monte Carlo math for millions of historical interactions of a wide range of stock and bond indexes. The program will give you a range of probabilities of outcomes, depending on the strategy you choose for both investing and withdrawing. (You'll find a fuller explanation in *The New Savage Number.*)

After running thousands of simulated interactions, the program will produce a range of probable outcomes and suggested strategies designed for your retirement planning. Each will have a different investment mix of stock categories and bonds, and perhaps even the promise of some income from a fixed annuity or other withdrawal schedules. And each scenario will have a different probability for success—defined as making your money last as long as you do!

If you are comfortable with an 80 percent probability that you won't run out of money before the end of your lifetime, then you can use that asset allocation and withdrawal strategy. Of course, you could get 100 percent assurance that your money would last your lifetime by using an immediate annuity, but then you wouldn't have the growth potential that a stock portfolio gives. It's all in the balancing act between growth and safety and in the withdrawal rate that the program advises.

Most mutual fund management companies, investment advisors, and financial planners now have access to Monte Carlo modeling tools for retirement planning. Not all will produce the same results, because they use different time periods for historical market returns, and because they may run a different number of simulations. We'll never know—until the far-distant future—which produced the best investment advice. But we do know that this type of modeling will produce a far better outcome than merely guessing or using averages to predict future returns and guide future retirement plan withdrawals.

STREAMS OF RETIREMENT INCOME

Most of us would like to have a stream of retirement income that will provide for our everyday lifestyle, *without* drawing down our principal. Then we could leave the balance for our children, grandchildren, or favorite charities. Unfortunately, that's unlikely to be the case for most people. They'll need to spend the principal over their remaining lifetime, in an intelligent plan provided by Monte Carlo modeling.

But you can minimize that use of principal if you can add to your income, either from your portfolio or from other sources. So let's examine how you might enhance a stream of income for your retirement lifestyle.

Annuities

If you wanted to make sure you had a check a month for life, beyond what Social Security promises, you could purchase an immediate annuity. (Annuities are described more fully in Chapter 7.) These insurance company contracts start paying a fixed monthly check that is guaranteed by the insurer to last as long as you live—or can continue over the life of your spouse. Of course, an annuity that covers two lives will pay a smaller monthly amount.

To find out how much income you could receive if you decided to purchase one of these annuities, go to **www.ImmediateAnnuities.com**. Or go to **Vanguard.com** and use their immediate annuity comparison service. Fill in the amount you have to invest, your age, gender, state of residence, and whether the annuity is for your lifetime or to cover two lives. You'll get an immediate quote from several major insurers offering annuity coverage.

But wait: Before you invest, you should understand the drawbacks of a fixed immediate annuity.

- First, you've decided on a fixed monthly check that will last your lifetime. But as already noted, inflation will cut into your buying power over time. That monthly check looks adequate now, but will it cover your living expenses in the future?

- Second, when you (or you and your spouse) die, any remaining balance in the annuity belongs to the insurance company. There is nothing left for your heirs even if you die just a short time after purchasing the annuity (unless you've purchased a *term certain* annuity, described in Chapter 7).

Annuities do offer the security of a monthly check that you cannot outlive. And so, many people will want to place a portion of their retirement funds in this type of product. But it certainly isn't where you would want to place *all* of your money, for the reasons just listed.

A Reverse Mortgage

A *reverse mortgage* turns your home into your pension, giving you either a lump-sum payout from the equity in your home or a fixed monthly check that will keep paying you as long as you live in the home.

A reverse mortgage is available to homeowners age 62 or older who have either paid off their mortgage or have a small remaining balance. The amount you can receive is determined by your age, the value of your home, and current interest rates. Basically, the older you are when you take out the reverse mortgage, the more money you can receive, either in a lump-sum or a monthly payout. And all the money you withdraw is tax-free, since it is the return of your own capital.

You don't need a credit check to qualify, and you retain title to your home. You won't have any mortgage payments, although you will be responsible for homeowner's insurance, property taxes, and upkeep on your home. But you'll now have a monthly check to pay for those expenses, or a pool of money in the bank to cover emergencies.

Basically, you are just borrowing from yourself, although you will be paying interest on that loan. But the interest is added to the amount of equity taken out of the home. When you sell the home, or die, the amount you have borrowed out of your home's equity must be repaid from the sale proceeds.

Most important, you—or your heirs—can never owe more than the home is worth. And you can never be forced out of your home because you've "run out" of equity. Eventually, when the home is sold, because you move or die, any proceeds (minus the withdrawals and interest and fees) are returned to you or your heirs. If the value of the home has dropped below the total amount taken out through the reverse mortgage, you or your estate are not liable to make up the difference.

There are basically two kinds of reverse mortgages, and they are offered by many banks. Since all of these mortgages are insured by the Federal Housing Administration, they must follow the same basic rules, although there could be some differences in cost. A reverse mortgage is called a *HECM loan*, which stands for Home Equity Conversion Mortgage. The two types of loans are the "Standard HECM" and the newer "Saver HECM." Each lets you borrow a different percentage of your equity and each has different fees.

The amount you can borrow on a reverse mortgage depends on the appraised value of your home. But no matter how valuable your home, the FHA has determined that the maximum amount of equity that will be considered for a reverse mortgage in 2011 is $625,500. (That limit is likely to increase in future years.)

The interest (which is taken out of your home equity) on either of these loans is calculated at a fixed or variable rate. These days, few lenders will promise a fixed monthly payment at a fixed interest rate for the rest of your life. Today, most reverse mortgage loans have a variable rate based on an index set by the FHA, and typically the interest is adjusted monthly. The initial interest rate on the Saver loan is slightly higher than on the Standard loan.

The Standard HECM loan allows you to access more money from your home equity than the Saver HECM, which gives you access to about 20 percent less equity. But, the Standard HECM requires a 2 percent upfront insurance premium, while the Saver has a tiny 0.01 percent upfront fee. Both loans also take a monthly insurance premium of 1.25 percent out of your equity to pay for the FHA insurance on these products.

(The FHA insurance protects the lenders so they don't lose money. Think about it this way: If the bank promises to pay you $2,000 a month for life through a reverse mortgage, and if you live to be 100 instead of the expected 85, the bank will lose out on the deal. The FHA insurance covers that possibility.)

The one place lenders do compete is in origination fees on these loans. The law allows banks to charge a maximum of $6,000 in origination fees, but many lenders today advertise that they will waive the entire origination fee. (They know they will make money on the loan interest over the years—as long as you don't live too long!)

If you're interested in knowing how large a lump sum—or what guaranteed monthly check—you could get through a reverse mortgage, go to **www.ReverseMortgage.org**, and use the online calculator. This site also has a search function to find reverse mortgage lenders in your area.

Income from Your Investment Portfolio

You could also structure your investment portfolio to receive income without selling stocks or digging into the principal. Here are a few strategies you might employ.

BOND LADDER

For example, you could create a *bond ladder* by purchasing high-quality bonds that mature in a staggered fashion over a number of years. If interest rates move higher, then as the bonds mature you will be able to invest in higher-yielding securities. And depending on the payment dates on the bonds you own, you'll receive a regular stream of income deposited directly into your bank account.

Just be careful to invest in high-quality bonds. Treasuries are particularly appropriate for this strategy (see Chapter 4), but you might want to use corporate or high-quality, tax-free municipal bonds as well. If you think interest rates are trending higher, keep your maturities short—perhaps spread out over only five years.

Also remember the lessons of Chapter 4 on bond pricing. When interest rates rise, bond prices fall. So if you need to sell your bonds, no matter what quality, in a period of rising rates, you could take a loss of principal. Finally, remember that bond pricing is typically opaque, and prices may jump significantly if you are purchasing only a small quantity. A bond ladder is a good strategy only if you have a substantial amount of money to invest, or if you use **TreasuryDirect .gov** to purchase Treasuries and automatically roll them over as they mature.

WRITING COVERED CALLS

Here's an interesting strategy that will require you to have a sophisticated broker to support your efforts. If you have a portfolio of high-quality stocks, you could write *covered call options* to get a stream of income without selling your stocks. The *premium* you collect increases your portfolio yield. Of course, the stock could be called away from you at the *strike price* of the option. But that simply means you have cash to buy more stock. And, of course, you collected the amount of the option premium. Equally likely, the stock will remain around the same level, or fall. Then when the option expires you have both the stock and the premium you collected.

That's a brief explanation of a strategy to increase portfolio income. To learn more, speak with a broker who has expertise in options, or go to **www.CBOE.com** and click on "Options Institute" where you can find simple explanations and courses to explain various option strategies. Also, check out *The Rookie's Guide to Options* by Mark Wolfinger (W&A Publishing, 2008).

THE BOTTOM LINE ON RETIREMENT PLANNING

I know financial planning for retirement sounds complicated, but there is plenty of competent help available. Your first job is to know how much is enough—and to save even more! The second challenge is to stick with your investment plan, once you know you've established reasonable goals. Then you'll face the challenge that comes with the realization that you are no longer contributing and must start withdrawing.

That's when you need sophisticated, professional advice about how to balance your investments and withdrawals so that you have the best chance of making it to the finish line with some money left over.

No one will take care of you in your old age if you don't make plans to take care of yourself. The government can't afford to keep you in the style you dream about. And your children will be busy facing the burdens of taxation and saving for their own retirement. By facing the problem as early as possible, you can have retirement security.

Only one disaster could completely disrupt your plans and I show you how to insure against that in the next chapter.

GETTING STARTED

There is no better time to get started than right this minute. Take the first step by going to www.ChoosetoSave.org, and then clicking on "Ballpark Estimate." Start filling out the short interactive worksheet.

Make some assumptions about your future wage increases, inflation, and investment returns. Then click to see how much more you should be saving—or how much your current lifestyle will be reduced if you don't save more.

Change your assumptions to see the impact of working longer, saving more, delaying withdrawals, or investing more aggressively. You might be surprised at the impact of even small extra contributions over time.

The first step in planning for the future is eliminating as much guesswork as possible and facing reality. This is the moment—and the place—to face up to your future.

TERRY'S TO-DO LIST

1. Get some perspective on your expected longevity by using the calculator at www.Livingto100.com.

2. Go to www.ChoosetoSave.org and use the "Ballpark Estimate" tool to figure out how much more you should be saving now to maintain your lifestyle in retirement.

3. Talk with a financial planner or mutual fund company about doing a Monte Carlo modeling scenario as you approach retirement age. My choice would be the service offered by T. Rowe Price at a cost of $250, or free if you have assets with them. Go to **www.TRowePrice.com/RIC** to access their online Retirement Income Calculator. You'll work with an individual planner if you use their advisory service.

4. Go to www.ReverseMortgage.org to see how much money you could withdraw from your home, tax-free, either as a lump sum or a monthly check.

CHAPTER

14

THE SAVAGE TRUTH ON LONG-TERM CARE INSURANCE

Insure Your Retirement Lifestyle

Even Superman needed long-term care! I thought that would get your attention. This chapter on long-term care insurance is not just for olde r people. It could have a direct impact on your own financial future—because you might be responsible for your parents' care. The time to start thinking about it is *now*.

Will you care for your parents—and your in-laws—in their old age? Will you invite them into your home, to use the bedroom your college kid just vacated, and will you provide them with help dressing and bathing? Or let's reverse the situation: Who will care for *you* in your old age? Will your children invite you to live with them and help you shower and take you to your doctors' appointments?

Think about it, because one way or another we're all going to be faced with this problem. If you're all alone, the situation might be even more dire. We don't like to think about needing help, and we haven't had much of an example of what a burden—financial, physical, and emotional—it is to have the responsibility for caring for an older loved one.

The boomer generation is living longer, healthier lives. But sooner or later, time will catch up. It's estimated that seven out of ten people turning age 65 today will need some long-term care, and one of five will need more than five years of care.

And that kind of care is costly, whether given in the home, or in assisted living, or in a nursing home. The cost of that care is not covered by Medicare (except for a limited number of days in a skilled nursing facility after a hospitalization), or by your Medicare supplement insurance. You, or your family, will have to spend a lot of money to provide that care, and those costs are rising faster than inflation. For example:

■ The average private-room nursing home now costs $90,155 per year.

■ Assisted-living facilities now cost nearly $40,000 a year, more if you have a cognitive problem.

■ Home health aides cost nearly $21 an hour. If you needed care nine hours per day, five days per week while your family care-giver is working, it would cost $49,140 per year.

Think about how those costs would add up over several years of care. Today there are 1.8 million Americans residing in skilled nursing facilities, and 12 percent have been there for five years or more! Of course, some of them are younger, victims of accidents or debilitating disease.

"Superman" (Christopher Reeve) was only 43 when he was paralyzed in a horse-jumping accident. Reeve lived for another nine years after the accident, surrounded by an array of expensive medical equipment and nursing talent. He did much to publicize the need for research into spinal cord injuries, and his experience serves as a warning to all of us about the need for this type of insurance.

Having *long-term care insurance* does more than just pay for your care. It keeps you from spending all your savings, so your spouse or family does not become impoverished. And it gives you the choice of where you want to receive that assistance—at home, in an assisted-living facility, or in a private nursing home.

If you have spent down almost all of your assets and can't pay for your care, the state Medicaid program will take over. You will likely be placed in a state-funded nursing home. Given the financial constraints on most state governments these days, and with due respect to those who work there, this is not the place you would chose to reside or would want your mother or father to spend their last days.

When it comes to planning for your future, long-term care insurance gives you peace of mind. Don't make the mistake of calling it by its old name: "nursing home insurance." Instead, consider it "nursing home *avoidance* insurance," since it will give you *choice*. Or consider it "retirement planning insurance" because you can live the retirement lifestyle you've planned without worrying about extended health-care expenses or caregiving being a burden on your spouse or family.

Long-term care insurance is a multigenerational product. It buys peace of mind for the person who is insured, and an equal portion of relief to family members who would otherwise be left with the financial burden of paying for care. Put simply, having a long-term care insurance policy allows those who care for you and about you to put financial considerations aside.

IN CASE YOU'RE WONDERING

I've given the subject of long-term care insurance a special chapter of its own, because I sense that the next looming social problem for our country will be the huge cost of caring for an aging population. But I've long been an advocate of LTC insurance because I've seen firsthand how costs pile up, and how desperately you want your loved ones (who cared for you as a child) to have the best care possible in their last years.

I paid for my grandmother's long-term care in the best private nursing home we could find. (Just visit a state-funded Medicaid nursing home as an alternative, and you'll see what I mean.) Her need for care came at the same time I was paying my son's college tuition. I have never seen money fly out of a checking account so fast.

I immediately purchased policies for my mother, my father, and myself. Yes, it was costly, but I remembered the old Savage Truth: *The lessons that cost the most teach the most!* Insurance seemed like a bargain compared to paying for years of care. My mother passed away a year ago without meeting the 90-day deductible to trigger her insurance. Thank goodness she didn't suffer long and didn't need extended care.

So, were those policy premiums a waste of money? Not at all. When my brothers and I were discussing her situation, before her death, the financial burden was mostly removed from our consideration. As for my dad, we're planning his 90th birthday this summer—and, thank God, he's still walking miles each day. And I'm still paying the annual premium, and hope to keep doing that for years to come.

Personally, I have two LTC policies: that first one, bought years ago, on which the annual premium remains stable, and another—a 10-pay policy—which I'll describe in this chapter. It will be fully paid up in just a few more years.

Yes, I know that not all of my readers can afford to be fully insured for long-term care. But even a small amount of insurance will get you into a private facility, where you may be able to remain if you use up your insurance benefits and require state aid. So please, read on.

UNDERSTANDING LONG-TERM CARE INSURANCE

If I've motivated you to consider long-term care insurance, you're probably wondering what these policies cover, how to purchase a policy, when to buy this coverage, and what it costs. This section will cover those topics, but first you should understand who can, and can't, qualify to purchase a long-term care insurance policy, as well as how and when your policy will start to cover the needed care.

The time to purchase a policy is when you're healthy and can qualify for the least expensive policy. Most LTC policies require a medical underwriting to determine that you are eligible and to set the price of your coverage. (Your employer might provide a group policy that has minimal underwriting questions.)

You might start considering LTC insurance at age 50, when prices will be lower. (Yes, that means you'd be paying premiums for many more years, but later in this chapter I'll explain 10-pay coverage, which can solve that problem.) And you're not too old to buy a policy at age 70, if you're still in good health. Premiums will be more expensive as you grow older, so don't procrastinate.

When it comes time to actually *use* your coverage, it's not simply a matter of calling the insurance company and telling them you need a caregiver. A physician must certify your inability to do *two or more of the basic activities of daily living* on your own, such as eating, bathing, dressing, toileting, transferring (walking), and continence—or the need for substantial supervision because of a severe cognitive impairment (e.g., Alzheimer's).

It's all stuff you don't want to think about because it's hard to imagine you might require a caregiver to assist you in doing those tasks. But when the time comes to access your policy benefits—either at home, or in assisted living, or in a nursing home—you'll be glad you can pay for the best care available.

In 2010, the 10 top long-term care insurers paid $10.8 million dollars *every day* to some 135,000 claimants. That amounted to $4 billion a year, according to the American Association for Long-Term Care Insurance. Overall, the industry is expected to pay out between $6 and $8 billion in 2011 claims, and the amount will grow each year as the nation's 8 million current policyholders grow older and increasingly need care.

If you need to use your coverage, it will be there for you. And most policies also provide a care coordinator who not only will help with the payout, but will assist you in finding appropriate care providers or setting. This is especially important if you're a senior on your own.

Here's one more Savage Truth: *Long-term care insurance is especially important for women!*

It's a fact: Women live longer than men. So you're likely to wind up on your own. If there was a man in your life at one point, he is likely to have used up the family's financial resources, as well as your energy in providing care and assistance. I ask all women to please at least consider whether they can afford some kind of coverage—and their daughters and sons to think about contributing to the cost of premiums.

Now, with those basics covered, let's take a look at what you should consider when purchasing a long-term care insurance policy.

Policy Coverage

Long-term care insurance policies typically cover nonskilled, skilled, and custodial care, as well as adult day care, either in your home or in an assisted-living facility or nursing home. All policies vary slightly in their coverage, so you will need an insurance agent who is familiar with these products to guide you through the purchase (more on that, later in this chapter). But you should know the basics, which follow.

ELIMINATION PERIOD

Just as you have a deductible on your car insurance, there will also be a deductible—called a *waiting* or *elimination* period—before your LTC coverage kicks in. Typically, this is a 90- or 100-day period. Choosing a longer elimination period can reduce the cost of coverage. But with full-time or nursing home care costing more than $7,500 a month these days, you might be relieved when the policy kicks in after about three months. In some major metropolitan areas, the monthly costs of care are much, much higher.

DAILY OR MONTHLY BENEFIT

Choosing a specific monthly benefit is the most common way to define the amount of coverage to purchase. You'll want to have at least $6,000 a month in coverage. But if that makes the policy too expensive, it's better to have a smaller amount of coverage than none at all. Remember, you will still have some income and assets of your own to contribute to your care.

LENGTH OF BENEFIT

Your policy could offer benefits for a period from two years to as long as you need care—sometimes called *lifetime* benefits, which is especially expensive. But you are not restricted to using up your benefits in the specific time period. If you need some care for a few months (after the elimination period) and then can go without care for a while before another period of needed care, the *pool of benefits* could last even longer. Check to make sure that you will not need to go through another elimination period if you resume use of the benefits.

The average stay in a nursing home is about three years—although Alzheimer's and stroke victims could require assistance for a decade or more. So compare the costs for a range of benefits and time periods.

INFLATION PROTECTION

The potential impact of inflation on care costs is a real concern when purchasing long-term care insurance. After all, you hope to use this coverage in the far-distant future, if at all. So you'll want to purchase some form of inflation protection when you buy the policy.

You'll be able to choose between *simple inflation*, which will adjust the benefit upward each year from the original cost based on a formula designed to keep up with the consumer price index, or *compound inflation* protection, which will increase your benefit more dramatically but is also very expensive.

There are always trade-offs, but if you forecast future inflation (as I do), then you might be better off buying a lower amount of daily or monthly benefit, and using compound instead of simple inflation. At least, ask your agent to demonstrate both the costs and benefits.

OPTIONAL RIDERS

Your agent may mention some optional riders to the standard LTC policy. Most policies have a *waiver of premium* rider, so that once you start using the benefits you can stop paying your annual premiums. Other policies offer a *return of premium* feature, which promises that if you die without using the coverage, a portion of the premiums you paid will be returned to your heirs. This coverage is costly, and you might be better off using the money to increase your basic coverage.

There is also an interesting *shared-care* rider available on most policies. It allows couples to utilize each other's benefit pool. This rider requires that each spouse purchase the exact same coverage. When one spouse dies, the remaining total lifetime benefit (if any) from the deceased spouse's policy will be added to the remaining spouse's total lifetime benefit. The premium for this rider will vary based on the age of the applicants and by carrier.

What Should It Cost?

The cost for your policy will depend on the features you choose, of course. Premiums are based on your age, your location (which determines the cost of care in your area), the features of your policy, and your health at the time you purchase the policy. All of these interact to determine the price you will pay.

A good agent will be able to draw comparisons and let you know of any discounts that might apply. For example, if both you and your spouse purchase at the same time, there could be as much as a 40 percent price discount on the second policy.

In Table 14.1, you'll see the annual premium costs for a policy that has a $6,000-per-month benefit, with a 90-day elimination period, and a four-year benefit period. In this example, created for an individual in good health, you can see how premiums are impacted by age and by your choice of inflation protection. Reducing the benefits to $150 per day would shave 25 percent off the premium. And remember, each spouse typically receives a 30 to 40 percent discount.

If you're thinking that this insurance is way too expensive for your budget, just think how much it will cost your family to pay for actual care, if you need it.

Table 14.1 LTC Price Comparisons

Age	No Inflation	3% Compound Inflation	5% Simple Inflation	5% Compound Inflation
40	$ 931.00	$1,557.00	$1,455.00	$2,181.00
50	$1,058.00	$1,741.00	$1,741.00	$2,491.00
60	$1,573.00	$2,679.00	$2,820.00	$3,509.00
65	$2,332.00	$3,628.00	$3,901.00	$4,676.00

Based on $200/day, 4 years, 90-day elimination, 100% home health care. Premiums vary based on benefits, age, health, and state of residence.
Source: Chart created by MAGA Limited, based on hypothetical client information.

For example, if you purchase the policy described in the example for Table 14.1, at age 50 with compound inflation, and if you pay premiums for 15 years before needing care, *it will take you only 152 days of care to recoup all the premiums you paid!* That means that just five months of covered care will repay you for all the money you spent on premiums.

If you purchase that policy at age 60, and pay for 15 years, it will take you 187 days of coverage, or less than 7 months, to recoup the premiums paid. And even if you start at age 60 and pay this premium for 25 years, not needing care until age 85, it will take you only 191 days of care to recoup the premiums you paid. The relatively shorter recovery period reflects the fact that you pay higher premiums when you buy later in life.

So before you give up on the possibilities, contact a qualified LTC insurance specialist to examine the possibilities and prices. And read on to the next section for tips that can lower the cost of your premiums or reorganize your assets to combine LTC insurance with life insurance or annuities to make the cost more manageable.

How to Buy a Long-Term Care Policy

I've always advised that you purchase your LTC policy from a financially strong insurance company. That makes sense, because you hope you won't use the coverage for many years.

That said, in the past two decades, many large companies have gotten into—and out of—the LTC insurance underwriting business. (Of course, an insurer is still required to support the policies already written, even if it is no longer selling the product.) Other insurers have found it necessary to increase prices, because experience with claims showed that more people were using their benefits for longer periods.

Since the price you pay for a policy is determined at the time of purchase, for many years buyers of LTC policies assumed premiums would remain the same for the life of the policy. And it's true that insurers cannot raise premiums on *your* individual policy. But they can go to state insurance commissioners and ask for an increase on everyone who purchased a certain class of policy. By now, the major companies that remain active in underwriting long-term care insurance have a strong basis on which to price their policies.

There are ways to limit your exposure to price increases, as I'll describe later.. But the place to start your search is with either an independent agent or a company that has a strong presence in the LTC insurance field. No single agent has access to all the leading insurers, so it is important for consumers to compare and ask the agent or broker which companies' policies they reviewed in making their recommendations.

Some companies (like New York Life and Northwestern Mutual) limit access to their policies to their own agents. Others, like Genworth and John Hancock (the two largest LTC insurers), make their products available through brokers, who typically also have access to other companies like Prudential and Mutual of Omaha. That said, here is a list of the major insurers that have demonstrated an intention to continue selling LTC policies.

Long-Term Care Insurance Companies

Genworth
John Hancock
MassMutual
Mutual of Omaha
New York Life
Northwestern Mutual
Prudential
Transamerica

Some of the companies listed here work through independent agents while others work exclusively through their own proprietary agents. LTC insurance is a specialty, and you want make sure you're working with an agent who understands the variables. Over the many years I have written about LTC insurance, I have come to know many excellent agents and they would all like to be listed in my columns and book. In the "Getting Started" box at the end of this chapter, I have listed a few of the larger organizations that I know will provide excellent service and advice.

MAKING LTC POLICIES AFFORDABLE

So far, I've written about the basic concept of long-term care insurance policies. But there are some steps you can take to qualify for a policy, reduce the cost, reposition existing assets, and limit your exposure to future premium increases. While these opportunities may not be appropriate or available for your situation or budget, it's worth examining how you can get a better deal on long-term care coverage.

Employer Group Plans

One place to start your search for coverage is with your employer. Many large companies are now offering group long-term care insurance for their employees and even employees' closest relatives. Some of these "true group" plans require little medical underwriting, which means that you could get coverage for your parents or spouse on a more favorable basis.

Of course, if you are younger and healthy, you might actually get individual coverage that is less costly. So it's worth making comparisons. Your company may ask you to pay the full premium, or it may share the cost.

Tax Breaks on LTC Premiums

If you are an owner of a business, you may be able to deduct some or all of the premiums for LTC insurance.

When a C-corporation (that's a form of corporate ownership) pays premiums for long-term care insurance, the cost is fully deductible to the company and is not considered to be income to the employee. A C-corporation can pick up the cost for any employees, but is not required to offer this benefit to all employees. As with all LTC insurance, when the employee actually starts receiving benefits, these payments are not considered taxable income.

Partnerships, and limited liability corporations (LLCs), Subchapter S corporations, and other entities that report taxable earnings to their owners can also deduct the premiums on LTC insurance for nonowner employees. But if the employee is an owner or partner, some of the premium must be taken as income, subject to some exclusions based on age.

Health savings accounts (HSAs) offer another way to get a tax break on paying LTC insurance premiums. If you use your tax-deductible HSA to pay the premiums, a qualified expense, you are effectively paying with pretax dollars.

There is a medical expense deduction for anyone whose medical expenses exceed 7.5 percent of their adjusted gross income in any one year. Long-term care insurance premiums are considered a medical cost to be included in this calculation, although only a portion of the premium may be considered depending on your age.

Many states also have tax deductions or credits for long-term care insurance purchases. Check with your accountant or tax advisor to see whether these are available to you.

10-Pay Policies

If you follow my advice to purchase your LTC insurance policy in your early fifties, you're exposed to the possibility of premium increases in future years. There's nothing more painful than having paid years of premiums, only to get an increase when you're retired and it's not in your budget.

There is a way to limit that exposure to future premium increases. You can do it by purchasing a policy that is fully paid up in 10 years. Of course, as you might expect, those policies are very expensive. But if you own a corporation, which can deduct the annual premiums, the cost becomes more bearable.

As an example, a 50-year-old man purchasing $6,000 of coverage for four years with simple inflation protection would pay anywhere from $7,200 to more than $11,000, depending on the insurance company. A few companies will even guarantee that the 10 years of premiums will remain level. Clearly this type of policy requires some comparison shopping.

Combining LTC with Life Insurance or Annuities

What if you never use your LTC insurance policy? Well, it did buy peace of mind, but it is still money that was spent for a product that was never used. Several large insurers have recognized this dilemma and have created policies that combine the benefits of life insurance and long-term care insurance. While each policy has its own features, the general idea is that if you don't use the money in the policy for long-term care costs, your heirs will receive a death benefit, so your money isn't wasted.

These combination policies are funded by a large, single-premium deposit into a life insurance policy. Typically, the money comes from savings that you don't plan to use in your lifetime but would otherwise leave to your heirs (unless you needed to spend it on long-term care). If some of the death benefit on the life policy is used for care, the balance goes to your heirs.

Buying one of these combo policies gives you leverage to get more long-term care coverage than simply self-insuring by keeping the money in savings. Here's an example of that leverage:

- A 55-year-old woman investing that $100,000 could get a $240,000 death benefit, or a $9,600 a month LTC benefit.
- At age 65, that $100,000 deposit would create $180,000 in death benefits, and an $8,400/month LTC benefit.

Withdrawals to pay for care costs are limited to 4 percent of the death benefit each month—with a 3 percent inflation increase. This combination policy buys you a lot more care than you could have received if you simply saved the $100,000 in case you needed care. Some policies offer an extended lifetime LTC coverage option for an additional premium.

Perhaps you don't need the life insurance, but you do want to reposition assets in an annuity. Then a combination *LTC/annuity* policy might be the solution. You can do a tax-free exchange of an existing annuity (including accumulated gains) into one of these combo life/annuity policies. Under recent tax law, if you need to access the money for custodial care, it will all come out tax-free—unlike most annuity withdrawals.

These combination products offer an interesting opportunity but they are not without costs. The "mortality costs" cover the death benefit promise, and, of course, there is a cost for the promise of long-term care coverage. But you know those costs up front, because they are baked into the promise of the death benefit and the care benefit, which won't change except for the inflation increases on the benefits.

Of course, you must have the cash to deposit into one of these policies. But once you make the purchase, you never have to worry about rising monthly premiums. You're locked in. Plus, you get the certainty that you (or your heirs) get something back from the policy—either the care benefits or the death benefits, or whatever is left over after you used some of the care benefits.

For more information, go to **www.OneAmerica.com** or **www.LincolnNational.com**. Each offers a variation on the combination policies. Or ask your agent for an explanation. As with traditional life or LTC insurance policies, there are underwriting standards you must meet to purchase these policies. So the time to consider it is when you're healthy and have the "extra" money to fund one of these products.

LIVING WITHOUT LTC INSURANCE

Despite the fact that the cost of long-term custodial care for an aging population threatens to overwhelm state and federal budgets, not much has been done to prepare for this eventuality.

The 2010 health care reform legislation created the Community Living Assistance Services and Support Act (CLASS Act). CLASS is a new voluntary government program under which individuals pay monthly premiums for modest future long-term care benefits. The program will primarily be offered through employers, although there are provisions that permit individuals to participate. Although provisions of the CLASS Act become effective in 2011, there are so many details to be worked out that most experts don't expect the plan will actually become available until 2013. Costs and benefit levels have yet to be determined. There is a five-year waiting period during which premiums must be paid before the participant becomes eligible to receive benefits.

The passage of CLASS does not negate the need for private long-term care coverage in any way. Two excellent sources for updated information are AdvanceClass, an advocacy organization (**www.AdvanceClass.com**), and the American Association for Long-Term Care Insurance (**www.AALTCI.org/class**).

Medicaid Planning

Many people mistakenly assume that Medicare will cover their nursing home needs, but it pays only for a limited number of care days after a hospitalization. Medicare supplement policies cover only the copayments for those limited days of care covered by Medicare. Instead, it is the jointly funded state and federal Medicaid program that covers care for indigent seniors. And it's a program that is already being swamped by conflicting needs in state budgets.

You must spend down most of your assets and apply almost all of your income before Medicaid will pick up the nursing home bills. You can't simply transfer assets to your children or a trust in order to qualify for Medicaid. Strict rules govern transfer of assets by the individual or spouse within five years of entering a nursing home. That's called the *lookback* period, and states are giving a much closer look at assets before picking up the tab. Not to mention the fact that a Medicaid nursing home might not be your long-term care alternative of choice.

Although the definition of Medicaid eligibility changes every year and varies from state to state, there are certain constants: A home of any value is exempted for singles (who are expected to return to the home) and for married couples. But Medicaid can attempt to recapture the cost of care after your death, preempting your plans to leave your home to your heirs. And if you receive a pension or Social Security, that income will be applied to the cost of your care.

Medicaid typically also exempts a prepaid funeral plan, cemetery plot, and certain personal items. Above those amounts, a married couple may be allowed a limited amount in resources to care for the spouse who remains outside the nursing home. Each state also has a monthly spousal allowance for the spouse who remains in the community.

But the bottom line is that states are going to get tougher about going after your assets if they have to pay for your care. There is no substitute for being able to pay. And the best way to ensure that you can pay for the care you want is through a long-term care insurance policy.

LONG-TERM CARE PARTNERSHIP PLANS

As part of a unique public–private partnership between insurers and states, a growing number of middle-income individuals are looking into *long-term care partnership qualified policies*. Partnership policies were first offered in just four states (California, Connecticut, Indiana, and New York), but today they are available in most states.

These policies provide limited benefits covering three or four years of care at reduced levels. But those who buy these policies are given a special added level of asset protection. As a buyer of a *partnership policy*, if you go on claim and exhaust the benefits of your long-term care insurance policy, you can apply for Medicaid under modified eligibility rules, including a special feature called an *asset disregard.*

This feature allows you to keep assets that would otherwise not be allowed. If you have a partnership-qualified long-term care insurance policy and receive $100,000 in benefits, you can apply for Medicaid and, if eligible, retain $100,000 worth of assets over and above the state's Medicaid asset threshold.

Partnership programs help both individuals and the state. Individuals can receive services they need without having to spend all of their assets. And, for the state, it can decrease the amount of Medicaid dollars used for long-term care services.

A Present for Your Parents

More and more adults are buying long-term care insurance policies for their parents. They buy the policies not only to preserve their inheritance, but to guard against spending their own retirement funds to take care of their parents. Seniors who have built up enough assets to cover their own long-term care needs may not require such a policy. But if paying for the care of one parent would leave the survivor penniless, adult children might want to make sure that both are adequately insured.

When looking into the subject of long-term care, those still in their fifties suddenly realize that the annual premiums are far more attractive for them than for their parents. Since one in four applicants for long-term care insurance is turned down, it's better to buy a policy while you are younger and in good health.

But how do you bring up the discussion with your parents, since it's not an eventuality that either of you wants to consider? Perhaps you and your siblings can join together to present a "certificate" for an appointment with an insurance agent as a Mother's Day or Father's Day present. Of course, the appointment is free, but you could announce that you're getting together to pay all—or half—of each year's premium.

You might be surprised that this starts a discussion about their plans for aging—something they hesitated to discuss with you. But no parent wants to be a burden on their adult children. We'll talk more about that in the next chapter on estate planning. And please don't skip that chapter because you think you're too young to worry. I'm superstitious, and I believe that planning is the best insurance against sudden disaster.

GETTING STARTED

It can't hurt to ask for a price quotation on LTC insurance for yourself or your parents. So pick up the phone and ask. Here are the names and contact information for trusted experts:

Long-Term Care Insurance Agencies/Brokers

www.MAGALTC.com	800-533-6242	Brian Gordon
www.CompareLTC.com	800-999-3026	Claude Thau
www.AALTCI.org	818-597-3227	Jesse Slome
www.LTCConsultants.com	888-400-1118	Phyllis Shelton

Or ask your employer about setting up a group LTC benefit for employees who choose to participate.

Remember, the time to buy is when you're young and healthy, and prices are affordable.

CHAPTER

15

THE SAVAGE TRUTH ON WILLS AND ESTATES

It Pays to Plan While You Can

It's the one subject people absolutely hate to talk about or think about. It's the one subject guaranteed to cause an argument or stop a conversation: *What would happen if you suddenly died tomorrow?* (See, you really wanted to skip this chapter!)

But like all other distasteful tasks, once you've made an estate plan—a simple will or living trust—you'll feel a whole lot better when it's done. You'll have the satisfaction of knowing that your loved ones will be taken care of and that the government will not be in charge of your assets. And the Savage Truth is that the entire process is easier and less expensive than you think.

IF YOU DON'T HAVE AN ESTATE PLAN, THE STATE WILL

Consider this: You're a young couple with no children and have put all your assets in joint name. On the way home from a party, there's a terrible accident. You die at the scene of the crash; your spouse dies a week later in the hospital. No will. You died first, so your assets pass to your spouse. When your spouse dies, everything goes to your mother-in-law!

If you die without any plan—*intestate*—state law will determine who gets your assets, who will raise your children, and even whether your pet will be given to a friend or an animal shelter.

Everyone Needs an Estate Plan

An estate plan is not only for those who have a sizeable estate. Your estate is everything you own. It includes your house or condo, mutual funds, savings accounts, company retirement plan, life insurance, clothes, and car—as well as your debts. It may not seem like much to you, but even your personal property might have some sentimental value to your family and friends.

Even if you have a very small estate, it makes sense to have a simple plan to distribute those assets at death. Think of the aggravation you'll spare your parents, children, and friends by organizing your financial affairs. And if you suddenly notice that your estate has grown into a sizeable amount over the years, think of the money you could redirect from the federal government to your heirs or charity just by planning.

Whether you're single or married, just starting out or in your retirement years, a parent or childless, you need to make a plan in case you die suddenly or are incapacitated and unable to make decisions for yourself. As you'll see, the plan can be a simple and inexpensive document that has a great deal of power to carry out your wishes.

Finally, accept this bit of superstition that passes for a Savage Truth: *If you don't have an estate plan, you're tempting fate.*

Joint Tenancy Is Not a Solution

Many couples title all their assets in joint name and make each other the beneficiary of their retirement plans at work. They figure this simple solution will save on the costs of making an official estate plan. But joint tenancy not only doesn't solve all your estate problems; it can create problems you never contemplated.

The most common form of titling property in the names of co-owners is *joint tenancy with right of survivorship*. It's simple to purchase real estate in this manner, or even to retitle a bank account with the name of a relative or friend. At the death of one of the owners, the entire property automatically passes to the co-owner, usually upon presentation of a certified death certificate to the bank or title company. There is no lengthy court procedure to transfer title or ownership in the account or property.

Although this may seem like a simple solution to distributing property, there are some drawbacks to joint tenancy with right of survivorship. When you enter into such an arrangement, you are exposing your portion of the property to the other person's creditors. If one owner is sued, the property held in joint name may be tied up in a court proceeding. For example, a parent who jointly titles property with an adult child could find that property involved in the child's subsequent divorce proceeding.

Similarly, joint tenancy restricts the right of one owner to sell the property. And if either party should become mentally incapacitated, a court proceeding might be required, with the court stepping into the role of the joint owner who cannot make decisions.

Placing an asset such as a home or savings account in joint tenancy after it has been owned by one person can also create a gift for gift tax purposes. Aging parents sometimes decide to add an adult child's name to a bank account for purposes of convenience, authorizing withdrawals on either signature. But adding a joint owner could impact the combined estate and gift tax when the money is withdrawn—if the amount exceeds the annual allowable gift (currently $13,000 per year). That shouldn't be a problem under the total current exclusion amount of $5 million.

Adding a child on stock or a brokerage account means the child assumes that parent's basis instead of getting the stock at death with a stepped-up basis. Unnecessary taxes will be incurred when the stock is sold.

Finally, placing property in joint tenancy ownership supersedes instructions that may be left in a will or revocable living trust. You may want a portion of your property to pass to your children, but if you've titled your home or investment account in joint tenancy with your spouse, that property will not become part of your estate covered by your will. It will pass directly to your spouse. And if your spouse remarries, he or she may leave the property to his or her new spouse, completely disinheriting your children.

Titling property in joint name may also preclude using some interesting strategies to avoid federal estate taxes. Thus, depending on the value of the property, joint tenancy may expose your estate to federal estate taxes, reducing the value of assets left to everyone else you care about.

A Will Won't Do

You've probably read this far and decided that it's worthwhile to make a simple will. But a will won't solve all the problems just described. Yes, a will can clearly direct how you want your property distributed at death, but before title to your property (your house or investment accounts, for example) can be changed to the name of your beneficiary, your will must pass through *probate*. That's the court procedure required to change title to your assets. A will guarantees that assets in your estate that are titled in your name go through the probate process.

Prevent Probate

Probate is simply the process of *retitling your assets*. But before that can be allowed, your assets must be made public to give your creditors a chance to file claims. The probate process makes your will an easy target for heirs who want to contest your will, causing additional delays and costs to your estate.

Probate has nothing to do with estate taxes, but it does take a long time—as much as a year or more, during which time your heirs may be restricted from transferring the property. Probate also costs money—fees for the lawyer handling the probate process.

When your will is filed with the probate court, it becomes a public document, exposing all your probate assets and the terms of your will to the public record. If you own property in more than one state, perhaps a vacation home, your will must go through probate in that state as well.

All property titled in your name must pass through probate, except for things such as retirement accounts or life insurance policies where you have named a beneficiary other than your estate. If you have named a minor beneficiary, the retirement funds will not be paid out. The beneficiary must have a court-appointed guardian to receive the funds, which are then tied up in probate court until the minor becomes 18 years old. Of course, property held in joint name with right of survivorship passes directly to the survivor, exposing it all to his or her creditors and taking future direction of these assets entirely out of your control.

There is a much better way than either a simple will or joint survivorship to plan for your hard-earned assets. A *revocable living trust* gives you control over distributions not only at death, but even beyond death. It protects your wishes while you are alive but incapable of making decisions on your own, and it can be the basis for protecting money that would otherwise have gone to the government.

But to understand all the advantages of the revocable living trust, first you must hear the sad and Savage Truth about estate taxes.

Nothing's Sure Except Death and Death Taxes—Unless You Plan Well

There's been a lot of headline political discussion about the "death tax" or estate tax in recent years. Some feel that the government should be entitled to a hunk of the assets you built over your lifetime. I disagree. If wealthy entrepreneurs want to vow to distribute their assets to good causes, that's entirely their decision. And it's nothing new. You wouldn't have the Rockefeller Foundation, the Ford Foundation, and dozens more philanthropies if wealthy people didn't understand the value of giving back to the society that enabled them to create such riches. But it's not a decision that should be forced by government.

You pay taxes all your life. You pay taxes when you earn money (income taxes), when you invest the money you earned (capital gains taxes), when you spend your money (sales taxes), and just for owning property purchased with your income (property taxes). Then you pay taxes again, whether you give the money away while you're alive (gift taxes) or when you die (federal estate taxes). Since you spend so much time and effort growing your wealth, it's certainly worth spending time planning to minimize those taxes.

The federal estate tax is a tax against wealth that you transfer to someone else at death, combined with the sizeable gifts that you make during your lifetime. At your death, under current law, if your estate is worth more than $5 million, you will pay estate taxes at a 35 percent rate. That was worked out as part of a tax compromise at the end of 2010, and it is scheduled to expire in 2012, when the exemption is supposed to return to $1 million with a top tax rate of 55 percent.

There is one other exemption to the unified estate and gift tax: Spouses can transfer an unlimited amount of wealth to each other (assuming each is a U.S. citizen) without incurring any tax. That looks like a handy planning device, until you realize that Uncle Sam could get an even bigger cut of your estate when the surviving spouse dies.

You may also transfer $13,000 per year to any number of people without reporting the gift or paying any taxes on it. A married couple could each give $13,000 per year, or a total of $26,000, to each of their children—or anyone else. In addition, each person may transfer, either by gift or at death, a total of $5 million without paying any federal estate or gift tax.

That should be enough for most of my readers to avoid estate taxes! But, when you total the value of your house, retirement plan, and the face value of life insurance if you are the owner, you can see that the estate tax has the potential to impact your planning, especially if lower limits return after 2012. Also, some states have their own higher tax rates, while most have laws that coincide with the federal rates and exemptions. Be aware that estate taxes are due and payable in cash within nine months from the date of death.

Estate Planning Is Not a Do-It-Yourself Project

In this era of instant access to current information, it is easier to make decisions and plans on your own. However, the one area that still requires qualified professional guidance is estate planning. Not only do laws change frequently, but state laws differ. It requires real expertise to deal with these regulations, not to mention crafting a plan structure that will be flexible enough to meet your changing life circumstances. I urge you to seek expert help in making an estate plan because the odds are you won't be around to fix errors in a self-made plan by the time your mistakes are discovered.

THE SAVAGE TRUTH ON REVOCABLE LIVING TRUSTS

The cornerstone of your estate plan should be a *revocable living trust*. The name is intimidating, but a revocable living trust is such a simple and flexible document that in the long run it actually eliminates a lot of legal work and costs. After all, assets in a revocable living trust completely avoid probate and probate legal fees!

But that's not all a revocable living trust does. It places your trust and your assets where they belong—in your hands, or the hands of someone you *trust*—not in the hands of the courts or the lawyers.

A revocable living trust is a trust you create and control while you are living. But it goes on, carrying out your instructions at your death or if you become temporarily or permanently incapacitated.

It is revocable because you may cancel it, change its terms, change the assets within it, or change its ultimate beneficiaries very easily at any time and for any reason. You may create the trust in your name (the Mary L. Smith Revocable Living Trust, Mary L. Smith, trustee) or in joint name (the Smith Family Revocable Living Trust, John and Mary Smith, cotrustees).

Because you are the trustee (or perhaps joint trustee with your spouse), you make all the decisions regarding your property or investments while you are alive. You also issue instructions that must be carried out by the person who is named successor trustee when you die or become incapacitated.

Once you've created a revocable living trust, if you ever become incapacitated by a stroke or coma, for example, your relatives won't have to turn to a court for permission and supervision to make decisions about your property. Your successor trustee, whom you name, can act immediately on your behalf. You should also make a health-care power of attorney and living will, which gives your instructions about end-of-life decisions (see the section on planning for health and wealth later in this chapter).

At your death, your successor trustee steps in immediately to follow your instructions regarding distribution of your assets. Your estate does not have to go through probate—the process of changing title from the name of the deceased—because you transferred title to your property to the trust during your lifetime. You avoid the fees, costs, and delays associated with probate because your successor trustee can act immediately according to your instructions.

A Revocable Living Trust Is Worthless If Assets Are Not Retitled

Once you create a revocable living trust, it's your responsibility to transfer title to all your assets into the name of the trust. The process is called *funding* the trust. For bank, mutual fund, or investment accounts, that's usually a simple matter of notifying the financial institution to change the name. If you hold stock certificates in your own name, you'll want to send them back to the brokerage firm to be transferred into your trust. The financial institution might ask for a copy of the first and last pages of the trust document to verify its existence and your authority to act as trustee. You will not be required to disclose any trust provisions relating to your personal estate plan.

If you own title to real property—a house, vacation home, rental real estate, or an expensive car—you'll have to make a special effort to have the property retitled. Your attorney can help with the procedure and may charge a small fee for each piece of property that is retitled. The title must be reregistered with the proper authorities, and you must notify the mortgage company that title has been changed. You should also ask your insurance company to add the trust's name as the insured.

You can simply assign all of your personal property—clothing, furniture, silverware, and china—to the name of your trust by preparing an inventory. If you have valuable artwork or collectibles, it is best to assign them specifically to the trust, using documentation your lawyer will provide.

If you really want your personal assets to be distributed according to your wishes, you must designate specifically in your revocable living trust. Simply placing a sticker on your artwork, or repeating regularly that your daughter gets the silverware, will not force your heirs to respect your wishes.

Some assets, such as retirement plans, cannot be retitled, but you might choose to name your living trust as the beneficiary in appropriate circumstances.

A Revocable Living Trust Has No Tax Impact

The revocable living trust will use your Social Security number, and it does not have to file its own tax return because you are the grantor of the trust. There is no tax consequence when you transfer assets into the trust. That is, if you purchased 100 shares of a stock at $2 a share, and it is trading at a much higher price when you transfer it into the name of your revocable living trust, there is no tax due, nor is there any change in your cost basis for the stock.

If you transfer your personal residence into a revocable living trust, you will still have the same cost basis. And you will still have a $250,000 capital gains exclusion ($500,000 for a married couple) on the sale of the house. In some states, the homestead exemption that protects the home from claims of creditors may be lost when title is held by a trust, so check with your attorney. If you own commercial property, the lender might have the right to accelerate the note when title is changed, something you should clarify in advance.

Any income from dividends or gains on the sale of property held by the trust will be reported on your personal or joint tax return, and you'll pay taxes at your personal or joint income tax rate. In other words, the revocable living trust is completely tax transparent while you're alive. And, by itself, the revocable living trust has no tax consequence at your death, either. Only when you combine your revocable living trust with more planning and additional trusts that may be funded at your death can you make an impact on your federal estate taxes.

You Can Easily Change Your Mind

You've heard about people adding codicils to their will to redirect their assets. It's an expensive and time-consuming process. But with a revocable living trust you can always change your directives with minimal cost and legal hassle. Selling an asset is as simple as calling your broker. Deciding to leave money to a charity or to change most provisions to a trust is a simple matter of adding an amendment to your document. But this must be done with the help of your attorney, not by simply writing a note on your trust document.

You'll Still Need a Pour-Over Will

When you establish your revocable living trust, you might keep some assets outside your trust. For example, your everyday checking account or your car will probably remain in your own name. You'll need a simple *pour-over will* that directs your representative to place these into your revocable living trust, where you've left instructions regarding their disposition. Since the assets outside your living trust will be minimal, probate won't cost much—or reveal anything about your bequests.

Although your living trust will give instructions about how your assets will be managed for the benefit of your minor children, a guardian must be named in a will. If you have young children, the pour-over will should accomplish that.

A Revocable Living Trust Does Not Protect Against Creditors

A revocable living trust has many benefits, but there are some things it will not do. A revocable living trust does not protect assets from creditors or give special protection in a bankruptcy. Since you are still in control of the assets, they are still vulnerable. Only when you create an *irrevocable* trust, from which you cannot withdraw or control funds, can you move your assets out of harm's way. Even then, property cannot be conveyed in this manner in anticipation of a lawsuit or bankruptcy.

However, if a trust is created at your death for the benefit of your spouse or your children, the assets in that trust could be protected from the creditors of your children, or from your child's spouse in the event of a divorce. Most states protect the assets in your revocable living trust from claims of unsecured creditors upon your death.

Singles, Single Parents, Domestic Partners, and Second Marriages May Benefit from a Revocable Living Trust

Singles and single parents often wonder whether it makes sense to have an estate plan. Perhaps more than anyone, they could benefit from a revocable living trust. If you're alone, this type of estate planning causes you to confront the issue of who would act in your best interests if you were unable to make decisions.

Although single parents generally rely on a surviving parent to care for children, there may be reasons to segregate the parenting responsibility from access to financial assets. A revocable living trust allows you to designate a successor trustee who is bound by your wishes and instructions in financial matters.

In the case of a second marriage, where spouses want to keep premarital assets separate, pursuant to a prenuptial agreement, a revocable living trust can serve as the vehicle for managing individual assets. In situations where adults live together but are not married, a revocable living trust naming a partner as successor trustee may help ensure that the wishes of the deceased are carried out according to instructions.

The Revocable Living Trust Is Only the First Step in Estate Planning

Now you know what the revocable living trust can do to protect your assets and your wishes while you are alive and after you die. There is no more practical or flexible instrument to cover the issues of privacy, legal fees, and control. But, by itself, the revocable living trust has no real impact on estate taxes. Only when used in conjunction with other trusts and strategies can you make an impact on potential taxes and assure a degree of control over how your estate will be spent.

Many people figure that if they buy life insurance, there will be enough money around to pay the taxes and keep everybody happy after their death. But unless you take special steps to protect that life insurance, it, too, could be subject to estate taxes.

THE SAVAGE TRUTH ON ESTATE PLANNING AND LIFE INSURANCE

The one thing everyone seems to know about life insurance is that it is tax-free to the beneficiary. That's just part of the truth. In fact, life insurance benefits do pass *income-tax-free* to the beneficiary. But if the deceased is the *owner* of the policy, the total amount of the life insurance is still part of his or her estate for estate tax purposes and could result in estate taxes being owed.

If you want to keep life insurance proceeds out of your estate, you have two choices. You can make someone else—your child or partner—the owner of the policy. You could give that person up to $13,000 a year to pay the premiums.

Or you could create an *irrevocable life insurance trust* to be the owner of the policy. You'll name a trustee who will be responsible for disbursing the proceeds after your death, either to pay for estate taxes or as you have directed. Each year you can make a gift to this trust, suggesting that the trustee might want to use the money to pay the life insurance premium.

In either of these scenarios, the proceeds of the insurance policy are kept out of your taxable estate. And having liquid assets might preclude the scenario of your heirs being forced to sell the family home or business if there isn't enough cash to pay estate taxes.

It's important to have the trust purchase a newly issued policy on your life. If you transfer an existing policy into the trust and then die within three years of the transfer, the proceeds would still be included in your estate.

SPOUSES AND ESTATES

The estate tax law allows married couples to leave an unlimited amount of assets to a spouse. That sounds like a simple way to plan, but it creates a problem down the road. The first to die will avoid estate taxes, but when the second spouse passes on, those combined assets might be subject to the estate tax, especially if the $5 million exemption is lowered in future years.

That's why estate planning attorneys for wealthy families typically create a trust designed to hold at least as much as the estate tax exemption. It may be referred to as a *bypass trust*, as it is designed to take advantage of the exemption from estate taxes. The rest of the money could pass directly to the spouse or other named beneficiaries.

Unfortunately, many estate plans create another trust to hold the assets designed to pass to the spouse, especially if the surviving spouse is a woman. This trust, sometimes called a *marital trust* or *QTIP* (qualified terminable interest property), is not an estate planning necessity. It simply reflects the desire of one spouse to retain control over the assets after death.

Many women who do not participate in estate planning sessions and ask questions find out too late that the money left to them is actually to be *administered* by trustees at a bank or law firm. A woman in this situation must ask for permission to withdraw cash, to change investment advisors, or to change the designation of what happens to the money after her death. It's a trust that demonstrates a lack of trust in the spouse who is the beneficiary.

To be sure, a wealthy woman could equally use this type of trust to restrict the use of assets by a spouse after her death. These trusts are often used in second marriages, where a wealthy spouse wants the surviving spouse to have use of the assets, but also wants to be sure that they ultimately go to his or her children at the death of the second spouse.

It's a legitimate technique, but let this serve as a warning that you should raise questions when an estate planning attorney starts talking legalese. Ask him or her to simply draw a chart of where the money goes—and who has control!

Grandchildren Are Not Little Tax Shelters

Once you realize how much tax might come out of your estate before it reaches your children, you might be tempted to pass them by. If you have enough money, or if your adult children are well off, you might be tempted to skip a generation and leave your assets to your grandchildren. Not so fast: The government stopped that ploy in the 1986 tax law by revamping the punitive *generation-skipping tax*.

As part of the tax compromise in December 2010, the exemption from this tax is raised to $5 million for 2011 and 2012.

I'm sure you're thinking that you wish you had an extra $5 million to hand off to your grandchildren! Well, you don't need an estate planning attorney and expensive trust to leave money to your grandchildren, especially if you want it to go to their college funds. Read Chapter 10 and learn about *529 college savings plans*, which allow you to give up to five years of the allowable ($13,000) gift to each of your grandchildren and watch it grow completely tax-free if the money is used to pay for college expenses. (And in case you change your mind about that gift, either because you need the cash or because of the child's behavior, you can take the money back, paying ordinary income taxes and a 10 percent penalty on the gains.) As well, you can pay college tuition directly to the school in an amount that exceeds the annual exemption, without any impact on ultimate estate taxes.

Be Careful Not to Gift Away Your Independence

While reducing estate taxes is an admirable goal, it must be pursued carefully. The life expectancy of the general population increases every year as new drugs and healthier lifestyles push back the barriers of age. So while it may be tempting to help an adult child with a gift of cash, and it may seem financially rational to remove assets from your estate, you never want to be in a position of requesting assistance from your children if you live longer than you expected or need additional assets to maintain your lifestyle. Consider the long-term consequences carefully before making gifts to your adult children, even in case of real need. You know what they say when you get on a plane: Put on your mask first, before helping others.

THE SAVAGE TRUTH ON CHARITABLE GIVING

It Pays to Give

Americans are the most generous people on the earth, giving about $300 billion annually to registered charities and educational institutions and countless more to friends, relatives, and even strangers on the street. Cynics say that much of this giving is motivated by tax considerations, but even when changes in the tax laws make it less attractive, the gifts continue. Still, it pays to take advantage of the tax laws that allow you to deduct charitable contributions from ordinary income up to certain limits (50 percent of adjusted gross income).

Make your contributions by check, but be aware that for each contribution over $250 you must have a written receipt from the charity in addition to your check. (If you're donating by text message, keep the phone bill as your receipt.)

If your total deduction for all noncash contributions exceeds $500, you must complete IRS Form 8283, along with your tax return. And if any donated item is valued at more than $500, you must have an appraisal. There are special rules that apply to contributions of cars, boats, and other items (such as art, jewelry, collections) with a claimed value of more than $5,000.

Under the Pension Protection Act of 2006, you can't deduct charitable donations of clothes or household items (such as furnishings, electronics, appliances, and linens) unless they're in "good" condition or better.

It's always better to make gifts of appreciated stock, assuming you have any, which avoids capital gains taxes.

As a reminder, you can't deduct a donation made directly to needy individuals who ask for assistance. You only get a deduction for contributions to registered 501(c)3 charities. Similarly, you don't get a deduction for your donation of services or the value of the time you contribute to charitable organizations. But you do get a very small deduction for miles driven on behalf of a charity.

You, Too, Can Be a Philanthropist

It really doesn't take a lot of money to become a philanthropist. Experts in estate planning can work dozens of variations on these charitable trusts or create individual foundations, which are often used by sports stars and other wealthy individuals to tax-manage their giving. But you don't have to pay legal fees to use these strategies.

Many financial services firms, including Fidelity Investments, Charles Schwab, and Vanguard, have created the *charitable gift funds* or *donor-advised funds*, which allow you to make a one-time, or annual, contribution to your own personal "foundation." That foundation is an account you set up in a charitable gift fund where the money is invested in a variety of mutual funds at your direction.

You, as donor, receive an immediate deduction for the contribution, but the money is invested to grow over the years as it is distributed gradually according to your instructions. Distributions can be made at your direction, only to registered charities. While the money remains in the investment pool it may grow in value, but those subsequent gains are not taxed. If you are seeking a large deduction, perhaps to offset a high-income year, a charitable gift fund gives you immediate tax benefit, continued growth of the assets, and a chance to do a lot of good.

THE SAVAGE TRUTH ON PLANNING FOR HEALTH AND WEALTH

When the subject of estate planning comes up, most people think about money. And if they don't have a lot of money, they figure they don't need a lot of planning. Think again. There may come a time when you would be better served by a good plan than a huge fortune.

Few people are willing to consider the possibility that they'll be disabled by an accident or a medical incident such as a stroke, or that they'll be one of the multitude of new cases of diagnosed Alzheimer's disease every year. Without a revocable living trust, which automatically designates a successor trustee to handle your decisions, your family will have to go to court to gain that power.

Young marrieds, without children, often don't see the need for an estate plan. They make each other the beneficiary of their retirement plans, and hold title to ther home in joint tenancy. But imagine the scenario of a terrible auto accident, in which you die first at the scene, while your spouse lingers on for weeks before succumbing to injuries. Without an estate plan, your assets pass to your surviving spouse. Then, when your spouse dies without a plan, *all* of those assets pass to your in-laws! See, you *do* need at least a simple will or revocable living trust.

No matter what your age, you owe it to your family and friends to be well organized and well prepared. Again, my inherent superstition plays a role in this advice. Could it really be a Savage Truth that fortune favors the well prepared?

Power of Attorney and Living Will

Even if you've created a revocable living trust and other documents to transfer your wealth and preserve your estate from taxes, you haven't finished planning until you execute some documents telling your loved ones and physicians how you want a health-care crisis to be handled and who has the power to make the decisions if you cannot.

We've all seen headlines about people languishing in a coma, or conflicted relatives debating in court about the care measures that should be taken for a patient. All of that would be resolved if the patient had created a *durable power of attorney for health care* and a *living will*. Even if you don't have a revocable living trust or a traditional will, these two documents are a must.

A *living will* is a written, legal expression of your desire to refuse medical treatment and life-sustaining procedures if you are in a terminal condition. Expressing your wishes relieves your closest relatives from the emotional trauma of making this decision or from debating among themselves about the best course of treatment. Make sure your physician has a copy of this document in your medical records, and give a copy to the individual you've chosen to be responsible for this decision.

The companion piece to a living will is a *health-care power of attorney* or *health-care proxy*. This document names a legal representative to make medical decisions on your behalf if you are unable to do so yourself. The person holding this power would be able to make decisions on your behalf about additional surgery or procedures.

Naming someone very close to you to act as your legal health-care representative places a tremendous burden on the designee. Think carefully about your choice. You'll want someone who is forceful in stepping into the medical process, cool under pressure, and smart enough to make careful choices.

The requirements for these documents vary from state to state, so if you're a snowbird who spends several months in a warm climate, you might need appropriate documents for each location.

Finally, if you are willing to donate your organs after your death, you should sign the back of your driver's license and tell a relative or close friend of your decision. This is also a statement that can be included in your living will.

An Organized Life Is an Unrecognized Virtue

If something were to happen to you tomorrow, would your family or friends be able to sort out your affairs, or is your financial life a mess? At the very least you should make a list of all the important names, account numbers, and telephone numbers related to your financial affairs. Or set up a filing system for your important account statements, stock certificates, and legal documents. Be sure to include a copy of your will (or instructions on where it may be found), title to your home and car, and a key to your safe-deposit box. Don't put your will in a safe-deposit box because it may not be accessible there.

Whether you've made a list or compiled all the documentation, tell a trusted relative or friend where to find this information. Being organized but secretive is no solution. If you're managing your finances with Microsoft Money or Quicken, all your data may be available with a click of a computer key, but did you remember to give your password to someone who could access the information?

If you go to **www.TerrySavage.com** and fill in the popup box with your name and e-mail, you will receive a link to my "Personal Financial Organizer" form. You can print out as many copies as you like and give them to friends and family. Not only will this information be available in case of emergency, the form will act as a checklist for organizing your financial life.

This Parental Talk Is Tougher than "the Birds and the Bees"

Parents don't owe their adult children a lot—certainly not money or an inheritance. One of the basic concepts of estate planning, though, is the desire to distribute material things after death. Still, many aging parents want nothing more than to avoid becoming a burden on their adult children. This desire to remain independent can create conflicts and anxiety in both generations.

There is much debate over how much to tell your heirs about your plans for their inheritance, but there is no doubt that parents should assure their children that there is, indeed, a complete and updated plan in place. A letter of instruction should be left with adult children or the attorney, detailing where the estate documents are held. Funeral and burial instructions should be left in this letter, as the estate documents are not usually examined until after the funeral. The documents for the health-care power of attorney, living will, and wishes regarding organ donation should be shared with those who will have to make the decisions.

If aging parents are unwilling to initiate this discussion, adult children must confront these issues squarely, perhaps by offering to pay for an estate plan as a Mother's Day or Father's Day gift. Parents should not take offense when the subject is raised. I know that's easier said than done, so pass this chapter around to all generations of your family.

TERRY'S TO-DO LIST

1. Think today about what would happen to your assets if you died tomorrow.

2. Before seeing an attorney, make a list of instructions you'd like to leave about your financial assets, guardians for your children, burial wishes, and mementos you'd like certain people to have. That list will organize your estate planning session.

3. Contact an estate planning specialist. A personal reference from a banker is a good start, but you can search for an estate planning specialist at **www .search-attorneys.com** or **www.naela.org**, the National Academy of Elder Law Attorneys, Inc.

4. Insist on consideration of a revocable living trust.

5. If you establish a revocable living trust, be sure to transfer title to all your assets into the name of the trust.

6. Make sure your life insurance is owned *outside* of your estate.

7. Use legitimate strategies to reduce estate taxes.

8. Remember to create living wills and health-care powers of attorney.

9. Have a serious discussion with your adult children. Details aren't necessary, but give them a general outline of your plans, and let them know where your documents are stored.

CONCLUSION ... AND BEGINNING

This is not the end of *The Savage Truth*. It is the beginning of your future, and your ability to exert control over the present. These Truths have survived market crashes and bubbles, and bull markets, too. They are the sound principles tested by time and based on history and hindsight. Sadly, it seems that each generation must learn them anew, because it's so easy to get carried away by emotion.

Once again, the Savage Truth: *The lessons that cost the most teach the most!*

If you're starting over, you now have a tremendous advantage. You've learned the lessons, and those mistakes are behind you. In front of you is opportunity. And if you are just starting out, I hope this book will save you some expensive tuition.

This is not to say that the markets and the economy can be predicted accurately. But they can be anticipated—if you will step back from current events and your own feelings about them.

Getting organized is the first step. Set up the system that works for you to track all your financial information. Technology such as online bill payment can help. And be sure to visit **www.TerrySavage .com** to sign up for a link to my Personal Financial Organizer form, which you can print out to guide you through the process.

When you fill out the pop-up box at my website, you will also join my list of "friends" and will receive my free e-mail newsletters, with updates on the markets and financial planning. And at my website, you can also post personal finance questions on my blog and check back for a prompt response.

Now it's time to start planning. As you've learned, good help is available. Take it one step at a time. Ask plenty of questions—and be sure to trust your own instincts. After all, no one cares about your money as much as you do!

Always remember that the one ingredient that only *you* can add is self-discipline—the determination to stick with that plan. Self-discipline is required on the upside, when you can easily get carried away by *greed*. And self-control is required on the downside of each market cycle, when *fear* can paralyze you or make you dump your plan in a panic.

Can you do this—gain control over your personal finances and your financial future? Yes, I firmly believe that you can—*if* you believe in yourself and in the future of our country. You've survived so far, and now you can move ahead.

America is the country in which you live, work, and hope to retire. As I said at the start, no one ever got rich betting against America. I'm not oblivious to our problems. But I'm optimistic that, as always, we'll rise to the challenge. By planning for a better future and working toward it, you are part of the optimism that has always moved this country forward.

America *will* survive and prosper—and so will you, if you plan, save, and invest. That's the Savage Truth.

ACKNOWLEDGMENTS

Over the years many individuals and organizations have contributed to the base of knowledge upon which I drew for this book. They have generously offered their time and resources to respond to my questions and read sections of the manuscript. I am indebted to them, while I take final responsibility for all the advice herein.

In the area of investments, special thanks go to Robert Benjamin and Heather McDonald at T. Rowe Price, John Woerth at Vanguard, and Steve Austin at Fidelity. For each of my books, Alexa Auerbach at Morningstar.com has generously provided the Ibbotson historical graphics, and special thanks to Jim Bianco at Arbor Research and Jim Stack of Investech.com for use of their research and unique graphics. Peter Gottlieb and his team have always patiently provided needed stock market advice and information.

The long-term care insurance chapter benefited from the major contributions of Jesse Slome, Claude Thau, Murray Gordon, Brian Gordon, Elaine Polisky, Bruce Moon, and Phyllis Shelton. I highly recommend talking to any of them for your LTC needs and have provided their contact information at the end of Chapter 14. Many thanks to Byron Udell of AccuQuote.com not only for providing commentary and numbers for the life insurance chapter, but for his efforts in restructuring my own personal coverage! For the property and casualty insurance section, Joan Walker and her team at Allstate gave me helpful access to Allstate's policy specialists.

It would be impossible to write anything about IRAs without the wisdom of Ed Slott at IRAHelp.com. Again this time around, Ed and his team have been accessible and knowledgeable about all the details. Special thanks to Dallas Salisbury of the Employee Benefit Research Institute, which created the best retirement planning tool on the Internet at www.ChoosetoSave.org. And deep gratitude to Dr. William Sharpe and Asma Emneina at FinancialEngines.com for their willingness to give my readers free access to a year of advice through the link at my website at www.TerrySavage.com.

When the subject is annuities, I always rely on Jeffrey Oster (Jeffrey .Oster@RaymondJames.com) for both my writings and my own investments. He always clarifies the differences between the good products and the costly ones, and always explains the hidden pitfalls. I trust him completely.

For information about the ever-changing landscape of student loans, I have access to the expert—Reecy Aresty at www.PayLessfor College.com. And when it comes to number-crunching, I appreciate the quick mind and calculator of actuary Nolan Frank.

Peter Bell, president of the National Reverse Mortgage Lenders Association (www.ReverseMortgage.org), keeps me updated on reverse mortgages, a product in which I was an early believer, and a concept that has only improved over the years. For estate planning updates, I rely on Michael Hartz of KattenMuchinRosenman, and for elder law issues, my thanks to Janna Dutton (www .DuttonElderLaw.com).

Special thanks go to Polly Smith, my editor at the *Chicago Sun-Times*, whose sharp eye and inordinate attention to detail have saved me many times. Also my appreciation to Howard Gold, my long-time editor at Moneyshow.com and Barrons.com, who has always expanded my horizons. Creators Syndicate distributes my column, and I appreciate their years of support. And once again, I benefited from Pat Stahl's precise, yet humane copyediting talent.

Thanks go to some special people who work tirelessly behind the scenes to support my work. Wes Welch (www.BusinessFirstBooks.com) has been a longtime partner in the distribution of my autographed books through my website and at my speeches. Robert Voigts (www .WordsworthDesign.com) is my forever website designer who always responds quickly and creatively to my incessant requests for change. Vinnie Sestito and Cathryn Armstrong of Experience Partners have moved me to the next level of marketing and technology.

And finally, thanks to all the editors at John Wiley & Sons, who have been so supportive and understanding. Joan O'Neil, Debra Englander, Adrianna Johnson, and Mary Daniello have worked on all of my books with patience and attention to detail. I am so fortunate to have them on my side.

Most of all, I send my appreciation to *you*, my readers. For many years, your responses to my columns, books, and newsletters have encouraged me to keep bringing you the Savage Truth on Money.

INDEX